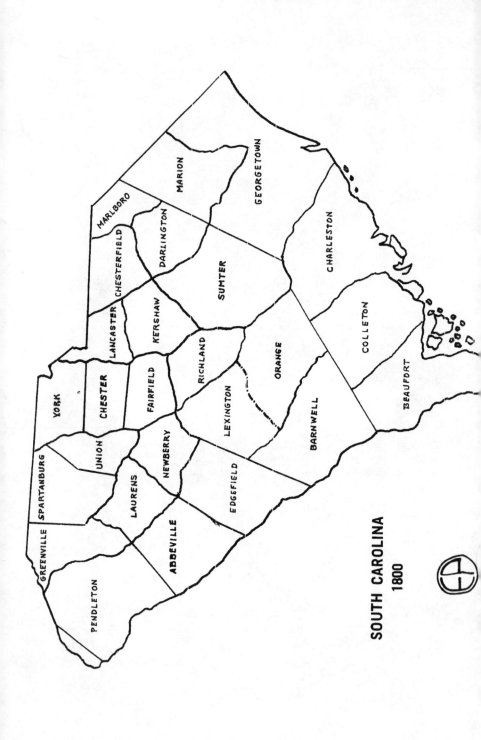

SOUTH CAROLINA
1800

INDEX TO
THE 1800 CENSUS
OF SOUTH CAROLINA

Compiled by

BRENT H. HOLCOMB

CLEARFIELD

Reprinted for
Clearfield Company, Inc. by
Genealogical Publishing Co., Inc.
Baltimore, Maryland
1997, 2000

Copyright © 1980
Genealogical Publishing Co., Inc.
Baltimore, Maryland
All Rights Reserved
Library of Congress Catalogue Card Number 79-93028
International Standard Book Number 0-8063-0884-2
Made in the United States of America

INTRODUCTION

The year 1800 brought a significant change to the court system of South Carolina. In that year most of the counties became known as districts. However, there were a few exceptions. In 1785 counties were laid out in all seven districts of the state: Camden, Ninety Six, Cheraws, Orangeburgh, Charleston, Beaufort, and Georgetown. The counties of Beaufort, Charleston, and Georgetown districts declined to function. Those of Orangeburgh District functioned only until 1791. In 1800 some of these counties were revitalized as small districts, with name changes: Liberty County became Marion District, Winton County became Barnwell District, etc. The counties of Salem, Claremont, and Clarendon combined to form Sumter District. In the 1800 census, in some cases, these non-functioning or then extinct counties were still designated within the district. For the simplicity of location in this index the district designations have been used, with the exception of Orangeburgh District, which is divided into Orange and Lexington counties (Barnwell District is clearly separated). This was done because Lexington was revitalized as a district in 1804. The districts of Charleston, Colleton (cut out of Charleston), and Beaufort were divided into parishes in this census, parish being an older division than county. The district of Georgetown carries both designations: Winyaw County (pp. 362-374) corresponds roughly to the later Georgetown District, Waccamaw Allsaints parish (pp. 376-380), Kingston County (pp. 380-392), later Horry District.

The map included here may be helpful. Now that the reader is thoroughly confused, he may find the names in the 1800 census most conveniently by using county (district) and page number as given in this index. In each case, the machine-stamped page numbers are used. The page numbers for Charleston District are somewhat out of sequence in the 200's, therefore for the latter part of that district the second set of machine-stamped numbers (60's) has been used. The abbreviations used are as follow:

Abb	Abbeville	Lan	Lancaster
Bar	Barnwell	Lex	Lexington
Bft	Beaufort	Mbo	Marlboro
Cfd	Chesterfield	Mrn	Marion
Chr	Chester	Nby	Newberry
Col	Colleton	Ora	Orange
Csn	Charleston	Pen	Pendleton
Dtn	Darlington	Spa	Spartanburg
Edg	Edgefield	Sum	Sumter
Fai	Fairfield	Uni	Union
Geo	Georgetown	Wil	Williamsburg
Gvl	Greenville	Yrk	York
Ker	Kershaw		

This index is offered in hope that it will make South Carolina ancestors easier to locate. Of course, no index is perfect, but every effort has been made to make this as accurate as possible. The following persons have contributed to this effort: Mr. Horace F. Rudisill, Mrs. A. O. Hendrix, Mrs. Morn M. Lindsay, Mrs. Wilma C. Kirkland, and Mr. Elmer O. Parker. Their aid was enlisted because of their familiarity with many names in certain counties and their ability to point out variations in spelling. For the less obvious spelling variants I have used "see" entries. Obviously, no one person or group of people can recognize all variant spellings. A knowledge of phonics and early pronunciations is the best guide. Where the interpretation of a name in the census is in doubt a question mark in parentheses (?) is placed after it. Doubtful surnames are placed at the beginning of the alphabet of that surname; e. g. *Smith (?), John* appears before *Smith, Allen*. The designation (2) after a name indicates its appearance twice on the same page or opening.

Please take note that on most of this census only alternate pages are numbered; therefore, the page before and after the numbered page should be examined. In the Winyaw County section of Georgetown District fourteen names are missing. In York District fourteen names are cut or torn from page 627 and thirteen from page 629. The Edgefield District census of 1800 is in very poor condition, and many surnames are obliterated or missing. Unfortunately, the entire 1800 census of Richland District is lost.

My thanks to the contributors mentioned above, and to Mrs. June Seay, Mrs. Billie Morris, Mr. Allan Shull, Miss Mary E. Boozer, and my brother and sister-in-law, Barry and Carol E. Holcomb, for their help in the task of alphabetizing.

Brent H. Holcomb, C. A. L. S.
Columbia, South Carolina

INDEX TO THE 1800 CENSUS
OF SOUTH CAROLINA

INDEX TO THE 1800 CENSUS
OF SOUTH CAROLINA

Thomas	Nby 65		Ezekiel	Pen 116
Adkins, Aaron	Ker 411		James	Csn 60
Francis	Nby 64		James	Nby 64
Hartwell	Yrk 630		Joseph	Abb 25
Hugh	Pen 152		Margret	Chr 89
James	Sum 591		Robert	Chr 89
John	Gvl 248		Thos.	Chr 76
Joseph	Pen 160		Akridge, Abel	Bar 43
Mary	Sum 597		Greenbury	Bar 43
Shadrach	Sum 591		Margaret	Bar 43
Thomas	Nby 64		Alan, Joseph	Bar 45
Wm.	Spa 168		Albergotie, Anthony	Bft 137
Adkinson, Duke	Sum 591		Albertson, Arthur	Dtn 125
Jesse	Sum 595		Albison, Elijah	Chr 76
William	Sum 595		James	Chr 76
Aertsen, Guilliam	Csn 112		Joshua	Chr 87
Affigne, Joseph	Csn 108		Albritton, Elizabeth	Uni 224
Aggnew, James	Bft 137		Mathew	Nby 65
Agnew, James	Pen 120		Alderson, Anne	Yrk 630
Agre, John	Abb 4		James	Yrk 630
Aiger, James	Csn 123		James C.	Yrk 630
Aikins, James	Fai 196		Jeremiah	Yrk 630
James	Fai 230		Aldrage, Elijah	Ker 407
Aikin, James Senr.	Fai 224		William	Ker 407
Aikins, John	Fai 203		Aldredg, Rebekh.	Pen 163
John	Fai 224		Aldredge, John	Edg 187
Aikin, Walter	Fai 224		Aldridge, Isham	Edg 187
William	Fai 219		John	Abb 9
Ainger, Edd.	Bft 84		Nathaniel	Abb 18
Edward	Csn 113		Samuel	Lex 571
Ainsworth, Jeremiah	Ora 529		Thomas	Dtn 121
John	Ora 529		Alewine, David	Nby 64
Leavin	Cfd 100		George	Nby 64
William	Cfd 100		Jacob	Nby 64
Air, Chas. Jas.	Csn 149		Micheal	Nby 64
James H.	Csn 166		Thomas	Nby 64
Aires, James	Fai 216		Alexander, Abel	Yrk 631
James	Fai 237		Abraham	Csn 146
Moses	Fai 227		Alexr.	Spa 188
Moses Junr.	Fai 227		Anguish	Uni 236
Stephen	Fai 219		Christian	Uni 232
William	Fai 219		Danl.	Pen 140
Airs, Ann	Csn 84		David	Csn 133
George	Csn 143		David	Pen 163
Ismael	Ora 541		Elias	Lan 2
John	Ora 541		Esther	Yrk 622
Margerett	Bft 98		Frances	Sum 609
Thomas	Wil 467		Harmond	Ker 399
William	Geo 377		Isaac	Ker 397
Aitken, John	Csn 183		James	Gvl 275
Aken, Frances	Pen 125		James	Pen 129
Aker, Peter Junr.	Pen 146		James	Pen 163
Peter Senr.	Pen 146		James	Spa 179
William	Pen 145		James	Spa 180
Akerman, S.	Col 385		James	Uni 237
Akin, Ann	Csn 145		Jane	Abb 40
Eleanor	Csn 88		Jno	Fai 207
John	Yrk 629		John	Dtn 122
Peter	Yrk 629		John	Dtn 127
Robert	Pen 109		John	Fai 234
Sarah	Csn 83		John	Gvl 273
Akins, Amos	Pen 104		John	Pen 129
Carter	Csn 149		John	Pen 146
David	Edg 133		John	Spa 187
George	Nby 64		John	Uni 237

John, Junr.	Yrk 622	John	Chr 94
John, Senr.	Yrk 622	John	Fai 204
Joseph	Gvl 275	John	Fai 217
Joseph, Rev.	Yrk 624	John	Ker 413
Josiah	Pen 161	John	Sum 597
Juda	Csn 144	Josiab	Chr 80
Lydda	Uni 236	Larkin	Yrk 628
Mary	Mrn 462	Lee	Pen 122
Obed	Yrk 631	Lydall	Lrs 42
Rachael	Csn 92	Micah	Gvl 272
Rany	Bar 59	Michal	Col 379
Reubin	Bar 60	Nancy	Geo 368
Samuel, Doctr.	Yrk 624	Rachel	Spa 182
Thomas	Lan 7	Relies	Lex 577
Thos.	Gvl 245	Richard	Ora 511
William	Csn 195	Robert	Abb 11
William	Fai 234	Robert	Edg 176
William	Nby 65	Robert	Pen 157
William	Sum 608	Saml.	Mrn 439
William	Yrk 624	Samuel	Csn 111
Willm.	Csn 82	Sarah	Sum 601
Alford, Arthur	Geo 389	Sarah	Wil 466
Jacob	Dtn 121	Squire	Pen 122
Jacob	Geo 382	Stokes	Abb 23
Jacob	Geo 389	Tabitha	Bft 120
James	Mrn 448	Thomas	Dtn 124
John	Edg 140	West	Lex 577
John	Geo 389	Will.	Lan 3
William	Geo 381	William	Csn 131
Alfred, James	Csn 93	William	Edg 142
Alison, Lemuel P.	Gvl 245	William	Mrn 439
Alkens, William	Fai 238	William	Pen 155
Alkins, Johnson	Fai 226	William	Pen 163
Allan, Asa	Bar 60	Wm.	Spa 182
John	Bar 50	Young	Edg 142
Allcorn, James	Fai 194	Allerpyer, Henry	Edg 148
Allen, --ury	Edg 147	Allin, David	Spa 203
Andrew	Fai 203	David	Spa 206
Ann	Ker 396	Isaac	Chr 87
Arthur	Dtn 123	James	Chr 77
Benjamin	Bar 45	James	Spa 189
Charles	Gvl 243	John	Chr 80
Charles Esq.	Lrs 13	John	Spa 188
Daniel	Spa 182	Richard	Chr 91
David	Lrs 19	Runnel	Spa 203
Drury	Edg 172	Saml.	Chr 74
Drury	Mrn 454	William	Mrn 459
Ezra	Sum 595	Willis	Spa 206
George	Chr 79	Wm.	Chr 83
George	Chr 82	Wm.	Spa 188
George	Gvl 254	Younge	Spa 206
Gersham	Pen 121	Allison, see also Ellison	
Hezekiah	Yrk 619	Allison, Francis	Lrs 19
Isaac	Pen 123	Hezekiah	Mbo 50
Isam	Ker 411	Hezekiah Jr.	Mbo 50
James	Abb 11	Jacob	Col 383
James	Edg 144	James	Csn 138
James	Pen 108	James	Lrs 13
James	Pen 158	James	Lrs 20
Jas.	Csn 163	John	Yrk 622
Jas. Est.	Col 381	John Dr.	Yrk 632
Jesse	Lex 577	Joseph	Lrs 15
Jesse	Lrs 42	Joseph	Mbo 50
Joel	Mrn 454	Lewis	Lrs 14
John	Chr 91	Mary	Lrs 13

Robert	Mbo	50		Alexr.	Spa	180
Samuel	Lrs	19		Allen	Edg	149
Thomas	Lrs	15		Allen	Lan	9
Thomas	Lrs	44		Amos	Abb	25
Thomas Senr.	Lrs	45		Amos	Abb	28
William	Lrs	45		Andrew	Lrs	39
Allisson, William	Ora	537		Archd.	Csn	147
Allmon, Benjn.	Csn	112		Charles	Lan	8
Allon(?), William	Nby	65		Charles	Mbo	50
Allport, John	Csn	93		David	Abb	29
Allrooks, William	Lrs	42		David	Edg	180
Allston, Benja.	Geo	377		David	Fai	202
Benja. Junr.	Geo	377		David	Geo	381
Josiah Wm.	Geo	378		David	Spa	167
Dr. Willm	Geo	371		David Maj.	Lrs	38
Wm., Estate of	Geo	377		Denney	Spa	191
Allwright, James	Csn	107		Elijah	Nby	65
Alman, Willis	Chr	75		Elijah	Uni	232
Alsbrook, Calbourn	Sum	609		Eliza	Pen	120
Alston, James	Fai	238		Elizabeth	Edg	168
Allston, John	Dtn	126		Elizabeth	Uni	244
Alston, Saml.	Mrn	461		Gabriel(2)	Nby	65
Samuel	Fai	198		George	Abb	25
William	Csn	118		George	Edg	149
William	Geo	379		George	Lan	2
Alsup, William	Fai	195		George	Pen	157
Altam(?), John	Nby	64		Henry	Geo	382
Alten, Jesse	Sum	585		Henry	Lex	565
Altman, David	Ora	531		Hezekiah	Gvl	281
James	Geo	382		Isaac	Lan	8
John	Mrn	437		Isaac	Pen	124
John	Ora	531		Isaac	Spa	179
Solomon	Ora	531		Jacob	Abb	25
Amaker, John Junr.	Ora	539		Jacob	Bft	112
Amberson,	Yrk	618		Jacob	Geo	380
Matthew, Junr.				Jacob	Pen	123
Matthew, Senr.	Yrk	618		James	Abb	27
William	Yrk	618		James	Bar	54
Amick, see also Adammack				James	Chr	88
Amick, Adam	Lex	568		James	Edg	172
Adam	Lex	574		James	Geo	372
Adamik	Lex	579		James	Gvl	256
Amison, Thomas	Sum	607		James	Gvl	275
Amison, Amos	Sum	607		James	Nby	64
Abraham	Sum	611		James	Pen	123
Jesse	Sum	608		James	Pen	153
Ammonds, Henry Junr.	Lex	567		James	Pen	157
Ammons, Joshua	Mbo	50		James	Spa	195
Thomas	Mrn	451		James	Sum	601
Wm.	Mbo	50		James	Sum	607
Amonet, Charles	Sum	603		James D.	Abb	40
Amos, Daniel	Spa	169		Jas.	Col	391
Amurettah	Bar	58		Jeremiah	Csn	74
(free black)				Jesse	Dtn	126
Ancrum, William	Csn	87		John	Bft	114
William	Csn	195		John	Abb	14
Anderson, Mrs.	Csn	149		John	Cfd	100
Aaron	Pen	122		John	Chr	76
Abell	Gvl	250		John	Dtn	117
Abraham	Pen	113		John	Dtn	126
Abraham	Pen	123		John	Edg	141
Abram	Ker	401		John	Edg	142
Agnes	Abb	18		John	Edg	172
Alexr.	Geo	364		John	Gvl	265
Alexr.	Ker	417		John	Lan	2

Arnolds, William	Lrs 42		Joshua	Abb 17
Arnot, John	Csn 109		Nathaniel	Bar 52
Arock(?), John	Sum 606		Nathaniel	Lrs 16
Aron(?), Toby	Edg 172		Thomas	Lrs 16
Aron, Henery	Ora 553		William	Abb 17
John	Ora 553		William	Bar 52
Philip	Ora 553		Ashlock, Richard	Pen 128
Arrasmith, John	Gvl 283		Ashmore, James	Gvl 280
Massa	Gvl 253		John	Gvl 280
Arrant, Jacob	Cfd 100		Wm.	Gvl 280
Peter	Cfd 100		Ashton, Catharine	Csn 86
Arrence, Harmon	Ker 396		Ashworth, James	Pen 138
Arrendel, John	Spa 171		Moses	Pen 141
Arrenton, William	Edg 163		Askew, Mrs. Senr.	Bft 126
Arrington, Benja.	Mrn 456		Askew, James	Pen 157
Burrell	Lex 565		Jesse	Mbo 50
Arronton(?), Arthur	Edg 183		John	Mbo 50
Benjamin	Edg 183		Mary	Bft 96
Arrowood, John	Spa 176		Young	Gvl 267
Arterberry, Bridget	Chr 77		Askin, Charles	Lex 564
Charles	Chr 75		James	Pen 155
Edward	Chr 84		Askins(?), John	Chr 89
John	Chr 92		Askins, Charles	Nby 65
Moses	Chr 84		Peter	Fai 241
Thomas	Chr 77		Aslin, Thomas	Edg 164
Thomas	Chr 92		Thomas	Edg 185
Arthur, George	Csn 163		Aspenal, Jesse	Nby 64
Hargrove	Lex 571		John	Nby 64
James	Yrk 617		William	Nby 64
Jesse	Lex 571		Astel, Joseph	Uni 238
Peter S.	Csn 173		Asten, Mary	Abb 8
Arthurs, Ambrus	Sum 608		Astin, Alexr.	Spa 178
Artist, John	Lan 10		Aston, James	Abb 4
Asbay, John	Uni 230		Atcheson, Wm.	Fai 204
William	Uni 230		Atkerson(?), Lettice	Mrn 447
Asbel, Aaron	Edg 145		Atkeson, Edward	Uni 239
Asbin, John	Chr 91		John	Uni 238
Philip	Chr 91		Atking, Stephen	Csn 60
Ash, Elizabeth	Csn 115		Atkins, Benjamin	Lrs 37
Hannah	Csn 118		Benjn.	Edg 155
John	Csn 122		Charles	Bft 126
Richd. C.	Col 367		Gabriel	Edg 156
Saml. Est.	Col 367		John	Edg 148
Ashby, Anthy. Est.	Csn 68		Samuel	Yrk 619
Thomas	Csn 149		Thomas	Edg 155
Ashcraft, Drury	Yrk 620		William	Lrs 36
Ashcroft, John	Yrk 620		Atkinson, Burrell	Ora 501
Ashe, John	Col 367		Eliza.	Mbo 50
John, Junr. Est.	Col 367		Henry	Fai 192
Robert, Junr.	Yrk 617		Henry	Sum 600
Robert, Senr.	Yrk 617		Isaac	Mrn 448
William	Yrk 617		James	Chr 76
Asher, Joel	Pen 108		James	Geo 371
Thomas	Uni 240		Jesse	Mrn 446
William	Pen 108		Mary	Csn 112
Ashford, George	Fai 236		Richd.	Dtn 127
George	Nby 64		Susanna	Mbo 60
Michael	Uni 230		Atmar, Ralph	Csn 140
Moses	Uni 231		Attaway, Elisha	Lrs 16
Ashler, John	Fai 231		Elisha, Junr.	Lrs 16
Ashley, John	Abb 17		James	Lrs 14
John	Bar 52		John	Lrs 16
John	Ker 413		John, Junr.	Lrs 15
John	Lrs 16		Joseph	Lrs 15
Jordan	Lan 5		Joseph	Lrs 16

Joseph	Lrs 16		Mary Mrs.	Csn 117
William	Lrs 17		William	Csn 113
Atteberry, Isaac	Ora 511		Ayers, Mary	Csn 60
Israel	Ora 515		Ayre, Lewis M.	Bar 69
Atwater, Isaac	Pen 116		Ayres, Joseph	Gvl 263
Isaac	Pen 117		Joshua	Nby 65
Titus	Pen 115		Martin	Gvl 283
Atwood, James	Lrs 28		Mary	Gvl 263
Auberry, George	Nby 64		Wm.	Gvl 263
Phillip	Nby 64		Ayris, James	Gvl 264
Augley, Conrod	Bar 55		Azevedo, Js. D.	Csn 142
Auglin, John	Lrs 23		Azube, Abraham	Csn 146
William	Lrs 23			
Augustus, Cesar	Pen 111			
Auldsbook, Landol	Cfd 100		B	
Aull, see Awl				
Austeen, John	Bft 98			
John, Senr.	Bft 98		B--nett, Samuel	Edg 185
Shadarich	Bft 98		Thomas	Edg 185
Solomon	Bft 96		Babb, Abner	Lrs 18
Austen, Betsy	Fai 213		James	Lrs 35
James	Fai 235		Joseph	Gvl 262
John	Fai 200		Joseph	Lrs 35
Joseph	Fai 215		Rhoda	Nby 68
Austin, Amos	Spa 206		Rody	Nby 68
Catharine	Csn 78		Sampson	Lrs 18
Cornelius	Abb 21		Thomas	Lrs 35
John	Lrs 21		Babler, Lemon	Fai 229
John	Uni 230		Bachelor, James	Geo 365
Nathaniel	Lrs 20		Backert, Yourith	Nby 67
William	Csn 94		Backler, John	Bft 130
Auston, Dickerson	Gvl 273		Backster, John	Ora 541
Drewry	Gvl 277		Bacot, Henry H.	Csn 126
Francis	Gvl 271		Laban	Dtn 116
John	Gvl 276		Samuel	Dtn 116
Mary	Gvl 277		Thomas	Bft 110
Nathaniel	Gvl 278		Thos. W.	Csn 125
Samuel	Gvl 278		Badger, James	Csn 152
William, Junr.	Gvl 278		Bagget, Abraham	Mbo 50
Wm.	Gvl 276		John	Mbo 59
Autery, Elizabeth	Spa 205		John	Mbo 59
Avant, Benja.	Geo 369		Baggett, James	Mbo 59
Francis	Geo 373		Nicholas	Ora 513
John	Mrn 443		Bagience, John	Sum 604
John	Mrn 446		Bagley, William	Ora 523
Jonathan	Mrn 443		Bagnal, Ebenezer	Sum 606
Joshua	Mrn 460		Isaac	Sum 605
Thomas	Mrn 443		John	Sum 600
Aveille, John B.	Csn 97		Bagshaw, Thomas	Csn 149
Avenne, Peter	Csn 154		Bagwell, Bevely	Spa 170
Avery, Charles	Gvl 268		Frederick	Lrs 43
Joseph	Lrs 43		Federick	Pen 145
Henry	Cfd 100		Hays	Spa 203
Richard	Bft 100		James	Spa 205
Thomas	Sum 605		John	Pen 145
Thos.	Gvl 268		John	Spa 174
William	Lrs 43		John	Spa 205
William	Pen 104		Littleton	Spa 205
Awbry, see Auberry			Wm.	Spa 205
Awl, George	Lex 579		Bailey, Absolem	Lrs 34
Philip	Lex 568		Allen	Abb 30
William	Edg 187		Benjn.	Col 385
Axon, Jacob	Csn 148		Benjamin	Gvl 247
Thomas	Csn 149		Benjamin	Pen 128
Axson, John	Csn 173		Canady	Lan 4

Daniel	Lrs 35	James	Sum 610
David	Csn 151	Jesse	Gvl 252
David	Lrs 33	Jesse	Sum 610
Elijah, Senr.	Yrk 622	Jessey	Edg 143
Henrey	Csn 132	John	Abb 25
Isaac	Bar 55	John	Abb 29
James	Lrs 30	John	Abb 34
Jesse	Edg 161	John	Cfd 110
John	Edg 161	John	Edg 143
John	Lrs 33	John	Geo 389
John	Lrs 35	John	Gvl 256
John	Mbo 59	John	Gvl 274
John	Pen 110	John	Lan 4
Joseph	Abb 27	John	Lan 9
Joseph	Abb 30	John	Mrn 457
Martin	Edg 162	Jonathan	Pen 127
Moses	Col 391	Joseph	Csn 94
Nathaniel	Abb 12	Leonard	Uni 226
Rueben	Fai 212	Margaret	Sum 610
William	Lrs 29	Peter	Gvl 251
William	Lrs 29	R. B.	Col 361
Zachariah Capt.	Lrs 34	Robert	Mbo 60
Zachariah, Junr.	Lrs 34	Robert	Pen 119
Bails, David	Edg 177	Samuel	Pen 119
Baily, Ely	Lrs 35	Thomas	Csn 116
William	Edg 167	Thomas	Csn 149
Bains, Robert	Edg 157	Thomas	Edg 181
Bainwell, Robert	Bft 94	Will.	Lan 9
Baird, Adam	Abb 24	William	Abb 27
Adam	Abb 28	William	Lex 561
Barbara	Nby 67	William	Mrn 436
Batt	Abb 34	William	Pen 127
David	Yrk 617	William	Pen 142
Elizabeth	Abb 40	William	Sum 595
Bailey, G. G.	Csn 125	Baldee, William	Abb 40
Baird, Hugh	Abb 25	Balden, William	Uni 223
James	Abb 34	Baldin, Eli	Gvl 275
James	Abb 39	Baldre, George	Nby 66
James	Lan 9	Baldwin, Isaac	Bft 138
John	Abb 3	Isaac	Lrs 16
John	Yrk 619	John	Gvl 278
Samuel	Abb 34	John	Gvl 280
Simon	Abb 24	John	Lrs 16
Thomas	Abb 34	Thomas	Pen 157
William	Dtn 124	William	Csn 150
William	Dtn 124	Bales, Jacob	Nby 65
Bairfield, Robt	Geo 391	John	Gvl 282
Baker, Amey	Csn 127	Baley, William	Mrn 451
Andrew	Lan 5	Balinger, John	Gvl 266
Andrew	Lan 10	Ball, Benjamin	Abb 18
Ann	Mbo 60	Elias	Csn 68
Archd.	Mrn 445	Elizabeth	Csn 126
Barthw.	Uni 226	George	Lrs 33
Caleb	Abb 34	J. C. Est	Csn 60
Cassilpey(?)	Edg 181	James	Abb 18
Charles	Pen 142	James	Lrs 33
Daniel	Mrn 454	John	Abb 18
David	Lan 5	John	Abb 23
Elisha	Lan 9	John	Bar 55
Frances	Csn 116	John	Csn 68
Henry	Pen 163	John	Csn 189
Jacob	Ora 527	John, Junr.	Abb 39
James	Abb 27	Ketherine	Abb 18
James	Edg 143	Peter	Abb 39
James	Geo 382	Peter	Lrs 31

Samson	Bft	122	Banner, Alfred	Bft	114
Thomas	Csn	128	Joseph	Lrs	32
William	Abb	17	Bannister, Abraham	Spa	177
William	Lrs	16	William	Pen	127
William	Lrs	30	Wm.	Uni	230
Ballad, Stephen	Pen	144	Banton, Lewis	Lrs	39
Ballantine, Mary	Csn	61	Bar, John	Sum	607
Wm.	Csn	60	Barbaree, Benajah	Gvl	258
Ballard, David	Ker	419	Barber, Allexander	Ora	543
Devereaux	Sum	597	Charles	Ker	421
Fanny	Pen	106	James	Fai	223
Jesse	Pen	161	John	Chr	80
John	Ora	517	John	Csn	153
John, Junr.	Ker	419	John	Fai	223
John, Senr.	Ker	419	John	Ker	421
Kellis	Spa	174	Moses	Ker	423
Robert	Lex	559	Nathel	Ker	421
Thomas	Ker	419	Robert	Fai	217
Ballenger, Edward	Spa	178	William	Bft	98
Edward	Spa	182	Barbant, Danl.	Geo	371
Francis	Spa	203	Barby, Elisha	Pen	159
James	Spa	182	Nancy	Lrs	37
James	Spa	207	Barclay, John	Lan	11
Ballentine, James	Lex	569	Thomas	Mbo	51
Ballew, see also Billue			Barefield, Mr.	Bft	98
Ballow, Thomas	Geo	363	Willis	Sum	603
Bals, Catherine	Nby	65	Bareno, Arthur	Wil	470
Balsy, Jonas	Mrn	451	Isaac, Junr.	Wil	474
Baltzegar, Margaret	Ora	541	Jean	Wil	471
Bamer, Zachariah	Lex	574	Barfield, Arthur	Mrn	439
Bampfield, Rebecca	Csn	140	Asa	Dtn	118
Sarah A.	Csn	100	Barrat	Mrn	439
Bamos, Manuel	Csn	148	Charles	Mrn	456
Banckston, Laurence	Spa	175	Daniel	Mbo	50
Bandy, Jesse	Chr	73	Darcas	Bar	51
Wm.	Chr	88	Elisha	Mrn	440
Banion, Benjn.	Edg	177	James	Edg	156
Banister, Balom	Abb	18	Miles	Dtn	118
Francis	Abb	18	Nathan	Mrn	458
James	Edg	146	Priscilla	Dtn	124
John J.	Sum	606	Priscilla	Mrn	439
Thomas	Abb	16	Solomon	Mbo	51
Bank, Hugh	Edg	160	William	Edg	156
Bankhead, Elizath.	Uni	248	Barfoot, John	Mrn	438
George	Uni	248	Baring, Charles	Col	393
Hugh	Uni	249	Baris, Samuel	Dtn	128
James	Chr	75	Barker, Beal	Fai	195
James	Uni	249	Benjn.	Fai	202
John	Chr	92	Colerien(?)	Chr	83
John	Uni	241	Elijah	Spa	197
John	Uni	249	Isham	Cfd	107
Robert	Fai	231	Isham	Cfd	109
Banks, Charles	Csn	130	James	Edg	186
Charles	Nby	66	James	Lrs	17
David	Nby	66	Jas, Junr.	Fai	217
George	Abb	32	Jesse	Lrs	17
James	Pen	107	John	Fai	195
John	Abb	20	Joseph J.	Csn	150
Levey	Abb	28	Laurens	Lrs	17
Samuel	Fai	192	Lewis	Cfd	101
Solomon	Pen	107	Moses	Geo	383
Thomas	Edg	177	Samuel	Fai	196
Vincent	Dtn	116	William	Bar	64
William	Csn	93	Barklay, Robert	Lan	9
Bankston, John	Spa	175	Barkley, James	Fai	213

Richard	Edg 173	Charles	Mbo 50
Thomas	Pen 106	Daniel	Abb 4
Barrett, Arther	Gvl 254	David	Gvl 253
Benjn	Edg 142	David	Pen 141
Esther	Csn 75	George	Csn 149
James	Csn 103	Henery	Pen 128
John	Gvl 251	James	Pen 138
Matthew	Edg 168	James	Pen 143
Rheuben	Gvl 254	John (2)	Pen 126
Thomas	Edg 169	John	Pen 138
William	Lrs 14	Joseph	Lrs 19
William	Wil 473	Joseph	Pen 137
Barringtine, Charles	Mbo 51	Joshua	Gvl 278
Jacob	Mbo 51	Joshua	Pen 136
Nancy	Nbo 51	Moses	Pen 138
Sarah	Mbo 51	Pressley	Pen 141
William	Mbo 50	Stephen	Pen 138
Wm., Jr.	Mbo 51	Thos., Jr.	Gvl 252
Barrom, Fielding	Sum 587	Thos., Senr.	Gvl 252
Barron, Alexr.	Pen 129	Will.	Lan 11
Alexr.	Csn 104	William	Bar 66
Archibald	Yrk 621	William	Pen 126
James	Mrn 450	Wm.	Spa 177
Jane E.	Csn 104	Bartrum, Robert	Abb 22
John	Csn 130	Baruch, William	Dtn 124
John	Yrk 621	Barwick, see Berwick	
Martha	Uni 225	Basket, Thomas	Nby 67
Thomas	Yrk 621	Baskin, James S.	Abb 9
William	Pen 129	John	Abb 9
Barrontine, James(2)	Edg 186	John	Abb 33
Barrot, Elisha	Edg 184	John	Ker 411
George	Nby 67	Prudense	Abb 9
John	Nby 67	Sarah	Abb 34
William	Nby 67	William	Abb 6
William	Sum 605	William	Abb 9
Barrott, Richard	Pen 108	Baskins, James	Ker 417
Barrow, Benjamin	Sum 609	John	Ker 415
Bennet	Sum 609	John	Ker 421
Taylor	Sum 609	M.	Lan 6
William	Sum 614	Basquen, Willm.	Csn 120
Barrs, Lewis	Ora 515	Bass, Ann	Csn 68
William	Ora 509	Benjamin	Sum 610
Barry, Andrew	Spa 203	John	Mrn 444
David	Csn 114	John	Wil 467
John	Lex 559	Joseph	Cfd 100
John	Spa 183	Joseph	Mrn 444
Nicholas	Csn 142	Phillemon	Uni 220
Richd.	Spa 185	Right	Mrn 445
Richd.	Uni 245	Thomas	Csn 89
Bartee, Jessie	Edg 152	Bassel, Smith	Pen 117
Thomas	Abb 23	Basset, George	Abb 40
Bartell, Mary	Mrn 453	Bassett, Eli	Bar 63
Bartin, Samuel	Bar 48	John	Bar 63
Thimoty	Ora 541	Lurana	Bar 64
Bartlet, Samuel	Pen 162	Bast, Sarah	Bar 56
Thomas	Sum 608	Bateman, Michael	Sum 593
Bartlett, --hardson	Edg 148	Thomas	Sum 610
Daniel	Yrk 630	Bates, Anthony	Spa 200
Sarah	Dtn 125	Drusiller	Bar 44A
Bartley, Agnes	Lan 2	Edy	Bar 51
Thomas	Lan 2	Elisabeth	Bar 60
Will	Lan 2	Elizabeth	Lrs 17
Barton, Amy	Bar 49	Fleming	Abb 39
Benjamin	Pen 113	Francis	Lan 10
Caleb	Pen 128	Henry	Gvl 252

Edward	Abb	21	John S.	Csn	140
Fuqua	Edg	170	Judge Thos.	Csn	131
Henry	Abb	32	Susan	Csn	60
John	Lrs	35	Thomas	Lex	569
Richard	Abb	32	Thomas, Junr.	Csn	102
William	Abb	32	William	Csn	116
William	Edg	165	Beek, Simon	Edg	184
William	Pen	138	Beekman, Elizabeth	Csb	90
Beasly, William	Abb	21	Samuel	Csn	152
Beason, Seal	Spa	196	Beesely, Charles	Dtn	121
Beatie, Robt.	Csn	124	John	Dtn	121
Beaty, see also Betty			Reuben	Dtn	121
Beaty, Elizabeth	Yrk	622	William	Dtn	121
James	Fai	213	Beets, Samuel	Nby	67
James	Geo	383	Begley, Jacob, Junr.	Lex	497
James	Pen	126	Behn, Arthur	Bft	130
John	Geo	389	Beird, Francis	Spa	196
John	Pen	142	James	Spa	186
John	Pen	149	Robert	Spa	195
Jonathan	Yrk	622	Bekley, Margaret	Lex	497
Mahaley	Uni	235	Belcher, Denis	Bar	47
Robert	Pen	136	Ferrel	Bar	65
Robert	Uni	235	Belew, Abraham	Gvl	256
Thomas	Pen	148	David	Gvl	256
William (2)	Pen	149	John	Gvl	256
Beauchamp, Henry	Mbo	51	Leonard	Edg	148
Beauford, Martha	Bar	69	Belfore, John	Spa	178
Beaufort, Charles	Csn	111	Belin, Allard	Geo	379
John	Uni	231	James, Senr.	Geo	374
Leeroy	Uni	232	Belk, Britain	Dtn	121
Beaver, Mary	Fai	205	Jeremiah	Dtn	121
Mathias	Csn	173	John	Lan	8
Wm.	Spa	205	John	Lan	10
Beavers, Sarah	Gvl	278	William	Dtn	121
William	Gvl	246	Bell, Agness	Chr	79
Beaws, Thomas	Abb	35	Abija	Csn	68
Beayne(?), Charles	Pen	134	Adam, Senr.	Lrs	24
Beazely, Adam	Fai	197	Alizander	Lex	570
George	Fai	219	Anne	Ora	523
John	Pen	137	Asey	Ker	407
Saml.	Pen	138	Charles	Lex	567
Beck, Charles	Bar	59	Daniel	Csn	108
John	Bft	114	David	Abb	25
John	Uni	236	David	Chr	82
Joseph	Bar	44A	David	Col	361
William	Abb	15	David	Csn	94
Becket, James	Csn	183	Duke	Abb	40
Beckett, James	Fai	213	Elisha	Ker	396
Petty	Bft	116	Elizabeth	Csn	173
Beckham, Dempsey	Edg	161	Federick	Sum	611
John	Edg	173	Francis	Ker	407
John	Uni	242	George	Fai	205
John	Uni	250	George	Chr	94
Philip	Chr	80	Israel	Nby	66
Wm.	Chr	90	James	Fai	199
Beckley, Joseph	Abb	6	James	Geo	375
Josh	Abb	6	James	Lrs	24
Beckman, Adolph	Csn	84	James	Pen	159
Beckum, Simon	Ker	417	James	Uni	220
Beckwith, Henry	Mrn	453	James	Uni	223
Bedenbaugh, see Pedimbox			James, Junr.	Fai	196
Bedford, James	Spa	176	Jane	Pen	161
Bedgegood, Malachi	Mbo	51	Jeremiah	Abb	12
Bedout, Judith	Geo	366	John	Abb	10
Bee, Eliza	Csn	82	John	Abb	19

John	Abb 39	John	Nby 65
John	Cfd 101	John	Sum 591
John	Chr 90	Jonathan	Fai 228
John	Csn 60	William	Nby 65
John	Fai 235	Belzer, Christian	Csn 60
John	Nby 66	Bembo, Edward	Nby 67
John	Sum 607	Benbow, Adam	Sum 606
John	Uni 223	Evan	Sum 606
John, Esqr.	Fai 239	Gershon	Sum 606
John, Junr.	Fai 220	Gressham	Sum 593
John N.	Chr 86	Martha	Sum 613
John W.	Spa 209	Benbridge, Wm.	Csn 60
Jonathan	Sum 602	Bender, George	Edg 154
Joseph	Abb 36	Benet, George	Bar 69
Joseph	Geo 376	Benison, William	Abb 8
Joshua	Lan 4	Benjamin, Samuel	Lrs 26
Lotterus	Sum 607	Bennan, Joshua	Ora 515
Malcomb	Cfd 109	Bennet, James	Chr 85
Mathew	Abb 3	John	Bar 53
Robert	Edg 172	John B.	Nby 67
Robert	Pen 124	Joseph	Chr 84
Saml	Spa 196	Joseph	Chr 89
Saml, Junr.	Spa 196	Legro (?)	Chr 87
Samuel	Bft 137	Margt.	Csn 163
Siles	Uni 226	Mary	Ora 533
Thomas	Dtn 123	Moses	Bar 53
Thomas	Ora 527	Peter	Csn 187
Thomas	Spa 187	Rhoda	Bar 69
Thomas	Uni 223	Richard	Nby 67
Thomas, Jr.	Dtn 125	Solom	Pen 163
Thomas, Junr.	Uni 223	Thomas	Csn 191
Thomas, Mrs.	Bft 137	William	Mbo 50
Valentine	Chr 77	Bennett, Betheina	Lrs 27
William	Abb 8	Cooper	Pen 145
William	Bft 122	Daniel	Spa 177
William	Edg 157	Elijah	Gvl 270
William	Fai 200	Elisha	Pen 158
William	Lrs 25	George	Pen 161
William	Pen 160	Hardiman	Pen 145
Wm.	Chr 86	Henrey	Csn 130
Wm.	Lex 565	James	Spa 199
Wm., Junior	Fai 200	James	Sum 605
William R.	Sum 608	John	Bft 118
Zacharia	Lan 4	John	Spa 177
Zacheriah	Bar 44	John	Spa 177
Zachs.	Bft 110	John	Yrk 631
Bella, free black	Wil 478	Joseph	Chr 85
Bellamee, John, Jr.	Geo 384	Minard	Mbo 51
John, Senr.	Geo 384	Stephen	Pen 158
Richd.	Geo 384	Thomas	Pen 161
Bellamy, Esther	Csn 129	Thomas, Junr.	Csn 104
Bellimee, Abraham	Geo 384	Thomas	Spa 177
Bellinger, B. B.	Bft 102	Thos.	Gvl 271
Ed:	Col 391	William	Ker 427
George	Col 391	Wm.	Csn 149
Isaac	Nby 67	William	Pen 145
J.	Col 393	William	Pen 160
Joseph	Bft 126	Wm.	Gvl 271
William	Bft 132	Winey	Edg 150
Bellune, William	Mrn 461	Bennicker, Charity	Ora 535
Belote, Peter	Abb 30	Benoit, Francis	Geo 368
Belser, Christian	Csn 98	Benoist, John	Csn 93
Belsher, Robert	Spa 205	Philip	Csn 68
Belton, Abraham	Ker 396	Samuel	Csn 68
Jesse	Nby 65	Benson, Benjn.	Gvl 285

Elizabeth	Spa 181	Joseph	Uni 229
Esthler	Fai 228	Joseph	Yrk 618
George	Bar 68	Joseph, Esq.	Abb 35
George	Spa 202	Majey	Yrk 628
Golden	Gvl 275	Nathaniel	Csn 84
Hannah	Chr 89	Oliver	Nby 67
Henry	Geo 392	Peter	Nby 67
Henry	Lrs 26	Robert	Abb 35
Henry	Spa 203	Robert	Abb 35
Isaac	Spa 180	Robert	Chr 90
Jaques	Dtn 114	Robert	Yrk 625
James	Chr 92	Robt.	Col 391
John	Chr 80	Samuel	Pen 107
John	Edg 175	Samuel, Junr.	Abb 10
John	Spa 203	Samuel, Senr.	Abb 35
Nathan	Spa 202	Thomas	Abb 10
Nicholas	Pen 134	Thomas	Abb 36
Patrick	Fai 234	Thomas	Csn 68
Robt.	Geo 392	Thomas	Edg 179
Samuel	Lrs 24	Thomas	Lan 7
Samuel	Uni 233	Thomas	Pen 132
Smith	Csn 149	Will	Lan 7
Thomas	Lrs 26	William	Abb 2
Thomas	Uni 235	William	Abb 35
Wiley	Pen 159	William	Abb 35
Wm.	Spa 179	William	Csn 166
Wm.	Spa 202	William	Edg 180
Bisshares, Bazle	Gvl 255	William	Lrs 28
William	Gvl 255	William	Yrk 617
Biter, Wm.	Spa 210	Blackburn, Ambrose	Gvl 267
Blanchard, Henry	Wil 469	Benjamin	Cfd 101
Jacob	Ker 429	Elias	Edg 139
James	Sum 587	John	Abb 5
Blanchert, Mrs.	Sum 585	John	Cfd 100
Isaac	Ker 409	John	Nby 68
Black,	Yrk 617	Joseph	Cfd 101
--[torn], Senr.		Steven	Geo 384
Adam	Lex 564	William	Abb 26
Alexander	Yrk 618	William	Nby 68
Annanias	Lan 8	Blackerby, Joseph	Lrs 28
Charles	Bft 137	Blackledge, Zackariah	Ora 545
Charles	Lan 8	Blackley, James	Lrs 22
Daniel	Pen 156	James	Wil 475
David	Abb 20	Jane	Wil 469
George	Yrk 624	John	Yrk 617
Hance	Gvl 280	John	Wil 469
Henry	Nby 68	John	Wil 474
Hugh	Lan 6	Blacklock, William	Csn 103
Jacob	Gvl 279	Blackly, John	Lrs 37
Jacob	Yrk 624	Thomas	Lrs 22
James	Abb 5	William	Lrs 22
James	Abb 35	Blackman, Benjn.	Mrn 446
James	Csn 127	Britain	Lan 5
James	Nby 67	James	Lan 5
James	Pen 132	James	Mrn 445
James	Pen 151	John	Lan 5
James	Yrk 617	John	Mrn 446
John	Abb 35	Joseph	Lan 5
John	Csn 133	Joseph	Ora 529
John	Edg 179	Solomon	Mrn 444
John	Lex 564	Thos.	Csn 68
John	Yrk 167	Will.	Lan 6
John	Yrk 624	Willm.	Mrn 445
Joseph	Pen 157	Blackmon, Benjn.	Csn 68
Joseph	Pen 158	Stephen	Bar 50

19

Blackstock, James	Gvl	266	Seth	Csn	124
John	Lrs	43	Blakely,		
Richd.	Spa	197	see also Blackley		
William	Yrk	619	Blakely, Benjamin	Lrs	21
Wm.	Spa	196	Jonathan	Lrs	21
Blackston, Isam	Bar	55	Nace	Lex	572
James	Bar	55	Robert	Csn	99
Blackwell, Abraham	Cfd	101	William	Edg	135
George S.	Edg	172	Blakeney, Hugh	Cfd	100
Hannah	Wil	477	James	Cfd	100
Isaac	Edg	143	John	Cfd	100
James	Edg	169	John, Jr.	Cfd	100
Joal	Edg	143	William	Cfd	100
John	Edg	173	Blakey, Elizabeth	Csn	126
John	Lrs	37	Elizabeth	Edg	169
John B.	Gvl	245	Blalock, Buckner	Edg	142
Josiah	Lrs	44	James	Edg	180
Moll	Edg	187	Jeremiah	Yrk	627
Morris	Mbo	60	John	Bar	49
Saml.	Geo	370	Lewis	Nby	67
Thorogood	Cfd	100	Richard	Bar	49
Urias	Cfd	101	Richard	Edg	180
Zach.	Spa	170	Blamyer, Willm.	Csn	88
Blackwood, James	Spa	179	Blan, William	Abb	16
Jno. Est.	Bft	104	Bland, Frances	Yrk	624
Margeret	Spa	179	Paton	Edg	139
Bladen, Thomas Q.	Csn	173	Richard	Bft	138
Blader, Isaac	Abb	16	William	Wil	474
John	Abb	16	William B.	Edg	151
Luke	Abb	16	Blankenship, Sarah	Yrk	630
Blagg, Caleb	Pen	131	Blankinship, John	Pen	160
Isreal	Pen	123	Blanks, John	Lan	8
James	Pen	159	Blanton, Claburn	Spa	180
Blain, James	Fai	219	Gudson	Edg	168
William	Abb	7	James	Mbo	50
Blair, see also Blare			William	Fai	214
Blair, George	Pen	142	Blare, Alexander	Chr	93
Hugh	Abb	36	James	Chr	73
James	Csn	130	James	Nby	67
James	Yrk	632	James	Nby	67
John	Lan	6	Margret	Chr	89
John	Uni	223	Thomas	Pen	151
John	Yrk	623	Wm.	Chr	89
Thomas	Fai	192	William	Nby	66
Will	Lan	2	Blasingame, James	Gvl	257
William	Csn	123	John	Gvl	263
William	Fai	238	John	Uni	216
William	Pen	148	John	Uni	216
Blake, Danl.	Col	385	John	Uni	217
John	Csn	103	Phillip	Uni	217
John	Csn	114	Thos.	Gvl	262
John	Csn	166	Thos.	Uni	217
John	Csn	173	Thomas	Pen	105
John	Lrs	29	Blayer, James	Pen	118
Joseph	Col	361	Blaylock, Hardin	Ora	537
Josh.	Bft	128	Richard	Ora	537
Robert	Lrs	29	Bleakley, Fields	Uni	238
Robert	Nby	67	Bledsoe, Abraham	Gvl	250
Thomas	Fai	215	Bartlett	Edg	133
Wm.	Bft	94	John	Edg	159
Wm.	Bft	94	John	Pen	107
Wm.	Col	383	Moses	Gvl	247
Blakelock, Harden	Lex	563	William	Gvl	247
Richard	Lex	563	Bleny(?), John	Edg	170
Blakeley, Saml.	Csn	124	Blessit, George	Chr	85

Blewer, John	Csn 60	Solomon	Uni 237
Blitchenden, Abraham	Ora 503	Spencer	Lrs 16
William	Ora 509	Spencer	Spa 194
William, Senr.	Ora 515	Spencer	Spa 194
Blitchington, Lucey	Bft 96	Bocey, Charles	Ker 403
Wm.	Bft 96	Bochet, John	Csn 173
Blitchinton, Abram	Bft 92	Michael	Csn 195
Blocker, James	Edg 139	Bochett, Rebrea(?)	Geo 366
John	Edg 139	Bockman, Samuel	Lex 487
Michall	Edg 162	Bocquet, Elizabeth	Csn 103
Stephen	Col 391	Body, Allen	Edg 157
Bloma, John	Csn 93	Hannah	Edg 171
Bloodworth, Betsey	Uni 234	Nathan	Edg 157
Bloom, John	Bar 66	Bodyford, Alexr.	Mbo 51
Blount, James	Bft 86	Bogan, Isaac	Uni 215
John	Bft 116	John	Uni 219
Lewis	Bft 116	Boggs, Aaron	Pen 116
Mary	Bft 110	David	Chr 77
Blue, John	Mrn 441	Elizabeth	Abb 29
William	Mrn 441	Jane	Yrk 621
William, Senr.	Mrn 454	John	Nby 66
Bluford, Bird	Uni 229	John	Spa 169
Bluitt, James	Csn 195	Mary	Abb 29
Blundel, Absolom	Spa 190	Robert	Abb 4
Blundell, Benjn.	Csn 83	Thomas	Yrk 622
Blunt, Benjamin	Bar 45	Bohannon, John	Lrs 31
Lemuel	Mrn 444	Boilston, George	Ora 511
Thomas	Geo 370	Johanna	Ora 511
Blyth, Joseph	Geo 379	Boineau, Michael	Csn 68
Blythe, Absolum	Pen 110	Stephen	Csn 195
Isabel	Abb 36	Bolan, Nancy	Lex 562
Jacob	Gvl 244	Boland, Robert	Gvl 271
Jonathan	Pen 109	Bold, John	Csn 130
John	Gvl 249	Boldright, Lewis	Mrn 435
Samuel	Csn 68	Thomas	Mrn 436
William	Gvl 249	Bole, Harvey	Abb 33
Wm	Gvl 264	Boles, Isaac	Abb 32
Blyther, William	Mrn 441	James	Pen 149
Boadley, James	Wil 474	William	Abb 33
John	Yrk 621	Boley, Shadrack	Edg 183
Benjamin	Yrk 621	Bolen, John	Bar 60
Boatman, Dinah	Uni 217	Sarah	Bar 67
Jesse	Uni 217	William	Nby 67
Robert	Uni 218	William	Ora 527
Boatner, Jacob	Sum 584	Bolin, Archabald	Pen 140
Jacob	Sum 587	Ebenezer	Pen 108
Boatner(?), Rebecca	Sum 584	James, Junr.	Geo 377
Boatright, C.	Col 391	John	Lex 568
Jacob	Mbo 59	John	Pen 109
Sabrey	Bar 44	William	Pen 113
Boatwright, Lewis	Cfd 100	William	Pen 140
William	Cfd 108	Boling, Able	Lrs 36
Boazman, David	Nby 66	Ellit	Gvl 285
Bobbett, Isham	Spa 178	John	Lrs 35
Bobbs, Elizabeth	Csn 141	Samuel	Lrs 43
Bobbit, Allin	Spa 174	Bollan, Benjamin	Yrk 629
Bobbitt, William	Edg 140	John	Yrk 629
Bobo, Absolum	Lrs 39	Bollen, Edward	Ora 525
Absolom	Uni 237	Bollough(?), Elias	Csn 148
Barram	Uni 235	James	Csn 149
Burrel	Spa 194	John	Csn 149
Kindred	Uni 236	Bolt, Abraham	Lrs 42
Levingston	Spa 194	Elizabeth	Lrs 16
Lewis	Uni 237	Rachel	Lrs 16
Samson	Spa 194	Bolton, George	Mbo 59

James	Mbo	50	Sheilds	Spa	209
James, Jr.	Mbo	59	Bookman, see Baukman		
Joseph	Lrs	40	Bookman, Robert	Lex	574
Matthew	Lrs	40	Booler, Rutherford	Nby	67
Salomon	Ora	551	Boomer, Dorah	Csn	142
Spencer	Ora	551	Boon, Danl.	Pen	139
Thomas	Ora	547	John	Ker	405
Boluler, Christopher	Edg	139	Nathan	Pen	139
Boman, Edward	Spa	202	Ratliff	Pen	140
Jesse	Pen	144	Sarah	Csn	163
Bonam, William	Col	381	William	Edg	147
Bond, Charles	Geo	370	Boone, Archibald	Cfd	108
Elijah	Edg	166	George	Cfd	108
Elisha	Uni	221	George	Lex	575
John	Uni	216	James	Col	367
Robert	Abb	4	James	Geo	382
Wm.	Uni	216	Thomas, Junr.	Geo	370
Bonds, Chapple	Ker	425	Thomas, Senr.	Geo	372
Dudley	Nby	65	Booner, Christian	Csn	138
James	Nby	65	Booth, Benjamin	Csn	95
Luke	Sum	603	James	Edg	148
Mrs.	Bft	138	James	Geo	391
Noah	Nby	67	Joseph	Chr	79
Richard	Chr	83	Stephen	Pen	104
Samuel	Ker	425	Thomas	Edg	154
Seth	Ker	425	Thos.	Geo	391
Solomon	Sum	603	Boothe, Benjn.	Dtn	118
Thomas	Fai	196	Edward	Mbo	51
William	Bar	54	John	Mrn	443
William	Edg	171	Mathew	Mbo	51
Wm.	Gvl	281	Joseph	Cfd	101
Bone, Daniel	Csn	90	Robt.	Mrn	456
George	Lex	489	Samuel	Dtn	115
James	Mbo	59	Booths, James	Edg	148
John	Cfd	108	Booser, Federick	Nby	66
John	Fai	199	Booyze, John	Nby	67
John	Ker	396	Boozman, John	Dtn	125
John	Mbo	51	Boozer, Frederic	Nby	67
John	Ora	539	Henry	Nby	67
Sarah	Ker	423	Jacob	Lex	567
Thomas	Csn	60	Borde, Augustus	Csn	150
Boner, Hugh	Chr	93	Borders, Peter	Gvl	268
Bonetheau, Elizabeth	Csn	83	Boren, James	Pen	112
Bonhom, James	Edg	133	John	Pen	112
Bonneau, Arnoldus	Csn	149	Borer, George	Uni	219
Arnoldus	Csn	175	Borin, Francis	Pen	112
Benjn. Est. of	Csn	149	Matthew	Pen	111
Elisha	Csn	175	Borough, Henry	Lrs	42
Elizabeth	Csn	175	Bourquin, William	Bft	124
Frances	Csn	115	Bosher, Isaac	Nby	66
Peter	Csn	149	Thomas	Sum	606
Bonner, Benjn.	Spa	168	Boseman,		
Brian	Spa	169	see Bozman, Boozman		
David	Fai	208	Boseman, Phil	Edg	174
Demsay	Spa	171	Bosman, Lemuel	Dtn	116
John	Fai	211	Bosner, Lewis	Edg	158
Philip	Bar	65	Bostick, Toliver	Edg	184
William	Fai	198	Bostic, Tristram	Dtn	127
Wm.	Spa	172	Bostick, Levi	Dtn	118
Bonsell, Elizabeth	Csn	145	Tristram	Dtn	118
Bonum, Jas.	Col	379	Wm.	Spa	207
Bonwell, Elenor	Csn	150	Richard	Bft	104
Booker, Bird	Uni	226	Stephen	Abb	39
James	Dtn	115	Bostion, Christopher	Bar	47
Thomas	Spa	208	Boswell, David	Edg	137

Robert, Senr.	Sum 605	Thomas	Lex 491
Robt.	Csn 60	Thomas	Lex 575
Samuel	Sum 604	Thomas	Pen 118
Thos.	Bft 88	Thomas	Pen 138
Bownen, Robert	Uni 250	Thomas	Yrk 632
Bowyer, Peter	Mbo 50	William	Abb 11
Box, Abraham	Lrs 42	William	Abb 40
Benjamin	Lrs 43	William	Bar 60
Edward	Lrs 40	William	Lrs 45
Edward, Junr.	Lrs 38	Wm.	Chr 85
Edward, Senr.	Lrs 38	Boyden, Danl.	Csn 166
Elijah	Lrs 41	Boyer, Jacob	Csn 109
Henry	Lrs 38	Jacob	Pen 104
Henry, Senr.	Lrs 39	Boyers, Matthew	Yrk 621
John	Lrs 43	Boykin, Burwell	Ker 399
Lewis	Col 387	Fanney	Fai 237
Margaret	Lrs 41	Lamuel	Mbo 50
Thomas	Bft 122	Matthew	Mbo 50
Boxton, J. W.	Col 391	Miles	Mbo 50
Boyakin, Drury, Junr.	Sum 611	Boyle, Jame--	Csn 76
Drury, Senr.	Sum 611	Boyles, Chas.	Col 367
Bayanton, Aaron	Bar 69	Danl	Col 367
Boyce,		John	Col 367
see also Buoyse		John	Fai 228
Boyce, Drury	Lrs 43	William	Fai 228
Boyd, Estate of	Wil 470	Boyls, Charles	Bar 63
Boyd, Alexander	Chr 75	John	Bar 46
Alexander	Chr 77	Boys, Robert	Abb 3
Andrew	Fai 231	Boyse, David	Abb 6
Andrew	Lan 2	James	Abb 6
Archer	Nby 67	Hugh	Abb 8
Benjamin	Csn 100	Boyt, Isabella	Geo 383
Benjamin	Bar 51	Bozeman, Agnes	Edg 150
Charles	Chr 93	Bozman, Elemuel	Csn 149
David	Chr 92	Jesse	Dtn 115
David	Nby 65	John	Csn 149
Elizabeth	Pen 113	Peter	Dtn 115
Elizabeth	Uni 227	Brabham, James	Csn 60
James	Lrs 31	Bracey, John	Csn 195
John	Abb 25	Jolly	Csn 126
John	Abb 38	Sach	Sum 587
John	Chr 92	William	Ker 397
John	Lrs 22	William	Sum 587
John (2)	Nby 65	Braceboy, Joshua	Mrn 449
John (2)	Nby 66	Bracker, William	Gvl 244
John	Nby 68	Brackenridge,	Abb 14
John	Fai 231	Elizabeth	
John	Pen 106	James	Abb 15
John	Pen 117	John	Abb 40
John	Uni 227	Brackin, James	Pen 108
John	Yrk 632	John, Junr.	Pen 108
John, Junr.	Pen 107	John, Senr.	Pen 108
John, Sr.	Nby 65	Bracknell, John	Edg 167
John, Senr.	Pen 107	Bradberry, Jemimah	Pen 123
John, Dr.	Sum 601	Bradbury, Thomas	Edg 166
Joseph	Uni 240	Bradcut, Richard	Pen 116
Josiah	Bar 65	Samuel	Pen 116
Reuben	Bar 65	Braden, David	Lrs 40
Richard	Bft 128	Saml.	Pen 149
Robert	Pen 116	Bradford, Charles D.	Fai 194
Nathaniel	Nby 68	Isham	Sum 610
Robert	Nby 68	James	Chr 92
Robert	Fai 209	James	Ker 419
Robt.	Chr 91	James	Yrk 626
Samuel	Bar 59	John	Abb 7

24

John	Gvl 281		Breaken, Sarah	Spa 191
John, Senr.	Gvl 281		Wm.	Spa 191
Lawrence	Gvl 281		Brebner, Archd.	Csn 129
Saml.	Gvl 275		David	Csn 145
Thos.	Gvl 281		Breed, Samuel	Ker 396
Thos., Junr.	Gvl 275		Breedon, James	Mbo 59
Thos., Senr.	Gvl 275		John	Mbo 51
Wm.	Gvl 266		Breeland, Elisha	Bft 118
Brasilton, John	Pen 153		Breeland(?), James	Csn 175
Brassel, John	Gvl 253		Breeland, William	Bft 122
Rachel	Edg 146		Breeler, Abm.	Bft 116
Brassiel, Willis	Edg 162		Absolum	Bft 116
Brassell, Britton	Edg 138		Amos	Bft 116
Braswell, Elizth.	Mrn 440		David	Bft 116
Henry	Mrn 441		Saml.	Bft 116
Bratcher, Benjn.	Spa 177		Bremar, Frances	Csn 145
John	Edg 165		Brenan, Eugene	Edg 144
John	Lrs 17		Joshua	Lex 572
Rachel	Lrs 16		Richard	Csn 78
Samuel	Nby 66		Suckey	Edg 186
William	Lrs 18		Brennan, John	Abb 12
William	Lrs 42		Brenningen, John	Abb 36
Bratton, James	Yrk 618		Brenyan, Henry	Abb 18
Jane	Yrk 623		Breshears, Wm.	Spa 184
John	Yrk 622		Henry	Spa 184
Mary	Yrk 623		Brevard, Joseph	Ker 399
Robert	Yrk 623		Brewer, Benjn.	Gvl 271
Robertson	Fai 210		David	Mrn 438
Thomas	Yrk 622		Jesse	Ora 545
William	Yrk 623		Royal	Ker 427
William, Colol	Yrk 617		Sarah	Sum 604
William, Doctr.	Yrk 626		Will	Lan 10
Braudeway, Alexander	Lrs 40		William	Edg 187
John	Lrs 38		William	Pen 160
William	Lrs 40		Brewton, David	Spa 186
Braudy, Ellenor	Lrs 41		Enoch	Spa 185
Braun, Samuel	Csn 105		George	Spa 186
Braveboy, Saml.	Cfd 101		Jonas	Spa 184
Braver, Dicey	Sum 601		Brial, James A.	Csn 60
Brawley, Thos.	Col 391		Brian, Gustavus	Yrk 632
Braxton, John	Bar 62		James	Yrk 632
Braysher, James	Gvl 264		Jesse	Mrn 452
Samuel	Gvl 281		Rd.	Col 391
Brazeal, Drury	Abb 31		Briant, John	Gvl 267
Elijah	Abb 31		John	Uni 216
Enoch	Abb 32		Lewis	Col 391
Brazeel, Cannon	Pen 160		Margaret	Ora 531
Elijah	Pen 143		Reuben	Spa 171
Joel	Pen 160		Richd.	Gvl 267
Brazelman, Peter	Nby 66		Wm.	Spa 172
Brazil, Vollentine	Nby 66		Brice, Alexr.	Uni 248
William	Lex 573		James	Fai 195
Brazleman, Peter	Lex 571		James	Pen 163
Brazzel, Nancy	Nby 66		Jennet	Spa 209
Brazzell, Jacob	Ker 403		John	Fai 239
William	Ker 403		John	Mrn 455
Breach, Peter Wm.	Csn 195		John	Pen 161
Breadwell, Jacob	Gvl 259		Saml.	Spa 168
Miley	Gvl 260		Thomas	Spa 168

William	Fai	238	Brisbane, John T.	Col	367
William	Pen	161	Mary	Ker	396
Brickell, Jas	Csn	68	William	Col	367
Bridge, Adam	Col	387	Briskey, Nicholas	Edg	169
Bridges, Abighail	Yrk	629	Brison, William	Edg	158
Benjamin	Gvl	246	Bristol, John	Mbo	59
Benjn.	Mbo	60	Bristor, Thomson	Gvl	270
Charles	Nby	66	Warrick	Gvl	270
Francis	Mbo	51	Britnal, James	Fai	222
James	Yrk	628	Joseph	Fai	221
John	Edg	132	Brit, Charles	Abb	30
John	Lex	565	John	Edg	179
John	Mbo	51	Brite, Caleb	Gvl	283
John	Nby	66	Britt, Amos	Spa	188
John	Spa	170	Heu	Edg	184
Joseph	Edg	159	James	Geo	373
Lydia	Yrk	628	John	Sum	611
Margaret	Lex	578	Phillip	Geo	373
Thomas	Yrk	628	Richard	Cfd	101
Thos.	Gvl	285	Thomas	Geo	365
William	Mbo	50	Brittin, Wm.	Spa	196
William	Yrk	628	Britton, Benja.	Geo	370
Wm.	Spa	175	Francis	Mbo	51
Bridie, Eleonere	Csn	121	Henry	Geo	373
Brient, Phillip	Uni	215	John G.	Mbo	51
Briggs, Elizabeth	Lrs	27	Moses	Mrn	460
James	Lrs	27	Steven	Mrn	435
John	Fai	196	Timothy	Mrn	460
John	Lrs	27	Wm.	Chr	87
Bright, Abraham	Bft	122	Broach, Abner	Dtn	116
Charles	Mbo	51	Broad, George Wm.	Csn	195
Ezekiel	Ora	501	Broadaway,		
James	Spa	199	see also Braudeway		
Jacob	Lex	568	Broadaway, Thomas	Sum	603
Iseiah	Spa	181	Broadfoot, ---	Csn	130
Jacob	Spa	181	Broadwater, Charles	Edg	163
Jacob	Lex	493	Scarborough	Edg	142
James	Spa	181	Broadway, John	Edg	181
Tobias	Spa	199	Brock, Charles	Uni	249
Brightman, Thomas	Abb	22	Christopher	Fai	218
William	Abb	22	David	Gvl	245
Brightwell, William	Edg	159	David	Uni	239
Brigman, Elizabeth	Mbo	51	Evins	Uni	248
Isaac	Mrn	451	Federick	Gvl	245
John	Mbo	51	George	Lrs	45
John, Jr.	Mbo	61	George	Yrk	630
Lewis	Mbo	61	James	Abb	3
Thos.	Csn	60	James	Cfd	101
Brigs, Henry	Edg	160	James	Edg	145
Brimer, Benjamin	Pen	147	James	Gvl	249
Briningham, Thos.	Gvl	264	James	Pen	143
Brinley, Jno George	Csn	175	Henry	Pen	145
Brinson, John	Geo	383	Isaac	Pen	143
John	Sum	603	Loyd	Pen	145
Matthew	Geo	376	Lucy	Sum	601
William	Geo	383	Matthew	Pen	106
Brinter, Jean	Sum	605	Majr.	Pen	162
Brisbane,			Reubin	Pen	145
see also Braisbane			Susanna	Cfd	109

27

Valentine	Cfd 101	William	Nby 65
Thomas	Abb 2	William	Pen 129
William	Pen 143	Zachy S.	Edg 137
Wm.	Uni 238	Brooksheir, Swift	Spa 198
Brockett, William	Yrk 619	Brookshier, John	Spa 174
Brockington, John	Wil 470	Broom, James	Lex 569
Brockinton, Richard	Dtn 115	Joel	Ora 511
William	Dtn 115	John	Fai 210
Brockington, Zerel	Sum 589	Luke	Yrk 630
Brockman, Henry	Gvl 278	Mathew	Fai 236
John	Lrs 20	Thomas	Edg 154
Brockway, Samuel	Csn 145	William	Fai 194
Brodie, Robert	Csn 122	Broomberry, Peter	Gvl 267
Thomas	Csn 89	Brooner, Michael	Edg 154
Brodgen, Joseph	Sum 604	Brosier, Andrew	Edg 141
Brodut, Francis	Geo 365	Bross, John	Csn 149
Brodway, Drury	Edg 182	Brotherer, John	Col 361
Brogdon, James	Cfd 101	Thos.	Col 361
John	Sum 605	Brothers, Cloe	Spa 169
Rachel	Mbo 60	Broughton, Alexr. Est	Csn 68
Broiske, Sarah	Csn 134	Ann	Col 367
Bron, John Peter	Csn 105	Ann	Csn 120
Bronddon, Meredith	Pen 138	Edward	Sum 584
Bronson, Daniel	Spa 191	Mary	Csn 68
Brook, James	Nby 66	Peter	Csn 68
Brooker, Joseph	Bar 55	Richd.	Bft 128
Unity	Bar 47	Thomas	Csn 68
William	Bar 55	Thomas	Edg 138
Brooks, Agnes	Nby 66	Willoughby	Pen 118
Archa	Gvl 284	Brouster, Hugh	Pen 157
Bartlet	Lrs 28	John	Pen 129
Charles	Edg 143	Samuel	Pen 156
Christopher	Abb 38	Sheriff	Pen 133
Daniel	Nby 68	Broward, John B.	Geo 375
Dudley	Edg 137	Browder, Arthur	Wil 475
Elisha	Nby 66	Browen, John	Col 367
Elizabeth	Cfd 100	Sarah	Csn 60
George	Gvl 274	Thos.	Col 361
George	Pen 151	Brower, Jeremiah	Csn 92
Edward	Edg 157	Brown, ---	Edg 148
Joab	Lrs 46	Brown, --ames	Edg 147
Job	Pen 122	Brown, --hua	Edg 147
John	Abb 20	Brown, Abner	Pen 114
John	Cfd 100	Alexander	Chr 81
John	Edg 170	Alexr	Pen 120
John	Edg 182	Alexr	Uni 233
John	Geo 370	Alphes	Dtn 118
John	Lex 565	Alpheus	Dtn 127
John	Nby 67	Ambrose	Pen 159
Jordan	Edg 163	Andrew	Abb 28
Moses	Edg 181	Andrew	Edg 181
Moses	Spa 208	Andrew	Pen 142
Peter	Uni 250	Ann	Chr 90
Richard	Nby 67	Ann	Csn 151
Robert	Edg 141	Ann	Sum 587
Robert	Edg 167	Archibald	Ora 503
Robert	Edg 168	Archibald	Yrk 617
Robert	Edg 178	Aris	Spa 208
Samuel	Edg 157	Barnaby	Pen 156
Sarah	Nby 68	Barnett	Geo 379
Simon	Edg 182	Bartlett	Bar 46
Thomas	Nby 67	Benjamin	Abb 36
Thomas	Spa 208	Benjamin Dtn 118,	Dtn 126
Thomas	Uni 216	Benjamin	Lrs 20

Burwell	Sum 593	James	Spa 171
Charles	Csn 86	James	Wil 463
Charles	Geo 373	James	Wil 465
Charles	Nby 65	Jeremiah	Mrn 455
Charles	Yrk 617	Jeremiah	Sum 593
Clabourn	Lrs 30	Jesse	Mbo 51
Clement Cles.	Csn 149	Jesse	Ora 519
Daniel	Cfd 101	Jesse	Pen 131
Danl.	Csn 129	Jesse	Spa 187
Daniel	Ker 399	Jesse	Sum 610
Danl. Capt.	Csn 127	Joel	Edg 182
David	Abb 7	Joel	Edg 185
Danl.	Csn 119	John	Abb 19
David	Bar 55	John	Bft 112
David	Lrs 35	John	Cfd 110
David	Pen 159	John	Chr 73
David	Spa 173	John	Chr 95
Duncan	Cfd 101	John	Csn 60
Edmond	Mbo 51	John	Csn 88
Edward	Uni 249	John	Csn 109
Edward	Mrn 436	John	Csn 149
Eli	Chr 73	John	Csn 149
Elish	Edg 153	John	Dtn 123
Elizth.	Mrn 457	John	Fai 196
Elizabeth	Sum 593	John	Fai 202
Elizabeth	Sum 611	John	Geo 375
Ezekial	Uni 218	John	Ker 415
Francis	Gvl 270	John	Lan 8
George	Chr 77	John	Lrs 15
George	Lrs 29	John	Lrs 27
George	Nby 66	John	Lrs 31
Godfrey	Sum 593	John	Mrn 457
Griffin	Pen 137	John	Pen 103
Hamilton	Chr 84	John	Pen 123
Heriot	Csn 113	John	Pen 124
Howell	Wil 473	John	Pen 146
Hugh	Chr 82	John	Pen 152
Hugh	Pen 142	John	Sum 591
Isaac	Spa 173	John	Sum 612
Jacob	Nby 68	John	Uni 248
Jacob R.	Nby 67	John	Wil 469
Jame(?)	Fai 214	John	Wil 463
James	Bar 62	John	Yrk 622
James	Bar 68	John H.	Cfd 100
James	Chr 74	John, Jr.	Dtn 123
James	Chr 82	Joseph	Abb 32
James	Csn 84	Joseph	Abb 37
James	Csn 187	Joseph	Cfd 100
James	Dtn 114	Jo[seph]	Chr 88
James	Dtn 118	Joseph	Chr 89
James	Dtn 126	Joseph	Edg 183
James	Dtn 127	Joseph	Ora 517
James	Edg 142	Joseph	Pen 121
James	Fai 198	Joseph	Pen 137
James	Geo 375	Joseph	Sum 595
James	Gvl 271	Joseph	Sum 597
James	Gvl 274	Joshua	Csn 100
James	Ker 397	Joshua	Fai 216
James	Ker 413	Joshua	Fai 240
James	Lrs 16	Joshua	Mrn 457
James	Lrs 23	Joshua	Pen 136
James	Nby 65	Judah	Ker 411
James (2)	Nby 66	Kader	Wil 469
James	Ora 519	Lami	Dtn 116
James	Pen 110	Larkin	Edg 184

29

Larkin	Pen 125	Thomas	Chr 91
Lewis	Cfd 100	Thomas	Dtn 128
Mariah	Csn 132	Thos.	Gvl 262
Margaret	Yrk 617	Thomas	Lrs 27
Margret	Abb 32	Thomas	Mrn 457
Mary	Csn 90	Thomas	Nby 66
Matthew	Lrs 28	Thomas	Pen 103
Moses	Sum 613	Thomas	Pen 123
Nathan	Nby 65	Thomas	Pen 125
Patience	Mrn 457	Thomas	Pen 145
Peter	Abb 33	Thomas	Pen 160
Peter	Ora 547	Thomas	Spa 171
Phadias	Dtn 121	Uriah	Sum 591
Phadias, Jr.	Dtn 121	Vincent	Lrs 15
Philip	Ker 413	Walter	Chr 79
Phillip	Sum 613	Walter	Lan 2
Pollard	Abb 34	William	Abb 5
Randolph	Pen 131	William	Abb 7
Rebecca	Ker 399	William	Abb 20
Reuben	Ker 423	William	Bar 43
Richd.	Mrn 458	William	Cfd 101
Richard	Yrk 625	Willm	Csn 86
Robert	Bar 67	William	Dtn 119
Robert	Chr 78	William	Edg 178
Robert	Chr 94	William	Fai 194
Robert	Dtn 123	Wm.	Gvl 260
Robert	Dtn 128	Wm.	Gvl 271
Robert	Ker 411	William	Ker 413
Robert	Lrs 30	William	Lrs 14
Robert	Nby 65	William	Lrs 19
Robert	Pen 159	William	Lrs 20
Robert	Sum 591	William	Lrs 21
Robert	Sum 605	William	Nby 65
Robert	Sum 609	William	Nby 66
Robert Esqr.	Lrs 27	William	Nby 67
Robt.	Col 385	William	Nby 67
Rob. John	Lan 8	William	Pen 114
Rody	Sum 613	William	Pen 155
Ross	Lrs 20	William	Sum 591
Sally	Lrs 19	William	Sum 595
Samuel	Abb 36	William	Sum 597
Saml	Geo 375	William	Yrk 620
Samuel	Gvl 274	William	Yrk 629
Samuel	Lrs 19	William, Junr.	Sum 591
Samuel	Mbo 51	Willy S.	Gvl 256
Samuel	Nby 65	Winn	Nby 66
Samuel	Ora 533	Zachariah	Mrn 437
Saml	Pen 137	Browne(?), Alexander	Edg 153
Samuel	Pen 137	Browne, Jesse	Pen 144
Samuel	Pen 143	Joseph	Pen 159
Samuel	Pen 160	William	Pen 145
Samuel	Yrk 617	Brownen, Chas.	Uni 218
Sarah	Ker 427	James	Uni 217
Serah	Ora 529	Thomas	Uni 218
Shad.	Mrn 436	Wm.	Uni 217
Shedrick	Abb 12	Brownfield, Robt.	Geo 367
Sims	Nby 65	Browning, Gideon	Col 363
Sinah	Sum 585	John	Csn 60
Solomon	Mrn 439	John	Ora 505
Spencer	Lrs 14	John	Spa 196
Stewart	Chr 90	P.	Csn 60
Susannah	Pen 137	Brownlee, James	Abb 9
Tarlton	Bar 57	John	Col 363
Thomas	Bar 61	John	Csn 102
Thomas	Cfd 100	Joseph	Lrs 36

William	Abb 12	Bruster, James	Lan 7
Brownlow, John	Pen 114	Bruton, Benj.	Geo 375
Broyles, Aaron	Pen 143	George	Ora 513
Joshua	Pen 146	Isaac	Spa 185
Bruard(?), John	Lan 3	Phillip	Spa 185
Bruce, Benjn.	Gvl 259	Saml.	Geo 375
Benjamin	Mrn 455	Bryan, Fedrick	Bar 46
Charles	Gvl 257	James	Abb 27
Charles	Pen 141	John	Csn 149
George	Pen 115	Joseph	Bar 46
James	Edg 140	Simon	Bar 46
James	Edg 183	William	Bar 46
James	Gvl 246	William	Bar 54
James	Gvl 254	William	Edg 165
James	Pen 115	Bryant, Ambrose	Ker 423
Jeremiah	Gvl 259	Aron	Pen 161
John	Dtn 114	Berry	Pen 111
John	Dtn 127	Burrell	Bft 112
John	Ora 519	Darby	Ora 531
John	Pen 141	Edward	Fai 192
Margaret	Ora 539	Frances	Dtn 126
William	Pen 109	Hardy	Dtn 115
Bruckner, Daniel	Csn 151	Hardy	Pen 120
Brumfield, Charles	Yrk 618	James	Bft 118
John, Junr.	Yrk 618	James	Fai 213
John, Senr.	Yrk 618	James	Pen 108
Brumley, James	Abb 26	James	Pen 111
Thomas	Sum 589	John	Bar 59
William	Abb 26	John	Csn 106
Brummit, James	Pen 117	John	Fai 224
Brummitt, Daniel	Uni 229	John	Lrs 40
Thos.	Gvl 250	John	Pen 120
Bruner, George	Ora 549	Kitty	Pen 117
Brunett, Joseph	Csn 138	Mary	Fai 192
Brunson,	Ora 509	Nancy	Dtn 122
Abraham, Junr.		Nancy	Gvl 267
Abraham, Senr.	Ora 509	Neadham	Pen 161
Charles, Jur.	Sum 601	Richard	Ker 411
Charles, Senr.	Sum 604	Richard	Ker 423
Daniel	Edg 167	Thomas	Bft 110
Daniel	Sum 600	Thomas	Cfd 110
David	Sum 604	William	Bft 110
George	Bft 110	William	Edg 181
George	Sum 600	Wm.	Dtn 115
Isaac	Edg 142	William	Fai 214
Isaac	Sum 584	William	Fai 220
James	Bft 110	Will.	Lan 7
James, Senr.	Bft 110	William	Ora 527
John	Csn 106	Wm.	Uni 216
John	Sum 606	Brymer, Joseph	Pen 144
Joseph	Edg 167	Brysan, Robert	Fai 193
Joseph	Ora 515	Bryson, Danl.	Pen 147
Josiah	Sum 603	John	Lrs 32
Peter	Bft 110	John	Pen 149
William	Ker 397	Leslie	Sum 606
William, Jur.	Sum 603	Robert	Fai 231
William, Senr.	Sum 603	William	Lrs 21
William Santee	Sum 605	William	Lrs 31
Brunston, Jacob	Bar 64	Buchanan,	
John	Bar 55	see also Buckhannon	
Mathew	Dtn 117	Buchanan, James	Nby 65
Mathew	Dtn 123	Jno	Fai 213
Brunt, Alexander	Fai 236	Samuel	Yrk 625
Mary	Fai 233	Buchannan, Benjn(?)	Cfd 101
Brussels, John	Chr 78	Mary	Ker 397

Thomas	Yrk 632	Buist, Geo., Revd.	Csn 123
Buchannon, Jacob	Csn 153	Bulen, Catharine	Csn 150
John	Csn 127	Bulgin, James	Csn 122
Buckaloo, George	Edg 163	Jno C.	Csn 149
James	Edg 159	Bull, Elvia	Col 393
John	Edg 163	Hannah	Csn 166
Buckanan, Creighton	Fai 209	John	Bft 86
Elizabeth	Geo 373	Jno	Bft 134
Buckannon, Alexander	Pen 150	Mrs.	Bft 86
Benjamin	Pen 150	Wm. Est.	Csn 166
Ebinezer	Pen 151	Wm. R.	Bft 104
John	Pen 151	Bullard, Gade	Mbo 59
John (2)	Pen 151	George	Cfd 100
Thomas	Pen 150	Joel	Cfd 107
William	Pen 150	John	Ker 419
Buckel, Margaret	Csn 115	John	Uni 226
Buckels, Richard	Lan 3	John	Uni 228
Buckett, Nazra	Sum 593	Jonathon	Gvl 285
William	Sum 593	Milley	Mbo 51
Buckley, Edward	Bar 59	Robt.	Mrn 442
James	Bar 59	Bullentin, John	Uni 224
Buckhalter, Abraham	Edg 159	Buller, Joseph	Csn 142
David	Edg 149	Bullion, Wm.	Gvl 283
Henry	Edg 141	Bullis, John	Lrs 41
Jeremiah	Edg 165	Bullock, Daniel	Edg 138
John	Edg 139	Daniel	Edg 139
Mary	Edg 162	James	Edg 174
Michael	Edg 141	John	Edg 174
Wm.	Edg 141	Mary	Edg 174
Buckhannan, James	Spa 197	Richard	Edg 175
Buckhannon, Benjamin	Nby 67	Richard	Lan 10
George	Nby 67	Richard	Pen 125
George	Nby 67	Bulman, George	Spa 205
Henry	Abb 33	Bulow, John	Csn 99
James	Abb 21	Bumburge, John G.	Bar 68
James	Nby 67	Bumpas, Gabriel	Spa 183
John	Edg 141	Robert	Lrs 41
Robert	Abb 7	Bumpass, James	Lrs 13
William	Abb 22	Bunch, Andw.	Csn 60
Wm.	Uni 223	Danl.	Csn 60
Buckhanon, Micajah	Nby 67	Gabriel	Yrk 629
Buckholt, Willm.	Mrn 444	Gideon	Csn 61
Buckholts, Jacob	Dtn 115	Henry	Nby 66
Buckle, George	Csn 81	Jacob	Csn 60
Buckner, David	Pen 117	James	Csn 60
Henry	Lrs 45	John	Csn 60
Budd, Abigail	Geo 365	Joseph	Fai 202
Rosanna	Csn 151	Lovit	Bar 63
Budden, Saml.	Wil 475	Mary	Csn 60
Solomon	Geo 370	Paul	Uni 241
Buddin, Jean	Sum 603	Selah	Csn 60
Buely, Jacob	Csn 99	Stephen	Bft 90
Buffington, Jacob	Yrk 623	Bundrick, Charles	Nby 67
John	Edg 181	John	Nby 67
Jonathon	Abb 34	Bunkley, Mary	Ker 401
Joseph	Edg 180	Bunn, Joham	Mrn 437
Richard	Edg 181	William	Mrn 439
Buffinton, Ezekiel	Pen 138	Bunt, John	Ker 396
Obern	Pen 138	Buntin, Benjamin	Edg 174
Buffking, Ben---	Geo 388	Bunton, William	Csn 114
John	Geo 388	Buoys, Alexander	Chr 77
Josiah	Geo 388	Buoyse, Alexander	Pen 104
Buford, Elizabeth	Csn 129	Burd(?), John	Geo 365
William	Wil 476	Burdeaux, Nathn.	Csn 60
Bug, Nicholas H.	Bar 64	Burdell, Robert	Csn 68

Burden, Isaac	Spa 199		John	Pen 125
Kensey	Csn 123		John	Pen 125
Portia	Col 367		Burke, Benjamin	Fai 217
Thomas	Nby 67		Joseph	Fai 216
Thomas	Uni 232		Judge E.	Csn 123
Burdeshaw, Peter	Abb 32		Randolf	Pen 125
Burdiet, Frederick	Lrs 15		Walter	Csn 91
John	Lrs 15		William	Dtn 120
Burdine, Henry	Pen 160		Burkes, Samuel	Pen 142
Jeremiah	Lrs 25		Burket, Abraham	Chr 86
John	Pen 107		Ann	Mrn 442
Nathaniel	Abb 25		Josiah	Mrn 457
Richard	Pen 107		Uriah	Mrn 457
Samuel	Pen 107		Cloe	Bft 92
Burdock, William	Edg 174		Burkett, Laml.	Mbo 51
Burell, John	Nby 67		Thomas	Mbo 51
Burbridge, Ricd.	Csn 60		Burkhalt, Jacob	Mrn 443
Thos.	Csn 60		Burkirk, Thomas	Sum 584
Burch, Henrey T.	Csn 130		Burkit, Joseph	Pen 122
Henry	Pen 140		Burks, Isham	Spa 181
Burch(?), John	Geo 365		Sarah	Lrs 14
Burch, Joseph	Mrn 450		Burlew, Moses	Bar 60
Burcher, E.	Csn 191		Burlow, Thomas	Edg 158
Burchfield, Adam	Pen 124		Burn, Elizabeth	Edg 186
James	Lrs 19		James	Csn 175
John	Pen 152		John	Gvl 262
Joseph	Pen 117		Burnell, Craddock	Edg 153
Thomas	Lrs 19		Burnes, James	Csn 127
Burckmyer, John	Csn 104		John	Gvl 274
Burford, Thomas	Pen 158		Larret	Gvl 274
Burg, Henry	Lan 7		Mary	Gvl 274
Burge, John	Ker 411		Burness, James	Csn 175
Jeremiah	Fai 221		Burnet, A.	Col 393
Richard	Fai 221		Anney	Abb 25
Burger, David	Csn 153		William	Abb 35
Burges, Edward	Csn 110		Burnett, Hezekiah	Edg 133
Elizabeth	Ker 403		James	Spa 178
James	Csn 151		John	Spa 177
James	Pen 128		Leonard	Spa 177
John	Ker 409		Luke	Spa 178
John	Uni 234		Stephen	Lrs 45
Joseph	Edg 176		Thomas	Edg 151
Richd.	Uni 236		Thomas, Senr.	Csn 104
Thomas	Spa 175		Winslow	Bft 137
William	Nby 66		Burney, Adam	Abb 8
Burgh, Henry	Ker 405		William	Pen 119
Burgess, Elijah	Lrs 38		Burns, Alexr.	Edg 164
James	Wil 463		Alexr.	Fai 233
Joel, Junr.	Lrs 36		Alexander	Pen 114
Joel, Senr.	Lrs 35		Anne	Yrk 624
John	Csn 189		Benjn.	Uni 233
John, Junr.	Sum 607		Charles	Gvl 266
John, Senr.	Sum 609		Creasay	Edg 175
Joseph	Sum 607		David	Edg 142
Josiah	Dtn 120		David	Edg 188
Burgin, Susanna	Csn 74		David	Lrs 23
Burgis, Mathew	Gvl 276		Dennis	Ker 399
William	Nby 66		Edmond	Lrs 14
Burgomaster, Christr.	Bft 108		George	Edg 175
Buril, Edward	Mrn 456		Han.	Lrs 28
Burk, Charles	Pen 125		James	Fai 227
David	Pen 108		James	Lrs 29
James	Bar 56		James	Spa 208
James	Lrs 27		Jeremiah	Edg 164
John	Gvl 257		Jeremiah	Lrs 24

John	Bft 126	Edward	Edg 135
John	Bft 128	Francis	Edg 144
John	Csn 94	Isaac	Bar 53
John	Edg 164	John	Bar 48
John	Ker 399	John	Edg 136
John	Lrs 14	Moody	Edg 137
John	Lrs 35	Philip	Edg 137
John	Pen 131	William	Bar 48
John, Junr.	Gvl 262	William	Edg 139
Lacklin	Yrk 620	Burtch, Michael	Sum 605
Lawrence	Ker 411	Burtchmore, William	Sum 602
Leeroy	Spa 181	Burton,	
Michael	Csn 119	see also Berton	
Panney	Edg 175	Burton, Allen	Abb 39
Robert	Lrs 25	Babester	Pen 150
Robert, Senr.	Lrs 24	Benjamin	Abb 39
Saml.	Spa 181	Charles	Nby 66
Samuel	Yrk 625	Charles	Spa 199
Tarrence	Lrs 25	Cutburt	Spa 199
Thomas	Fai 196	David	Spa 182
William	Csn 183	Francis	Mrn 452
William	Fai 212	George	Pen 128
William	Pen 114	Hutchins	Lrs 36
William	Yrk 619	James	Nby 68
William	Yrk 625	John	Abb 38
Burr, Nathaniel	Csn 82	John	Bft 137
Burrel, Hezekiah	Spa 200	John	Pen 145
Walter	Spa 200	Joseph	Abb 39
Burrell, Jesse	Pen 147	Josiah	Abb 16
Thomas	Lrs 26	Nat	Spa 198
Walter	Gvl 253	Robert	Edg 132
Burress, Joshua	Pen 147	Robert	Lrs 19
Thomas	Pen 147	Samuel	Pen 128
Burret, Joseph	Edg 162	Thomas	Lrs 37
Burris, see also Baris,		Thomas	Spa 202
Burrows, Burroughs,		Thomas, Senr.	Lrs 44
Burress		William	Edg 174
Burriss, Anthony	Pen 141	William	Nby 67
Edward	Pen 134	William	Pen 128
Burris, John	Edg 139	Wm.	Spa 204
John	Pen 134	Burtz, Fredrick	Lrs 37
Burrow, Green	Uni 242	Busbee, Benjamin	Lex 489
Wm.	Spa 191	Benjn.	Ora 529
Wm.	Spa 210	John	Lex 489
Burrows, A. slave of	Wil 473	Keziah	Lex 489
Elizth.	Wil 472	Nathan	Lex 493
Frederick	Csn 92	Needham	Lex 487
George	Wil 472	Sherard	Lex 489
George, Sr.	Wil 473	Busbie, Benjamin	Lex 577
George W.	Csn 88	Drusilla	Lex 575
Jane	Dtn 117	Elisha	Lex 578
Joseph	Wil 463	Frederick	Lex 578
Joseph	Wil 472	Ferryby	Lex 578
Robert	Yrk 617	John	Lex 575
Samuel	Dtn 126	Micajah	Lex 574
Willm.	Csn 130	Nathan	Lex 568
William	Yrk 617	Nathaniel	Lex 574
Bursh, Jacob	Lex 568	Needham	Lex 574
John	Lex 568	Robert	Lex 574
Burnsides,	Lrs 36	Sherrod	Lex 574
Andrew Capt.		Busby, Jacob	Nby 66
James	Lrs 32	Jeremiah	Nby 65
John	Edg 154	John	Bar 62
William, Capt.	Lrs 31	Mark	Fai 236
Burt, Armstead	Edg 135	Miles	Edg 156

Sion	Fai 206	James	Fai 204
Sion	Pen 140	John	Csn 166
Stephen	Abb 21	John	Edg 154
Thomas	Nby 66	John	Nby 67
Zachariah	Edg 157	John	Edg 149
Busey, Benjn.	Spa 187	John A.	Gvl 256
Saml.	Spa 187	Joseph	Csn 166
Bussey, Dempsey	Edg 160	Joseph	Edg 153
George	Edg 160	Josiah	Edg 151
Joshua	Edg 171	Kader	Wil 472
Zadock	Edg 160	Malechiah	Lrs 17
Bush, Bibby	Edg 135	Moses	Lrs 28
Daniel	Edg 168	Rueben	Nby 67
Edward	Bar 59	Robert	Edg 187
Isaac	Bar 59	Sampson(?)	Edg 187
Isaac	Csn 183	Seamon	Fai 220
John	Bar 61	Thomas	Bft 100
John	Bar 65	Thomas	Edg 133
John	Edg 141	Thomas	Gvl 277
Bush(?), John	Edg 145	William	Abb 5
Bush, Jacob	Lex 493	William	Edg 132
John, Junr.	Bar 65	William	Gvl 276
Prescot	Edg 140	William	Mrn 441
Providence	Csn 183	William	Pen 144
Richard	Edg 136	Willis	Gvl 279
Richard	Edg 141	Butt, John	Pen 126
William	Edg 145	Thomas	Edg 136
William	Pen 111	Butterton, Joseph	Csn 96
Bushall, Thomas	Csn 166	Butterworth, Stephen	Gvl 267
Bushart, David	Fai 196	Buzard, Henery, Senr.	Ora 551
Randolph	Fai 207	Henery, Junr.	Ora 551
Busholong, James	Abb 3	Jacot	Ora 553
John	Abb 3	Buzbay, Micajah	Spa 180
Butchers, John	Col 361	Buzby, Isaac	Nby 67
Butler, ___	Geo 379	John	Nby 67
Butner, --mes, Junr.	Edg 149	Jacob	Pen 162
Butler, Aron	Mrn 440	Molly	Bft 104
Aaron, Junr.	Mrn 440	Buzzard, Elizabeth	Nby 66
Abnor S.	Gvl 262	Jacob	Nby 66
Agron	Nby 67	Philip	Nby 66
Anderson	Gvl 256	Byas, James	Spa 168
Andrew	Edg 153	James	Spa 170
Anthony	Edg 140	Joseph	Spa 170
Anthony	Sum 584	Nathan	Spa 170
Benjamin	Abb 21	Thomas	Spa 170
Benjamin	Gvl 279	Wm.	Spa 171
Benjamin	Nby 66	Byce, Elijah	Spa 206
Benjamin	Nby 66	Elisha	Spa 206
C. P.	Csn 137	Enoch	Spa 203
Chas.	Col 383	John	Spa 169
Butler(?), Chas.	Col 383	Jonathan	Spa 206
Butler, Chaziah	Sum 611	Byden, Daniel	Csn 191
Daniel	Nby 66	Byerly, Gasper	Fai 234
Elisha	Mrn 441	Byers, David	Yrk 625
Elizabeth	Fai 201	David	Yrk 625
Enoch	Fai 220	Edward	Yrk 625
Ephraim	Fai 220	Robert	Csn 93
Evin	Edg 167	William	Yrk 626
Henry	Nby 67	William, Senr.	Yrk 625
Isham	Mrn 440	Williamson	Yrk 625
Jacob	Nby 67	Byke, Peter	Csn 125
James	Csn 175	Bynum, Isaac	Pen 116
James	Dtn 113	Jesse	Pen 117
James	Dtn 119	Jessey	Abb 3
James	Edg 136	John	Lex 571

35

Byram, John	Lrs 45		Henry	Csn 183
Henry	Lrs 38		Moses	Ker 407
Byrd, Benjamin	Lrs 21		Peter	Mrn 452
Elizabeth	Ora 505		Samuel	Lrs 44
John	Ker 409		Caldwell, Andw.	Abb 35
Nancy	Ora 523		Charles	Abb 5
Nathaniel	Ora 545		David	Ker 419
Natl.	Ora 543		David	Abb 36
William	Lrs 27		David	Lan 7
William	Ora 503		David	Lrs 33
Byrnes, Joseph	Csn 95		David	Lrs 40
Patrick	Csn 90		David	Pen 158
Byrum, Jesse	Lrs 39		George	Fai 197
Byter, Moses	Lrs 15		Henry	Abb 5
Bythewood, Danl.	Csn 85		Henry, Jr.	Csn 126
Thos.	Csn 85		Henrey, Senr.	Csn 129
			James	Abb 10
			James	Abb 34
C			James	Fai 196
			James(2)	Uni 232
			John	Abb 21
Caaps(?), William	Gvl 252		John	Chr 76
Caborne, George	Csn 166		John	Csn 142
Cabos, John	Csn 125		John	Lrs 31
Cabourne, Robert	Bft 102		John	Nby 68
Caddell, Thomas	Pen 118		Joseph	Nby 68
Cade, Stephen	Mbo 52		Joseph	Nby 69
Cadwell, James	Pen 136		Robert	Pen 162
John	Pen 157		Samuel	Csn 108
Caff, Ned S.	Wil 472		Samuel	Fai 197
Caffery, Burnet	Edg 139		William	Abb 35
Cage, Nathaniel	Chr 94		William	Fai 209
Cahusac, John	Csn 195		William	Nby 69
Cail, John	Bft 124		Calem, Job	Csn 68
Cain, Abijah	Lrs 24		Cales, William	Geo 371
Abner	Uni 233		Caley, William	Fai 230
Alexander	Uni 224		Calfrey, Lewis	Bft 104
Archibald	Sum 584		Calhoon, James G.	Wil 470
Barbery	Lrs 24		John	Lrs 44
Harrold	Uni 234		Calhoun, Alexander	Nby 70
Hugh	Yrk 626		Andrew	Abb 24
James	Ker 405		Ezekiel	Abb 33
John	Lrs 24		Henry	Csn 118
John	Yrk 626		Hugh	Abb 12
John	Yrk 628		James	Abb 10
Mary	Dtn 123		James	Csn 85
Michal	Abb 36		John	Abb 22
Patrick	Abb 34		John E.	Csn 68
Paul	Col 369		John E.	Pen 121
Saml.	Col 369		Joseph	Abb 11
Samuel	Yrk 624		Martha	Abb 10
Snoden	Gvl 258		William	Abb 22
Thomas	Csn 81		William	Abb 34
William	Abb 32		William	Csn 115
William	Sum 584		William, Junr.	Abb 10
Cains, Elizabeth	Csn 195		William, Senr.	Abb 2
Caits, John	Lex 561		Calk, James	Edg 177
Calabuff, Isaac	Csn 149		John	Lex 579
Calahan, Josiah	Gvl 247		Call, James	Lex 497
Margaret	Lrs 23		Callaghan, John	Csn 132
Morris	Edg 167		Morris	Edg 187
William	Gvl 244		Morris	Lex 577
Calcut, James	Mrn 445		Callaway, Francis	Pen 129
James	Wil 463		Joseph	Gvl 253
Calder, Archibald	Csn 183		William	Gvl 254

Daniel	Spa	176	Cornelius	Lrs	39	
Isaac	Spa	176	John, Senr.	Lrs	37	
Isaac	Spa	176	John Allen	Lrs	25	
James	Pen	115	Magnes	Mbo	52	
James	Spa	176	Thomas	Lrs	37	
John	Spa	175	Carley, Joseph	Yrk	621	
John	Spa	176	Carlile, John	Bar	56	
John	Spa	176	John	Geo	379	
John	Spa	181	William	Bar	48	
John	Spa	190	William	Geo	380	
Joseph	Pen	115	Carlin, John, Junr.	Gvl	249	
Moses	Spa	176	John, Senr.	Gvl	249	
Reuben	Spa	176	Carlisle, Benjamin	Bar	47	
Richd. (2)	Spa	176	Colman	Uni	229	
Stephen	Pen	115	Francis	Abb	9	
Thomas	Pen	107	Phebe	Mbo	60	
Cantwell, Adam	Gvl	249	Richard	Mbo	60	
John	Gvl	249	Carloss, Robert	Mbo	52	
John, Senr.	Gvl	285	Carlton, Joseph	Pen	112	
John	Spa	206	Carmachel, Arther	Nby	72	
Peter	Gvl	252	Carmackel, Patrick	Nby	70	
Sarah	Gvl	246	Carmand, Peter	Csn	148	
Thos.	Gvl	250	Carmical, Elenor	Abb	3	
Woody	Pen	123	Joseph	Abb	3	
Canty, ---	Ker	405	Robert	Abb	3	
Cantzon, Moses	Lan	2	Carmichael, Danl.	Mrn	448	
Canucan, Peter	Csn	75	Dougald	Mrn	440	
Capdeville, Peter	Csn	76	Dougald, Junr.	Mrn	440	
Cape, Brian	Csn	79	Neil	Mrn	440	
Bryan	Csn	108	Carmichal, Robert	Abb	4	
Thomas	Csn	187	William	Abb	37	
Thos.	Gvl	280	Carmichel, James	Ora	555	
Capehart, George	Pen	131	Carn(?), J---	Edg	183	
Jacob	Pen	129	Carn, John	Csn	85	
Capers, Gabriel	Csn	151	Lewis	Ora	551	
George S.	Csn	175	Carna, Ely	Gvl	259	
Sinclair	Sum	593	Carnahan(?), Adam	Lan	3	
William	Geo	369	Carnahan, Robt.	Fai	204	
Caple, Littleton	Sum	614	William	Yrk	628	
Cappleman, John	Nby	68	Carnal, Curtis	Lrs	32	
Caps, John, Senr.	Sum	605	Carne, Jacob	Lan	5	
Matthew	Edg	160	Thomas W.	Csn	95	
Samuel	Sum	603	Carnes(?), Robert	Lan	8	
Capson(?), John	Lan	3	Carnes, Alexander	Lan	8	
Car, Isham	Bar	69	Frederick	Lan	9	
John	Bar	69	Hubbard	Gvl	244	
William	Bar	55	Jacob	Lan	9	
Joseph	Bar	67	James	Gvl	244	
Carawey, Charles	Bar	63	John	Geo	366	
Carbou, Joseph	Edg	142	Laurence	Csn	106	
Carden, Jane	Fai	195	Samuel	Csn	140	
Leonard	Spa	177	Sarah	Col	369	
Carder, George	Pen	162	Carney, Absolum	Gvl	260	
Nimrod	Pen	160	--eddick	Edg	144	
Cardoza, David	Csn	118	Lot	Gvl	260	
Care, Adam	Sum	601	Pynerby	Gvl	260	
Caredaeux, J. B.	Csn	149	Rebeckah	Fai	208	
Carey, Benjamin	Bft	106	Carns, Susanna	Csn	95	
Benjamin	Pen	155	Carold, Benjn.	Gvl	259	
Joseph	Csn	91	Carpenter, Burwell	Pen	145	
Thomas	Spa	169	Dan	Ker	397	
Thos.	Pen	135	Joseph	Csn	107	
Cargell, John	Gvl	276	Ruben	Edg	167	
Cargile, Clement	Edg	143	Carr, Charles	Geo	368	
Cargill, Clement	Edg	178	Isaac	Abb	31	

James	Csn 109	Samuel	Yrk 625
John	Csn 85	Thomas	Edg 159
Julian	Geo 366	Thomas	Yrk 617
Martha	Sum 601	Uriha	Pen 106
Moses	Abb 32	Wade	Abb 37
Nancy	Lrs 30	Walter	Yrk 625
Robert	Chr 78	Walter, Junr.	Yrk 625
Richard	Csn 133	William	Csn 122
Carrack, John	Pen 161	William	Csn 187
Carradine, Thomas	Pen 124	William	Edg 158
Carraway, Elijah	Dtn 121	William, Junr.	Yrk 625
Ezekiel	Dtn 121	William, Senr.	Yrk 625
John	Dtn 122	Carsson, Henery	Ora 535
Thos.	Ker 423	Cart, John	Csn 103
Carrel, Daniel	Uni 222	Carter, ---h	Edg 148
Delena	Abb 31	Carter, Alexander	Chr 88
Jacob	Bar 66	Alexr.	Uni 244
James	Abb 31	Anne	Yrk 630
Nat M.	Spa 178	Benjamin	Ker 399
Thomas	Bar 66	Benjamin	Lrs 36
Thomas	Chr 74	Blake	Chr 87
Daniel	Csn 154	Charles	Edg 179
Sterling	Pen 124	Churchwell(?)	Chr 77
Thomas	Wil 471	Daniel	Lex 572
Carrere, Charles	Csn 89	Daniel	Sum 595
Carrick, James	Pen 164	David	Pen 163
Carrier, Elizabeth	Ora 513	Edward	Gvl 261
Carrington, John	Lan 10	Elisabeth	Bar 66
John	Yrk 633	Elja	Col 393
Carrold, George	Gvl 259	Fedrick	Sum 605
Carroll, Alexr.	Geo 389	Geor. Doctr.	Csn 141
Barthomew	Csn 111	George	Col 393
James	Pen 123	George	Mbo 51
James P.	Col 367	Giles	Dtn 127
Jeremiah	Yrk 620	Griffin	Spa 207
James	Yrk 622	Henry	Chr 85
John	Pen 124	Isaac	Ora 517
John	Yrk 620	Isham	Bar 47
John	Yrk 621	Jacob	Col 393
Joseph	Yrk 621	Jacob	Edg 153
Joseph, Junr.	Yrk 626	James	Spa 175
Joseph, Senr.	Yrk 631	Jayles	Dtn 118
Leonard	Pen 117	Jesse	Col 393
Mary	Yrk 622	Jesse	Chr 90
Moses	Yrk 620	Jesse	Gvl 263
Saml.	Geo 389	Jesse	Mrn 437
Samuel	Yrk 631	Joel	Lrs 35
Thomas	Bft 84	Joel	Yrk 630
Thomas	Spa 178	John	Chr 77
Thomas	Yrk 621	John	Chr 87
William	Mrn 451	John	Dtn 124
Carrothers, William	Abb 3	John	Edg 152
Carsey, Stephen	Pen 150	John	Edg 179
Carson, James	Csn 113	James	Edg 179
James	Edg 182	John	Fai 194
James	Pen 131	John	Lrs 35
John	Abb 24	John, Junr.	Lrs 35
John	Edg 162	John	Sum 606
John	Yrk 617	Josiah	Mrn 453
John	Yrk 622	Moses	Bft 86
John	Yrk 625	Naboth	Sum 606
Robert	Abb 30	Rachel	Lrs 35
Robert	Ora 533	Reubin	Lrs 21
Robert	Yrk 625	Robert	Gvl 258
Samuel	Yrk 617	Robert	Lrs 35

Ron	Edg 186	Casley, John	Lan	6
Saml.	Cfd 109	Cason, Benjamin	Lrs	34
Samuel	Cfd 101	Elizabeth	Lrs	28
Samuel	Ora 519	Giles	Lrs	28
Samuel	Edg 137	John	Lrs	28
Sarah	Edg 150	Joseph	Edg 158
Sarah (free Negroe)	Sum 606	Laban	Fai 223
Thomas	Chr 80	Larken	Edg 158
Thomas	Dtn 118	Thomas	Edg 167
Thomas	Edg 150	Thomas	Edg 167
Wille	Ker 423	Thomas	Lrs	23
William	Bft 86	Triplet	Edg 134
William	Edg 182	William	Abb	28
William	Fai 207	William	Edg 158
William	Geo 384	William	Edg 172
William	Lrs 30	Casper, Henry	Edg 168
William	Lrs 34	Jacob	Edg 168
William	Bar 54	Caspper, James	Abb	13
William	Mrn 453	Cassels, Henry Minr.	Sum 608
William	Sum 607	Henry, Junr.	Sum 607
Willm.	Mrn 437	Henry, Senr.	Sum 608
Wm.	Spa 170	John	Sum 611
Zimry	Lrs 34	Lidia	Sum 612
Cartledge, John	Cfd 101	Cassells, John	Geo 372
Samuel	Edg 167	Cassity, James	Sum 587
Cartlight, Sarah	Dtn 125	William	Cfd 101
Cartor, Anne	Pen 135	William, Jr.	Cfd 101
Cartright, Paul A.	Bft 82	Zach	Cfd 108
Caruth, Adam	Gvl 280	Cassles, Benjamin	Chr	87
Caruthards, Nathl.	Cfd 101	Castalow, Henry	Bar	59
Carveil, James	Uni 228	James	Bar	58
Carville, Peter	Geo 366	Caster, John	Col 393
Carver, Joseph	Spa 180	Castillo, William	Edg 152
Joseph	Spa 180	Castillou, William H.	Edg 151
Richd.	Spa 180	Castle, Benj.	Lan	5
Thomas	Spa 180	Samuel	Nby	69
Thomas	Spa 180	Castleberry, Marke	Pen 137
Carvine, Barthow.	Geo 369	Mary	Uni 219
Carwile, Zachariah	Abb 21	Odam(?)	Pen 137
Carwiles, William	Abb 10	Paul	Spa 187
Cary, Merki	Bar 57	Wm.	Spa 187
Simon	Nby 69	Castlebery, William	Pen 137
Case, George	Pen 136	Castler, Jobe	Nby	70
Isaac	Nby 70	Caston, James	Lan	7
John	Mrn 455	John	Lan	4
John	Spa 172	Saml.	Lan	5
Michal	Abb 6	Wilk.	Lan	5
Casey, Abner	Spa 193	William	Ker 397
Aron	Spa 192	Castro, John	Csn 144
Benjamin	Csn 151	Cate, Aaron	Nby	68
Elisha	Lrs 43	Isaih	Nby	68
Jacob	Spa 194	Thomas	Edg 155
John	Pen 126	Thomas	Nby	68
John	Spa 193	Cater, Thomas	Bft 102
John	Spa 194	William	Bar	54
Joseph	Spa 192	Cates, Henry	Nby	68
Levi	Nby 68	Joseph	Edg 133
Moses	Spa 192	William	Edg 156
Moses	Spa 194	Cathorn, Thomas	Lan	4
Moses, Junr.	Spa 192	Catledge, Edmund	Edg 143
Randle	Spa 193	John	Edg 168
Wm.	Spa 192	Cato, Elenor	Nby	68
Cash, Benjn.	Spa 174	George	Sum 597
Caskey, Thomas	Fai 235	Mary	Nby	68
Casky, Samuel	Lan 8	Starling	Lan	10

Benjamin	Lrs	35	John	Col 367
George	Sum	612	John	Edg 174
Isaac	Abb	38	John	Gvl 270
Isaac Doctr.	Csn	116	John	Gvl 274
Israel	Nby	70	John	Spa 202
James	Dtn	118	John W.	Col 393
James	Nby	68	Joseph	Fai 193
James	Pen	130	Joseph	Fai 230
Jesse	Nby	69	Joseph	Nby 70
Joel	Edg	140	Joseph	Pen 113
Joel	Nby	68	Nancy	Nby 69
John	Dtn	118	S. Est.	Csn 166
John	Lrs	30	Shadrack	Lrs 16
John	Nby	68	Thomas	Lrs 33
John	Nby	69	Thomas	Nby 72
John	Pen	114	Thomas	Sum 603
Josiah	Gvl	274	Threshly	Cfd 101
Josiah	Lrs	29	William	Cfd 109
Meshack	Uni	219	William	Edg 182
Rial	Nby	71	William	Pen 115
Robt.	Fai	205	Chappel, John	Lex 570
Robert	Fai	234	Chappell, John	Lex 489
Shadrick	Pen	130	Mary	Chr 83
Samuel	Sum	612	Rachell	Geo 385
Thomas	Sum	612	Charles, Andrew	Csn 102
Timothy	Lrs	19	Martin	Nby 72
Zacheriah	Gvl	274	Michael	Nby 72
Chandlon, George	Sum	591	Chartin, Mariah	Csn 101
Samuel	Sum	591	Chace, Abram	Lan 2
Chandlor, Agnas	Gvl	272	Chase, James	Csn 85
Jesse	Gvl	270	Chassereau, John	Bar 68
John	Gvl	269	Chasteen, Abraham	Gvl 255
John, Jr.	Gvl	270	Chatham, Thomas	Mbo 61
John	Gvl	272	Chavers, John	Mbo 59
John	Gvl	284	Joseph	Bar 61
Shadarack	Gvl	272	Chaves, Wm.	Gvl 275
Solomon H.	Gvl	273	Chavis, Margret	Abb 14
Timothy	Gvl	270	Chavos, Anes	Bar 54
Wm.	Gvl	270	Elisha	Bar 63
Wm.	Gvl	284	Hannah	Bar 58
Wm. H.	Gvl	273	Cheatum, Robert	Abb 39
Chanely, Jerh.	Col	393	Chechester, Jno Doctr	Csn 124
Chaney, David	Dtn	122	Check, Ely	Lan 7
Levi	Ora	537	Jere.	Lan 7
Chanlor, James	Dtn	126	Jesse	Lan 7
Chapel, William	Edg	182	Randle	Lan 7
Chaplin, Benjn.	Bft	138	Widow	Lan 7
Darcus	Csn	146	Cheek, Elizabeth	Lrs 16
John, Junr.	Bft	138	Ellis	Lrs 15
John, Senr.	Bft	138	James	Lrs 17
Thomas	Bft	138	Lewis	Lrs 15
Thomas, Senr.	Bft	138	Nancy	Lrs 16
Thomas	Csn	183	Silas	Yrk 631
Wm.	Bft	138	William	Lrs 13
Wm. F.	Bft	138	Willis	Lrs 15
Chapman, Abraham	Nby	72	Cheeseman, Aaron	Sum 591
Allen	Cfd	101	John	Sum 591
Catharine	Csn	121	Nathaniel	Sum 591
Isaac	Spa	207	Cheeves, Alexander	Csn 144
Jacob	Edg	179	Chenett, Anthony	Geo 386
James	Pen	119	Cheney, John	Edg 135
Jesse	Lan	9	Cherrey, George	Uni 230
Joel	Nby	69	Cherry, George	Chr 80
John	Cfd	101	Jacob	Ker 401
John, Jr.	Cfd	101	John	Chr 92

John	Ker 403	Abraham	Sum 602
Letty	Chr 92	Ezekiel	Geo 390
Noah	Bar 44	John	Csn 124
Peter	Yrk 621	Chisholm, Adam	Uni 243
Sarah	Mbo 60	Alexr.	Csn 118
Simon	Mbo 52	George	Csn 127
Thomas	Chr 90	Chisiah, John	Lan 5
William	Sum 603	Chism, William	Gvl 249
Cherrytree, Jacob	Csn 149	Chisolm, Alexander	Bft 86
Chesney, Richd.	Spa 195	John	Bft 122
Robert	Uni 246	Rebecca	Bft 122
Chesnut, James	Chr 74	Robert	Csn 183
John	Ker 399	William	Csn 195
Chesnutt, Danl.	Geo 383	Chitty, James	Bar 68
Robt.	Geo 383	John	Bar 68
Chesser, John	Bft 120	William	Bar 69
Prissy	Bft 120	William K.	Csn 94
Wm.	Bft 120	Choice, Wm.	Gvl 273
Chester, Abel	Ora 501	Choir, James	Abb 4
David	Ora 501	Choswood, Jonathon	Uni 242
Martin	Bar 66	Chouler, J.	Csn 167
Chesterson, William	Gvl 285	Chouler, Joseph Doctr	Csn 78
Chetem, John	Edg 163	Chovin, Alexr.	Geo 372
Chetum, Gutridge	Edg 163	Chas. Estate	Csn 175
Jonathon	Abb 31	Chrisman, George	Lan 5
Robert	Abb 30	Michael	Lan 10
Chevas, Mary	Bft 96	Christ, Alexander	Fai 230
Chevers, Elijah	Ora 519	Christi, Peter	Nby 70
Chevilliette, John	Ora 521	Christian, Gidion	Edg 188
Chew, Samuel	Lrs 17	Jesse	Edg 181
Chick, Burwell	Nby 69	Lewis	Lrs 36
Chiffells, Ann	Col 367	William	Csn 98
Thos.	Col 367	William	Edg 183
Childers, David	Spa 189	Christie, Alexander	Csn 153
David	Spa 190	Christmas, Richard	Edg 136
Jacob	Yrk 629	Christopher, Ephraim	Lrs 27
Patterson	Pen 107	Chumler, Mary	Spa 196
William	Abb 38	Thomson	Spa 195
William	Pen 152	Wm.	Spa 195
Wm.	Spa 190	Chuning, Elizabeth	Sum 591
Childres, ---omas	Edg 147	Chup, Jacob	Lex 572
Childres, Jesse	Lrs 18	Chupien, Lewis	Csn 132
John	Lrs 18	Church, Benjn.	Spa 178
John	Lrs 42	Thomas	Geo 363
John	Lrs 43	Cimbess, Saml.	Fai 229
Mary	Pen 121	Cisholm, John	Mrn 462
Richard	Lrs 18	Cison, Stephen	Edg 149
Thomas	Lrs 18	Cithcart, Mary	Fai 207
Childress, John	Pen 121	Cizzem, Joshua	Uni 247
Joseph	Pen 121	Cizzim, Turner	Uni 246
Childs, Benjamin	Abb 25	William	Uni 246
Benjamin	Abb 39	Clabrook, Richard	Csn 89
James	Abb 23	Clage, Cammel	Edg 158
John	Abb 23	Jonathan	Edg 159
John	Abb 38	Clairman, Jacob	Pen 137
Judea	Abb 39	Claimour, Thomas	Pen 137
Judy	Abb 23	Clakely, Cutlip	Lex 572
Milly	Abb 39	Elizabeth	Lex 572
Nimrod	Abb 39	John	Edg 150
Richd.	Spa 202	Claland, James	Nby 70
Rubin	Abb 10	Clampet, Samuel	Fai 193
William	Abb 7	Clanch(?), Jacob	Lan 8
Chiles, Joel	Gvl 285	Clanton, David	Sum 608
China, Levi	Lex 562	Ephraim	Ker 409
Chinners, Abraham	Mrn 461	Ephraim	Ker 421

Gilliam	Ker 423	James	Csn 132		
John	Ker 421	James	Edg 161		
John, Senr.	Ker 419	James	Edg 161		
Nathl.	Ker 421	James	Edg 169		
Richard	Sum 608	James	Mbo 59		
Saml.	Ker 421	James	Pen 111		
Sion	Uni 239	James	Spa 203		
William	Ker 419	James	Sum 605		
Clap, Jacob	Nby 72	James	Uni 239		
Joseph	Nby 72	James	Yrk 627		
Clarday, Smith	Pen 103	Janet	Gvl 268		
Clardy, Benjamin	Pen 104	Jesse	Uni 220		
Elliott	Pen 104	Joel	Dtn 125		
James	Lrs 28	Joel	Dtn 128		
James	Lrs 40	John	Abb 32		
John	Pen 104	John	Bft 86		
Claret, Joseph	Csn 107	John	Bft 138		
Clark, Aaron, Junr.	Edg 140	John	Chr 86		
Aaron, Senr.	Edg 173	John	Edg 154		
Abdon	Sum 593	John	Edg 181		
Abnor	Edg 170	John	Fai 192		
Alexander	Yrk 623	John	Fai 222		
Anne	Sum 584	John	Lan 5		
Archibald	Mbo 59	John	Nby 68		
Aron	Abb 16	John	Pen 132		
Asa	Geo 371	John	Uni 220		
Azariah	Nby 69	John	Spa 177		
Barnabas	Mbo 59	John	Yrk 631		
Benjn.	Spa 177	John, Junr.	Sum 605		
Bolin	Pen 111	John, Senr.	Sum 605		
Braxton	Gvl 257	Joseph	Edg 169		
Burgess	Yrk 626	Joseph	Geo 372		
Cooper	Mbo 59	Joseph	Wil 476		
Daniel	Cfd 101	Joseph	Yrk 629		
Daniel	Lan 5	Joseph	Yrk 631		
Daniel	Nby 69	Lavias	Gvl 269		
Daniel, Senr.	Lan 11	Lee	Spa 198		
David	Csn 121	Lewis	Bar 48		
David	Edg 149	Lucretia	Csn 87		
Dinah	Spa 186	Mary	Mbo 59		
Elisha	Lan 5	Mary	Spa 177		
Elizabeth	Csn 106	Mary	Uni 234		
Elizabeth	Edg 150	Micaji	Pen 111		
Ethy	Sum 605	Molley	Abb 29		
Fereby	Mbo 52	Moses	Csn 175		
George	Abb 16	Moses	Edg 158		
George	Col 393	Moses	Edg 159		
George	Chr 85	Nicholas	Bft 88		
George	Mrn 453	Nicholas	Lrs 40		
George	Nby 68	Rachel	Lan 5		
Gregg	Lex 559	Robert	Csn 80		
Hardy	Mbo 61	Robert	Ker 421		
Hardy, Jr.	Mbo 52	Robt.	Gvl 276		
Henry	Geo 378	Salley	Spa 171		
Henry	Uni 234	Saml.	Fai 239		
Henry, Junr.	Gvl 257	Saml.	Spa 203		
Henry, Senr.	Gvl 257	Samuel	Abb 16		
Herod	Ker 413	Samuel	Edg 177		
Isaac	Mbo 52	Samuel	Sum 587		
Jacob, Junr.	Abb 39	Sarah	Csn 111		
Jacob, Senr.	Abb 10	Solomon	Yrk 623		
James	Bft 138	Stephen	Csn 195		
James	Bft 138	Susannah	Bft 86		
James	Chr 81	Thos.	Edg 178		
James	Csn 87	Thomas	Geo 373		

Thomas	Nby 68	Cleland, Robert	Nby 70
Thomas	Nby 70	Robert	Nby 70
Thomas	Pen 150	Clem, John	Edg 168
Thomas	Spa 188	Clemons, Aaron	Gvl 268
Thomas	Uni 220	Clement, James	Dtn 124
Thomas, Senr.	Geo 365	John	Csn 137
William	Abb 40	John	Pen 146
William	Cfd 101	Obadiah	Edg 166
William	Fai 220	Stephen	Edg 137
William	Pen 142	Zepheniah	Edg 139
William	Pen 148	Clements, Benjamin	Pen 161
William	Yrk 622	Benjamine	Pen 160
William	Yrk 624	Charles	Pen 159
William	Yrk 631	James	Pen 159
Willm.	Wil 468	John	Csn 163
Wm.	Chr 76	Thomas	Dtn 127
Wm.	Col 393	Reubin	Pen 159
Wm.	Uni 220	William	Csn 117
Clarke, Daniel	Sum 593	Clemmens, John	Fai 222
David	Pen 139	Clemment, Isaac	Pen 145
George	Pen 148	Clemments, Arthur	Sum 605
Hariot	Ker 423	James	Sum 605
Henry	Sum 595	Clemmons, Benjn.	Pen 162
James	Ker 397	Cully	Pen 162
John	Sum 591	Edward	Spa 177
Jonathan	Pen 121	Clemon, Stephen	Edg 163
Joseph	Pen 121	Jacob	Lrs 39
Joseph	Pen 124	James	Lrs 35
Micajah	Pen 115	Clemons, Vardemon	Bar 69
Clarksay, William	Csn 94	Zepheniah	Edg 163
Clarkson,		Clenahan, Robert	Yrk 620
Willm., Senr.	Csn 138	Clendening, Thomas	Yrk 617
Clary, Ann	Bar 53	Clerk, Elizabeth	Csn 183
Daniel	Nby 70	James	Csn 183
James	Nby 72	Cleton, Alexr.	Fai 230
Vachel	Edg 159	Isham	Fai 202
William	Nby 69	William	Fai 202
William	Nby 70	Cleveland, Aaron	Bar 64
Class, Frederick	Lex 560	Benjamine	Pen 126
Clastrier, John	Csn 119	Daniel	Pen 126
Classtrier, Maxn.	Csn 107	Edward	Bar 63
Claxton, Charles	Sum 614	Edward	Bar 63
Clayburn, Len	Gvl 254	James	Bar 59
Clayter, Laurence	Mrn 460	Jerimiah	Pen 126
Clayton, ---	Scn 151	Jeremiah	Pen 128
Augustin	Spa 203	John	Pen 128
Charles	Spa 209	Neel	Pen 123
Edmon	Spa 196	William	Pen 128
Gowen	Gvl 255	Clifford, R. G.	Pen 141
James	Ora 515	Clifton, George	Bft 88
James	Spa 194	James	Chr 80
John	Bar 58	William	Bft 88
Joseph	Ora 511	Wm.	Chr 80
Warren	Pen 124	Clime, Martin	Csn 100
William	Ora 547	Cline, George	Bar 69
William	Pen 118	Philip	Chr 79
Cleapor, Charles	Csn 84	Cling, G., Junr.	Col 381
Cleare, Adam Perry	Bft 83	George, Senr.	Col 381
Michl Perry (2)	Bft 83	Clinton, James	Yrk 621
Cleary, John R.	Csn 147	John	Yrk 621
Cleburn, William	Ker 413	Joseph	Csn 175
William, Junr.	Ker 413	Joseph	Yrk 631
Cleckler, Jacob	Edg 172	William, Capt.	Yrk 622
Cleckley, Lewis	Ora 535	Clissey, Raymond	Csn 125
Clegg, Richard	Nby 69	Clitheral, Jas.	Col 385

Solomon	Lrs 37	Robert	Edg 172
Susannah	Fai 203	Sarah	Dtn 121
Thomas	Fai 203	Sarah	Geo 364
Wiley	Fai 230	Sarah	Spa 189
William (2)	Dtn 116	Solomon	Sum 593
William	Dtn 126	Stephen	Bar 58
William	Edg 178	Thomas	Mrn 459
William	Lrs 34	Thomas	Yrk 628
Wm.	Uni 237	Walter	Ker 417
Wm.	Uni 242	William	Abb 16
Coley, John	Lrs 19	William	Ker 413
Colford, George	Csn 87	William	Lrs 20
Colhoon, John	Bar 63	William	Mrn 461
Colhoun, Ezekial	Abb 10	Wm.	Uni 239
John	Abb 5	Collom, Stanford	Pen 126
Collens, Martha	Edg 142	Staca	Gvl 274
Coller, Mons.	Csn 152	Colly, William	Cfd 101
Colleton, Elizth.	Bft 128	Colman, George	Geo 370
James	Bft 116	George	Nby 72
Joseph	Bft 128	Lusy(?)	Csn 152
Colley, James	Yrk 617	Thomas	Ora 533
John	Ker 417	James	Bar 46
Mary	Lan 7	Colsen, Dread	Col 393
Saml.	Spa 210	C.	Ora 535
William	Fai 205	James	Dtn 125
William	Pen 161	Leah	Edg 171
Collier, Edward	Abb 30	Lewis	Ora 535
Elizabeth	Nby 71	Colsworth(?),	Csn 76
John	Lan 9	Theophilus	
Rachel	Ora 547	Colter, Archibald	Chr 74
Thomas	Ker 407	John	Chr 74
William	Nby 71	Robert	Chr 74
Collins, Ann	Bar 69	William	Uni 241
Charles	Abb 21	Coltharp, Henry	Yrk 630
Daniel	Csn 75	Colton, John	Abb 25
Danl. O.	Fai 197	Colum, Uriah	Edg 156
David	Nby 69	William	Edg 170
Davis Revd.	Yrk 632	Colvin, Daniel	Chr 92
Demsey	Mrn 436	Hannah	Chr 82
Edmund	Ker 427	John	Chr 82
Edward	Ker 419	Nicholas	Chr 82
Elias	Geo 374	Thomas	Chr 82
Elizth.	Mrn 459	Wm.	Chr 82
J. M.	Csn 82	Colwell, William	Nby 70
James	Bar 48	Colzy, Charles	Csn 125
James	Lan 2	Combe, John	Csn 107
James	Sum 595	Thomas	Ora 525
Joab	Edg 167	Combess, John	Chr 94
John	Chr 89	Combs, Bennett	Pen 114
John	Pen 135	William	Ora 531
John	Spa 168	Come, Isaac	Edg 156
Jonathan	Mrn 458	Comer, John	Uni 221
Joseph (2)	Bar 54	Joseph	Uni 230
Joseph	Ker 419	Robert	Uni 229
Joseph	Spa 168	Saml.	Uni 221
Joseph	Yrk 628	Stephen	Uni 229
Lewis	Ker 419	Thomas	Lrs 30
Lewis	Yrk 628	Wm.	Uni 219
Lewis, Sr.	Ker 401	Wm., Junr.	Uni 219
Lucy	Nby 70	Comerland, John	Lex 484
Martha	Edg 166	Mary	Lex 484
Mary	Bar 50	Commander, Joseph	Sum 607
Mary	Csn 147	Obediance	Sum 611
Nelly	Csn 149	Saml.	Geo 371
Robert	Chr 78	Saml., Senr.	Wil 465

Thos.	Geo 369	William	Csn 195
Commitee, J.	Col 363	William	Ora 547
Compton, Isaac	Sum 597	Willis	Mrn 442
Luke	Gvl 272	Connerly, John	Nby 71
Robert	Sum 585	Mary	Nby 71
Saml.	Sum 597	Conners, Charles	Sum 601
Samuel	Nby 69	Samuel	Sum 595
William	Nby 70	Connoly, Charles	Col 369
Con(?), George	Chr 84	Joseph	Bar 62
Conant, Hardy	Lrs 29	Connor, Brian	Csn 76
Jeremiah	Lrs 31	Isaac	Sum 601
Keziah	Lrs 30	John	Abb 6
Conaway, Caleb	Pen 146	Mary	Ora 545
James	Lrs 21	W.	Col 361
Cone, Charles	Nby 70	Conoly, Henry	Bar 55
Neal	Edg 152	James	Bar 63
Conedrey, John	Abb 12	Conrad, Scipio	Mbo 61
Coneway, Charles	Lrs 14	(free black)	
Congo, Benjamin	Pen 107	Consoler, James	Pen 121
Conn, Benjamin	Lex 493	Constant, John, Junr.	Yrk 624
George	Abb 11	John, Senr.	Yrk 624
James	Abb 25	Conte, Seignout	Csn 96
John	Chr 94	Conway, Edward	Nby 69
John	Mbo 52	John	Lex 559
Richard	Ora 529	Robt.	Geo 380
Connel, George	Spa 204	William	Ker 405
Giles	Spa 204	Conwell, Benjamin	Nby 69
James	Dtn 118	James	Nby 70
Jesse	Edg 180	Joseph	Nby 69
Connell, James	Dtn 128	William	Nby 69
John	Ker 415	Conyares, ---	Lex 565
Simon	Dtn 128	Conyer, Edward	Lex 571
William	Dtn 128	Conyers, Elizabeth	Csn 119
Connelley, Wm.	Spa 176	James	Sum 600
Connelly, George	Csn 116	John	Sum 606
Mary	Dtn 117	Mary	Sum 614
Mary	Dtn 126	Straughn	Sum 613
Patrick	Yrk 618	Thomas	Dtn 123
Connely, Amhurst	Csn 61	William	Csn 89
Ann	Col 393	Coock, Jediah	Gvl 275
Elizabeth	Csn 92	Moses	Gvl 275
Thomas	Spa 189	Robt.	Gvl 252
Conner, Benjn.	Edg 138	Wm.	Gvl 268
Benjamin	Fai 238	Coocksey,	Gvl 283
Barbary	Mrn 459	Andrew, Senr. (2)	
Catlett	Edg 188	Cournelius	Gvl 282
Edward	Geo 381	Josiah	Gvl 282
George	Abb 20	Coocy, John	Abb 29
James	Mbo 52	William	Abb 29
Isam	Chr 84	Coogler,	
John	Abb 20	see also Cugler	
John	Mbo 59	Coogler, Cattarine	Lex 484
Joshua	Spa 209	John	Lex 484
Lewis	Abb 20	Mathias	Lex 487
Lewis	Mbo 51	Uriah	Lex 487
Lewis, Jr.	Mbo 61	Cook, Mrs.	Cfd 110
Martin	Gvl 285	Abraham	Cfd 101
Maxmilion	Gvl 285	Abraham	Ora 533
Nancy	Mbo 51	Amos	Uni 227
Robert	Spa 209	Benjamin, Senr.	Yrk 622
Samuel	Csn 141	Burrell	Fai 212
Thomas	Chr 88	Charles	Fai 238
Thomas	Mbo 51	Charles	Ker 405
Thomas, Jr.	Mbo 61	Charles	Yrk 620
Widow	Pen 118	Cornelius	Lrs 43

David	Spa 205	William		Csn 151
Deanbery	Edg 151	William		Pen 148
Dudley	Abb 33	Cooker, Leonard		Gvl 269
Elisha	Pen 152	Cooley, George		Pen 106
George	Cfd 101	Jacob, Junr.		Gvl 268
Greenbery	Edg 148	Jacob, Senr.		Gvl 266
Honor	Mrn 448	Cooly, John		Dtn 118
Hugh	Uni 247	Coombs, John		Yrk 624
Isaac	Uni 228	Coon, Benjamin		Lex 568
Isias	Dtn 119	Francis		Lex 497
Jacob	Nby 69	George		Fai 205
James	Lrs 28	Henry		Lex 487
James	Mbo 51	Henry		Lex 576
Jedediah	Edg 165	Henry		Nby 69
Jehu	Spa 198	John		Bar 55
John	Bft 86	John		Col 361
John	Cfd 101	Cooner, Jacob		Ora 543
John	Fai 227	Mary		Ora 539
John	Lrs 34	Coonrod, Peter		Chr 86
John	Mbo 51	Cooper, Aaron		Geo 389
John	Pen 122	Abner		Uni 219
John	Spa 205	Adam		Fai 204
John	Yrk 620	Agrippa		Abb 22
John, Jr.	Dtn 128	Benjamin		Lrs 37
John G.	Edg 137	Benjamin		Ora 525
Joseph	Abb 23	Charles		Edg 137
Joseph	Nby 69	Charles		Edg 175
Levi	Uni 227	Elizabeth		Spa 169
Lewis	Ker 421	Ezekiel		Geo 389
Lucy	Dtn 126	George		Sum 607
Martin	Edg 166	Hadley		Edg 148
Martin	Nby 69	Hugh		Yrk 617
Mary	Dtn 117	Hugh		Yrk 633
Mathew	Dtn 126	Jacob		Chr 79
Meriman	Edg 160	Jacob		Lrs 20
Mary	Chr 76	James		Geo 368
Mary	Nby 70	James		Gvl 263
Nathan	Fai 212	Jesse		Mrn 454
Randolph	Lrs 14	John		Bft 94
Reubin	Mbo 52	John		Bft 106
Samuel	Edg 135	John		Chr 75
Sarah	Cfd 101	John		Csn 87
Susannah	Abb 27	John		Dtn 113
Susannah	Edg 173	John		Mbo 52
Thomas	Edg 148	John		Mrn 439
Thomas	Mbo 51	John		Mrn 443
Thomas	Mbo 61	John		Spa 172
Thomas	Spa 185	John		Spa 182
Thomas	Uni 238	John		Uni 231
William	Cfd 101	John		Uni 235
William	Dtn 116	John		Uni 245
William	Dtn 126	John		Wil 465
William	Edg 148	John		Yrk 622
William	Edg 168	John, Senr.		Yrk 622
William	Ker 399	Joseph		Dtn 114
William	Ker 409	Joseph		Geo 389
Willm.	Mrn 446	Joseph		Lrs 27
Wm.	Uni 228	Joseph		Mrn 439
Wilson	Bar 48	Joseph		Ora 525
Wiot(?)	Edg 188	Joseph		Uni 232
Wright	Nby 69	Mary		Col 393
Cooke, Eli	Uni 227	Nathan		Uni 232
J. G.(?)	Csn 151	Nusom		Uni 245
Jonathon	Uni 227	Powdre(?)		Edg 148
Saml. D.	Bft 138	Robert		Yrk 622

Samuel	Lrs	44	Samuel	Pen	110
Sion	Spa	168	Corbit, Isaac	Edg	136
Susanna	Uni	217	James	Sum	602
Stacey	Uni	232	Susannah	Sum	601
Thomas	Csn	195	Corby, Leonard	Pen	104
Thos.	Gvl	263	Corder, Ephraim	Chr	88
William	Uni	232	Morgen	Chr	73
Wm	Spa	211	Wm.	Chr	74
Wm.	Uni	219	Cordery, Mary	Bft	100
Wm.	Uni	245	Cordes, Catharine	Csn	69
Willm. James	Wil	464	Catharine	Csn	195
Coopper, Anthony	Abb	28	Elizabeth	Csn	68
Elizabeth	Nby	70	Rebecca	Csn	195
Elizabeth	Nby	71	Thomas	Csn	195
Cope, Jno	Bft	130	Cordier, Peter	Csn	109
Copeland			Cordle, Jesse	Lrs	19
see also Coupland			Sampson	Lrs	20
Copeland, Elizabeth	Lrs	22	Corgle, Henry	Lex	569
George	Lrs	22	Cork, Elizabeth	Fai	232
J---	Edg	144	Samuel	Fai	193
James	Nby	70	Corker, Thomas	Csn	88
John	Lrs	23	Corley - see also		
John	Yrk	628	Cauley, Cawley		
Reuben	Pen	114	Corley, Bartolomew	Ora	521
William	Pen	104	Charles	Lex	573
William	Yrk	628	David	Lex	578
Copelin, Ambrose	Abb	3	Elizath.	Gvl	266
Jacob	Bar	68	Jeremiah	Ora	517
Jarrett	Pen	120	Valentine	Edg	180
Copey, Gabriel	Bft	138	Cormick, Thomas	Csn	79
Wm. H.	Bft	138	Cornehan, Joseph	Mbo	51
Copland, Alexr.	Spa	178	Cornelison, John	Lrs	37
Nicholas	Cfd	101	Cornelius, Austen	Pen	130
Coplin, Caleb	Sum	610	Wm.	Gvl	252
Isaac	Bar	68	Cornet, Hardy	Edg	142
Riply	Sum	610	Cornut, John	Edg	170
Coppock, Benjamin	Nby	70	Cornwell, Daniel	Spa	177
Isaac	Nby	70	Edward	Spa	181
Jane	Nby	70	Elijah	Pen	127
John(2)	Nby	70	Elisha	Spa	180
John	Nby	70	Ely	Chr	84
John Sr.	Nby	70	Wm.	Chr	93
Joseph	Nby	70	Coroy, John	Edg	159
Thomas	Nby	70	Corre, Charles G.	Csn	136
Copray, Wm.	Gvl	264	Correll, Tunis	Lex	558
Coram, Frances	Csn	103	Corrie(?), John	Csn	121
Thomas	Csn	139	Corrie, Nicholas	Uni	240
Coran, Samuel	Gvl	267	Samuel	Csn	106
Corban, Matt.	Col	387	Correl, Alexander	Csn	79
Corben, Arthur	Bft	132	Corrothers, James	Abb	10
Benjamin	Bar	57	Cortes, Thomas	Csn	83
Corbet, John	Bar	56	Cortman, Christopher	Lex	579
Mary	Bar	57	Cosby, John P.	Mbo	52
Corbett, Edward	Bft	88	Robert	Abb	13
Edward	Dtn	119	Cosey, Allen	Edg	166
Isham	Edg	186	Coskrey, Charles	Csn	75
James	Dtn	118	Cosnay, John	Csn	139
James	Dtn	127	Costine, John	Csn	118
John	Ora	529	Cote, Henry	Nby	70
Samuel	Csn	150	John	Nby	69
Thos Junr.	Csn	68	John Sr.	Nby	69
Thomas Sr.	Csn	83	Marmaduke	Nby	69
Corbin, Isaac	Gvl	259	Mary	Nby	69
John	Pen	116	Nancy	Nby	69
Peter	Chr	94	Samuel	Nby	69

William	Nby 69	Countz, Adam	Lex 493
Cotes, James	Edg 186	John	Lex 493
John	Edg 182	Peter	Lex 495
John	Edg 186	Coupland, Aaron	Cfd 108
John	Lrs 46	Ann	Cfd 101
Josiah	Bft 126	Nicholas	Cfd 109
Moses	Nby 70	Ripley	Cfd 101
Cothron, Alexander	Nby 70	William	Cfd 108
Samuel	Nby 70	Cournand, Peter	Csn 92
Cotny, Benjamin	Bar 64	Shadrack	Csn 153
Cotney, William	Edg 177	Cournie, Charles	Csn 96
Cotrel, Henry	Chr 86	Course, Isaac	Cfd 101
Cott, John S.	Wil 466	Lydia	Csn 93
Cotten, David	Gvl 266	Coursey, Elizabeth	Edg 142
James W.	Csn 149	Mary	Edg 141
Molley	Edg 175	Courson, Delila	Csn 114
Reb---	Edg 187	Courtenay, Ezra	Dtn 118
Cottingham, Charles	Mbo 52	James	Dtn 118
Charles, Jr.	Mbo 52	Courtnay, John	Dtn 118
Dill	Mbo 52	Courtney, Edward	Csn 78
Edward	Mbo 51	Ezekiel	Sum 591
Jonathan	Mbo 52	Humphrey	Csn 138
Lydia	Mbo 59	James	Csn 138
Thomas Jr.	Mbo 51	James	Pen 138
Turbeth	Mbo 51	Johnatan	Ora 529
Thomas	Mbo 51	Jonas	Sum 591
Cottington, Danl.	Mbo 51	Robert Junr.	Sum 591
Cotton, Abner	Abb 25	Robert Senr.	Sum 591
Alexander	Abb 25	William	Yrk 623
Asa	Edg 138	Courtor, Mary	Csn 76
David	Abb 29	Courturier, John	Csn 195
David	Edg 173	Courty, John	Csn 75
Siars	Abb 25	Cousar, David	Lan 2
Thomas	Edg 141	James	Lan 2
Wm.	Gvl 266	James	Lan 8
Couch, Aaron	Gvl 248	John	Lan 8
Benjamin	Gvl 249	Nathl.	Lan 8
Benjn.	Spa 211	Richard	Lan 7
Drury	Spa 193	Richard	Lan 8
Isaac	Gvl 248	Will.	Lan 7
Israel	Lrs 39	Cousart, Thomas	Lan 8
James	Gvl 248	Coussins, Elizabeth	Csn 124
James	Spa 193	Couturier, Isaac	Csn 69
John	Edg 168	Philip	Csn 69
John, Junr.	Gvl 247	Coveney, Thomas	Csn 91
John	Gvl 247	Coville, Jacob	Yrk 628
John	Spa 193	Covington, Febey	Abb 40
Joseph	Lrs 18	Francis	Gvl 251
Mathew	Spa 193	Henry	Mbo 59
Moses	Lrs 27	John	Edg 187
Wm.	Uni 237	[C]ovington, Joseph	Edg 187
Councill, Jesse	Mbo 52	Covington, Sarah	Mbo 61
Cough, Milinton	Abb 37	William	Mbo 52
Coughman, Andrew	Lex 564	William Jr.	Mbo 61
Christopher	Lex 565	Wm. Jr.	Mbo 51
Cougler, Catherine	Lex 576	Wm. N.	Mbo 61
Ulrick	Lex 576	Cowan, Andrew	Abb 33
Countryman, James	Yrk 625	Lazarus	Abb 30
John	Yrk 625	Coward, Benjamin	Ker 419
Rhoda	Yrk 625	Edward	Bar 52
Counts, Adam	Lex 569	Elisha	Mbo 52
Christopher	Edg 153	Ephraim	Mrn 452
Henry	Nby 70	Esikiel	Bar 52
Jacob	Nby 72	Hardy	Bar 53
John	Nby 72	Isam	Bar 52

James	Mbo	51	John	Lrs	37
Jessee	Bar	52	John	Lrs	46
Joel	Mbo	52	John	Pen	129
John	Wil	469	John	Pen	150
Jonathan	Pen	111	John	Uni	234
Lewis	Ker	419	Jonathan	Lrs	45
Lewis	Mrn	451	Jono: Est.	Col	383
Needham	Bar	53	Joseph	Csn	98
Wm.	Mbo	52	Joseph	Geo	376
Zachariah	Bar	53	Joseph	Lrs	30
Cowden, Thos.	Gvl	262	Joshua	Gvl	259
Cowen, Andrew	Spa	183	Judith	Mrn	442
David	Lrs	16	Kitty	Edg	139
Isaac	Abb	14	Marcy	Mbo	61
James	Spa	183	Marcy	Mbo	59
John	Abb	14	Mary	Pen	151
John	Bft	132	Nancy	Edg	143
John	Chr	79	Phillip	Pen	139
John	Csn	74	Richd	Uni	225
John	Gvl	256	Robert	Gvl	248
Joseph	Gvl	255	Samuel	Mbo	59
Rachel	Uni	240	Samuel	Mbo	61
Robert	Chr	79	Sarah	Dtn	128
Cowley, Robert	Chr	89	Simon	Pen	112
Cowser, John	Chr	85	Susanna	Mbo	51
Nancy	Chr	84	Susannah	Mbo	52
Cowzzins, Mary	Csn	74	Susannah	Pen	122
Cox, Abraham	Gvl	265	Thomas	Lrs	22
Absolom	Abb	28	Thomas	Lrs	29
Allen	Nby	70	Thomas	Uni	225
Barbary	Mrn	452	Thomas Senr.	Lrs	29
Benja	Mbo	59	William	Abb	21
Benjamin	Lrs	21	William	Dtn	119
Benjamin	Mbo	61	William	Edg	143
Charles	Gvl	276	William	Edg	145
Charles	Lan	9	William	Geo	376
Christopher	Edg	169	William	Gvl	248
Conney	Gvl	282	William	Lrs	46
David	Lrs	45	William	Mbo	51
Edward	Lrs	26	William	Mrn	442
Edward	Pen	122	William	Pen	122
Elisha	Geo	384	William	Pen	146
Elizabeth	Pen	129	William Senr.	Edg	169
Emmanuel	Mbo	52	Wm.	Gvl	281
George	Gvl	249	Wm.	Pen	136
George	Mrn	462	Wm.	Spa	183
Henry	Edg	135	Coy, William	Pen	151
Henry	Pen	135	Cozby, James	Abb	4
Isaac	Gvl	278	Crabtree, Joshua	Pen	135
James	Csn	119	Samuel	Lrs	25
James	Edg	139	Samuel	Nby	69
James	Nby	68	Craddock, Bat.	Lrs	30
James	Pen	151	Daniel	Lrs	30
Jesse	Edg	144	Cradock, David	Lrs	45
Jesse	Mbo	60	John	Bar	56
John	Csn	100	Crafford, Alexander	Chr	90
John	Csn	101	David	Gvl	281
John	Csn	111	Edward	Lan	3
James	Csn	127	James	Lan	2
John	Dtn	119	John	Sum	608
John	Geo	376	Moses	Gvl	269
John	Geo	384	Robert	Lan	2
John	Gvl	255	Samuel	Gvl	264
John	Gvl	259	Wm.	Gvl	271
John	Lrs	29	William	Pen	105

Rody	Chr 83		John	Uni 246
Thomas	Mrn 442		Crowson, Thos	Geo 386
Wm.	Chr 84		Croxton, Benjamin	Lan 4
William	Pen 131		Crozier, Andrew	Abb 32
Croskee, William	Sum 603		Samuel	Abb 27
Croskey, Jas.	Col 385		Cruce, Isaac	Gvl 264
Crosley, George	Uni 220		Cruckshanks, Willm.	Csn 132
Cross, George	Csn 92		Cruger, Fredk. D.	Csn 120
James	Csn 143		Mr.	Bft 114
Johanna	Csn 80		Nicholas	Csn 97
John	Bft 138		Cruise, Jesse	Bar 65
John	Csn 61		Joseph	Edg 175
John	Geo 364		Richd.	Spa 173
Mathew W.	Csn 79		Stephen	Spa 211
Susanna	Csn 95		William	Abb 21
Thomas	Spa 188		Crum, David	Ora 541
Crossby, Henery	Ora 507		David	Ora 543
James	Ora 507		E.	Col 361
Crosset, Wm.	Chr 79		Frederick	Ora 541
Crossett, Andrew	Fai 209		Jacob	Ora 547
Crosskeys, Elizath.	Csn 191		John	Ora 541
Crossland, Edward	Mbo 51		John	Ora 541
John	Fai 210		Magdalen	Ora 541
Crosswhite, Jacob	Nby 70		Crumbley, Hugh	Pen 157
Croswell, Gilberd	Sum 610		Crumley, Martin	Ora 553
Crotwell, George	Nby 72		Crumly, Hannah W.	Nby 72
Crouch, Isaac	Edg 176		Benjamin	Nby 72
Jeremiah	Geo 382		Samuel	Nby 72
Thos.	Gvl 247		Crump, Ruth	Abb 18
Toliver	Edg 140		Crumpton, Bazel	Spa 199
Crout, Michael	Edg 171		James	Pen 151
Crovat, Peter	Csn 76		John	Lrs 13
Crow, Charles	Nby 68		Joshua	Uni 225
Charles	Nby 72		Samuel	Uni 225
Charles Jr.	Nby 70		Thomas	Spa 199
Easter	Gvl 280		Crumsna, S.	Col 393
Isaac	Spa 195		Crutchfield, Amos	Lrs 14
Isaac	Spa 195		Cruthers, Nathan	Dtn 128
James	Spa 186		Cryder, John	Ora 549
James	Spa 195		Crymer, George	Gvl 276
Jonathan	Spa 195		Cubet, David	Chr 85
John	Dtn 128		Cubstead, Mary	Ora 553
John	Spa 195		Cud, John	Uni 248
Levi	Spa 193		Cudd, Jonathan	Spa 175
Levy	Spa 188		Jonathon	Uni 231
Mary	Spa 193		Zach	Uni 249
Randle	Spa 193		Cudworth, Benjn.	Csn 140
Samuel	Edg 182		Nathl.	Csn 95
Saml.	Spa 193		Cugler, John	Lex 575
Thomas	Pen 103		Mathias	Lex 575
Thomas	Pen 159		Culbertson, David	Spa 181
William	Pen 121		James	Lrs 30
William	Spa 185		Josiah	Gvl 260
Wm	Spa 186		Robert	Lrs 45
Crowder, James	Pen 149		Saml.	Spa 211
James	Spa 198		Culbreath, John	Edg 156
John	Lan 9		Culbud, Joseph	Edg 136
John	Pen 114		Culclazer, David	Ora 555
Mary	Gvl 282		Culhoon, Dixon	Bar 43
Robt.	Gvl 273		Micajah	Bar 43
Crowell, William	Ora 555		Samuel	Bar 52
Crowley, William	Cfd 101		Cullah, Benjamin	Ora 555
Crowney, Johnson	Edg 138		Cullahan, William	Abb 12
Crownover, Benjn	Uni 246		Cullee, James	Sum 595
Daniel	Uni 246		Culle, Jesse	Ker 423

Cullee, John	Ker 425	Samuel	Abb 16
Lear	Ker 425	Cunningham, Agnis	Edg 162
Culliat, David	Col 367	Artr.	Ker 421
J. A.	Col 387	Arthur	Wil 463
Culliatt, A.	Col 383	Arthur	Uni 243
James	Csn 142	Charles	Csn 98
Cullins, Charles	Abb 20	Elizabeth	Abb 36
John	Abb 19	Francis	Abb 34
William	Abb 6	Francis	Pen 148
William	Abb 20	Henry	Uni 244
Cullwell, James	Nby 70	James	Abb 33
Cully, William	Bar 64	James	Uni 248
Culp, Augustine	Lan 7	John	Csn 99
Benjamin	Lan 7	John	Csn 108
James	Yrk 623	John	Lrs 39
Sarah	Sum 605	John	Uni 220
Thomas	Sum 584	Joseph	Edg 150
William	Ker 415	Joseph	Edg 180
Culpeper, John	Lex 561	Mary	Wil 477
Culpepper, Benjn	Edg 133	Matthew	Lrs 13
Joseph	Lex 560	Polly	Edg 175
Culwell, Daniel	Nby 72	Robt.	Ker 421
Elizabeth	Nby 70	Robert	Spa 210
Helen	Yrk 627	William	Abb 5
James	Nby 70	William	Ker 399
James	Nby 71	William	Pen 129
John	Nby 70	William	Pen 131
John	Nby 70	Cunnington, Elizabeth	Csn 110
Joseph	Nby 70	Cureton, James	Lan 6
Joseph	Nby 72	John	Lrs 30
Robert	Nby 70	John Senr.	Lrs 34
Samuel	Nby 71	Curl, Henry	Nby 69
William	Nby 72	Curley, Wm.	Gvl 278
William	Nby 70	Currence, John	Yrk 621
William	Yrk 627	Currenton, Henry	Pen 132
Cumbaa, John	Ora 525	Currey, James	Abb 40
Cumberlander, Barbary	Lex 575	John	Abb 36
John	Lex 575	Currie, Archibald	Dtn 128
Cumbers, Winney	Edg 146	Daniel	Dtn 124
Cumings, Thomas	Lrs 34	John	Dtn 128
Cummings, David	Mrn 456	Currier, James	Yrk 629
John	Lrs 34	Richard	Yrk 624
Moses	Ora 505	Currington, Thomas	Pen 115
Cummins,	Abb 11	Curry, Charles	Yrk 617
Francis Revd.		Danl	Fai 232
Harmon	Pen 147	Dudley	Fai 235
James	Lrs 33	Francis	Yrk 625
John	Csn 100	Gawn	Fai 203
Thomas	Pen 147	Jacob	Bar 48
Cumpton, Amos	Uni 226	John	Dtn 122
Stephen	Uni 226	John	Edg 150
Cuningham, Daniel	Lrs 20	Joseph	Fai 197
George	Lrs 44	Laughlan	Mbo 52
James	Lrs 44	Nathan	Lrs 18
John	Chr 90	Samuel	Fai 210
John	Lrs 44	Samuel	Yrk 625
Matthew	Lrs 22	Stafford	Fai 197
Robert	Lrs 22	Stephen	Ora 521
Samuel	Lrs 44	Will	Lan 3
Thomas	Lrs 45	William	Fai 198
William	Lrs 22	Curtess, James	Pen 142
William	Lrs 44	Curtis, Fielding	Uni 216
Cunningan, Jane	Abb 39	Frances	Csn 61
Cunningem, Margaret	Abb 23	Frances	Csn 103
Robert	Abb 23	Henry	Spa 197

John	Dtn 114	Joseph	Uni 244
Owen	Dtn 113	Margaret	Cfd 107
Richard	Nby 72	Saml.	Uni 241
Richd	Uni 232	Thomas	Spa 210
Robert A.	Csn 80	Wm.	Geo 366
Tabitha	Cfd 108	Wm.	Spa 170
William	Nby 72	Wm.	Uni 243
Willis	Edg 142	Davie, Joseph	Edg 183
Darden, David	Cfd 102	Davies, Benjn	Ora 539
David	Cfd 109	Francis	Lex 578
James	Cfd 102	Isaac	Lex 565
John	Cfd 109	Davis, ---	Edg 185
Dargan, Ann	Dtn 117	Abia	Mrn 435
Timothy	Dtn 113	Abraham	Ora 501
Darin, Dolly	Bft 122	Adam	Pen 145
Dark(?), Timothy	Wil 468	Adam	Uni 249
Darlington,	Bar 60	Agnes	Sum 604
Christopher		Alexander	Abb 40
Job	Bar 57	Andrew	Gvl 244
John	Bar 58	Ann	Bar 51
Darnel, Daniel	Nby 73	Ann	Ker 423
James	Nby 73	Argent	Bft 96
Darnal, Major	Uni 233	Aron	Uni 246
Morgan	Spa 187	Arthur	Bar 57
Darnold, Isaac	Uni 236	Augusten	Abb 14
Darr, Peter	Csn 151	Benjamin	Mbo 52
Peter	Csn 175	Benjamin	Sum 605
Darrell, Ann	Csn 113	Benjamin Junr.	Geo 392
Edwd Coll.	Csn 136	Benjamin Junr.	Mrn 434
Darragh, John	Pen 160	Benjamin Senr.	Mrn 436
Darrell, Kezia	Csn 127	Benjn.	Gvl 254
Robert	Csn 105	Brook	Pen 128
Dart, Emelia	Csn 126	Caleb	Chr 83
Isaac M.	Csn 146	Caleb	Lrs 20
Dashields, Thomas	Lrs 27	Charles	Bft 86
Daslass, Mathew	Csn 137	Charles	Uni 241
Dastas, Mathew	Csn 152	Chesley	Nby 72
Daugharty, James	Nby 72	Damsey	Ora 511
Dauton, Matthew	Edg 187	Daniel	Bar 57
Dauson, William	Edg 142	Daniel	Lrs 22
Davenport, see also		Daniel	Dtn 123
Devenport		Daniel	Dtn 123
Davenport, Wm.	Chr 87	Danl.	Col 363
Daverson, John	Nby 73	David	Spa 208
David, Daniel	Spa 182	David	Sum 605
Fed	Pen 107	Edward	Ker 401
Isaac	Sum 600	Edward	Pen 148
Joshua	Mbo 52	Eli	Pen 127
Josiah	Mbo 52	Elijah	Yrk 630
Peter	Sum 606	Elisabeth	Bar 64
Robert	Pen 143	Elizabeth	Pen 163
William	Pen 126	Elizabeth	Sum 600
Davidson, Elias	Yrk 623	Enos	Uni 234
Gilbert	Csn 133	Evin	Spa 203
James	Fai 213	Felia	Chr 90
James	Wil 470	Francis	Edg 177
Jane	Lan 3	Francis	Ker 415
Jesse	Spa 171	Francis	Mrn 455
John	Lrs 25	Francis	Pen 116
John	Nby 73	Federic	Uni 247
John, Junr.	Yrk 623	Gabriel	Yrk 633
John, Senr.	Yrk 623	George	Spa 196
Robert	Yrk 623	George	Yrk 633
Wm.	Chr 81	Guardiner	Bar 50
Wm., Junr.	Spa 170	Halse	Yrk 619

Harman	Csn	87	Joseph	Pen	139
Harmon	Nby	73	Joseph	Uni	232
Harmon Senr.	Nby	73	Josiah	Mrn	438
Harrison	Ker	413	Kesia	Mrn	455
Henry	Lrs	26	Levy	Fai	199
Henry	Uni	246	Lewis	Edg	177
Henry Junr.	Mrn	455	Lewis	Pen	128
Henry Senr.	Mrn	435	Lewis	Pen	146
Henson	Ker	427	Lewis	Pen	162
Hezekiah	Pen	144	Machlin	Abb	39
Hugh	Spa	197	Mark	Gvl	269
Israel	Abb	38	Mary	Mrn	435
Israel	Csn	145	Mary	Spa	209
Jacob	Spa	170	Moore	Sum	608
James	Bar	50	Moses	Pen	109
James	Bft	88	Mosey	Abb	38
James	Edg	176	Nathan	Pen	113
James	Edg	187	Nathaniel	Yrk	619
James	Fai	195	Nathl	Pen	130
James	Ker	413	Nicholas	Gvl	276
James	Lrs	24	Pan C.	Pen	143
James	Mrn	435	Rachel	Ker	423
James	Ora	531	Rezin	Bar	66
James	Sum	605	Rhuebin	Gvl	268
James	Sum	611	Richard	Bft	122
James	Uni	221	Richard	Pen	159
James	Uni	232	Reason	Nby	73
James	Yrk	623	Robert	Abb	7
Jane	Lrs	25	Robert	Abb	35
Jesse	Bft	122	Robert	Edg	180
Jesse	Csn	61	Robert	Edg	185
Jesse	Edg	186	Robert	Ker	425
Jesse	Gvl	254	Robert	Lan	2
Jesse	Pen	144	Robert	Lan	6
Jesse	Spa	179	Robert	Pen	110
Jeremiah	Chr	83	Robert	Uni	222
Joel	Ker	427	Saml.	Chr	90
John	Abb	26	Samuel	Edg	153
John	Abb	31	Samuel	Edg	180
John	Csn	151	Samuel	Pen	108
John	Dtn	121	Sarah	Bft	92
John	Edg	176	Sion	Edg	176
John	Edg	178	Surry	Gvl	285
John	Gvl	254	Terry	Edg	178
John	Gvl	259	Thomas	Abb	22
John	Mbo	52	Thomas	Abb	4
John	Nby	72	Thomas	Cfd	102
John	Nby	73	Thomas	Csn	61
John	Pen	108	Thomas	Dtn	114
John	Pen	146	Thomas	Edg	178
John	Spa	209	Thomas	Fai	221
John	Spa	209	Thomas	Nby	72
John	Uni	240	Thomas	Pen	162
John	Uni	249	Thomas	Sum	603
John	Yrk	624	Thomas	Uni	232
John B.	Chr	78	Thomas	Yrk	631
John Esq.	Lrs	30	Thomas Senr.	Sum	609
John M.	Csn	134	Thos.	Col	363
John Mrs.	Col	397	Tollifario	Uni	235
Jonathan	Gvl	276	Vincent	Uni	246
Jonathan	Pen	116	William	Abb	18
Jonathan	Spa	206	William	Abb	29
Joseph	Chr	90	William	Abb	34
Joseph	Gvl	259	William	Bar	44
Joseph	Mrn	435	William	Bar	52

Joshua	Yrk 629	Wm.	Gvl 272
Samuel	Pen 110	Devereaux, Paul	Csn 119
Samuel Senr.	Pen 110	Devine, George	Spa 204
Depass, Abram	Csn 117	Thomas	Gvl 255
Ralph	Csn 146	Deviney, John	Pen 155
Depau, Frances	Csn 95	Devinport, Charles	Abb 38
Depestie, Hector	Csn 111	Susannah	Abb 38
DePestre, Hector	Csn 151	Devlin, Charles	Abb 27
Deprey, Hugh	Sum 589	James	Abb 2
John	Sum 589	John	Abb 2
Deramus, Anne	Ora 539	Patrick	Lan 2
Elizabeth	Ora 539	Devore, John	Edg 149
Derby, Josiah	Uni 232	Devour, Matthew	Edg 151
Phillip	Uni 232	Dew, see also Due	
Zadock	Yrk 632	Dew, Mr.	Mrn 435
Derham, Charnel	Fai 228	Needham	Bar 54
John	Yrk 621	Dewall, Cesar	Nby 73
Joshua	Fai 200	John	Csn 129
Nathaniel	Fai 216	Dewalt, Daniel	Nby 72
William	Yrk 621	Dewar, Robert	Csn 121
Derkheim, Myer	Csn 76	Dewees, William	Csn 111
Derrick,		Deweese, Samuel	Gvl 270
see also Dehrick		Dewett, Daniel	Fai 195
Derrick, Barbary	Lex 575	John	Geo 376
George	Lex 575	Dewey, Samuel	Sum 591
John	Lex 574	Dewit, Charles	Mrn 450
Thomas	Lex 573	Chas.	Col 363
Derrum, Arthur	Abb 16	S.	Col 363
Stephen	Abb 17	Dewitt, Frederick	Cfd 101
Derwin, George C.	Yrk 629	Harris	Mbo 52
James	Yrk 629	John	Mbo 52
John	Yrk 629	John, Jr.	Cfd 102
Wm.	Spa 207	Martin	Dtn 124
DeSaussure, Henry W.	Csn 126	Micaga	Mrn 444
Desbeaux, John	Csn 83	Nancy	Dtn 116
Deschamps, Francis	Csn 175	William	Dtn 125
Joseph	Csn 175	Di---, Henry	Abb 39
Mary	Csn 175	Dial, see also Dyall	
Desel, Charles	Csn 116	Dial, Haistings	Lrs 44
Deshazo, William	Edg 170	James	Gvl 264
Despain, Benjamin	Gvl 247	Jeremiah	Nby 72
Desportes, Peter	Csn 95	Isaac	Lrs 45
De Tollenare, Chas.	Csn 69	John	Dtn 118
Detollenare, Sarah	Csn 61	John	Lrs 18
DeTollenare, Sarah	Csn 91	Martin	Lrs 18
Detto, James	Cfd 108	Dias, Boland	Edg 140
Devaul, Betsey	Edg 149	Henry	Bar 65
Michal Junr.	Abb 30	Joel	Edg 140
Michal Senr.	Abb 30	Dias, Edward	Spa 187
Samuel	Edg 154	Dick, Charles	Uni 249
Devaut, John	Bft 138	Elizabeth	Edg 153
Deveaux, Barnwell	Bft 138	James S.	Geo 362
Israll D.	Ker 397	Mary	Geo 367
Jacob Senr.	Csn 121	Dickenson, Frances	Csn 83
Devees, Sarah	Bar 45	Joseph	Csn 128
Devega, Moses	Csn 141	Dickerson, Elizabeth	Gvl 265
Devenport, David	Nby 73	John	Gvl 282
Francis	Nby 73	Thompson	Gvl 267
Isaac	Nby 73	Dickert, Christopher	Nby 72
James	Nby 73	Michael	Nby 72
John	Lrs 39	Peter	Nby 73
Joseph	Gvl 272	Dickeson, Anthoney	Pen 133
Ransom	Lrs 38	Charles	Pen 119
Thomas	Lrs 39	Ellender	Pen 131
William (2)	Nby 73	James	Uni 229

William	Mbo 52	Donald, Hesikiah	Chr 84
D'Lashment, Jack	Spa 190	John	Abb 14
Doane, Joseph	Csn 108	Donaldson, Hugh	Uni 243
Doar, Jacob	Csn 175	Mathew	Abb 40
John	Csn 175	Robert	Uni 244
Dobbin, Jennet	Wil 470	Thomas	Abb 17
Dobbins,		William	Pen 134
see also Dawbins		William	Yrk 622
Dobbins, James	Pen 158	Done, James	Uni 243
John	Pen 158	Doney, see Donor	
John	Fai 234	Donnelly, James	Yrk 627
Thos.	Col 393	Donnorn, Isaac	Lan 3
Dobbs, James	Abb 4	Donnahoe, John	Bft 120
Lodwick	Pen 142	Donnally, James	Bft 98
Nathaniel	Gvl 246	Donnalson, James	Csn 125
William	Lrs 40	Donnelly, Pat.	Geo 362
Dobins, Starrett	Pen 134	Donoho, Timothy	Lrs 34
Dobs, Josiah	Uni 248	William	Lrs 35
Dobson, Henry	Pen 126	Donohoe, John	Lrs 34
Henry	Pen 143	Donor, Peter	Dtn 115
John	Yrk 632	Donoven, Isaac	Csn 110
Robert	Bft 84	Donum, Ebenezer	Csn 175
Doby, John	Lan 9	Dooley, William	Ker 396
Joseph	Lan 9	Doolin, Elizth.	Spa 208
Dodd, Edward	Uni 236	Dooling, John	Dtn 120
Jesse	Uni 236	Sarah	Dtn 120
Richard	Pen 161	Doolittle, Benjn.	Edg 161
Sarah	Gvl 246	Nancy	Edg 161
Wm.	Uni 236	Doorne, Willm.	Geo 368
Dodds, Hough	Pen 135	Dopson, James	Bar 46
James	Fai 212	Joseph R.	Bft 84
James	Fai 235	Doran, James	Pen 142
John	Fai 204	Dorch, Mary	Bar 54
Saml.	Fai 195	Thomas	Bar 54
Thomas	Fai 198	Dority, James	Gvl 253
Doddson, Charles	Pen 139	Dorkins, Elijah	Nby 73
[D]odgen, Olomon	Edg 185	Dorman, John	Mrn 455
Dodgen, William	Edg 183	Dorn, John	Edg 159
Dodgens, William	Nby 73	Peter	Edg 165
Dodson, Dillingham	Pen 139	Dorough, Hugh	Chr 91
Enoch	Abb 13	James	Lrs 43
Hightower	Yrk 628	John	Lrs 43
William	Abb 13	William	Lrs 43
Dodd, William	Sum 601	Dorrill, John	Csn 151
Doer, Thomas	Csn 175	Jonathan	Csn 151
Doggen, Henry	Csn 151	Rebecca	Csn 151
Dogherty, Samuel	Ker 403	Robert	Csn 151
Doherty, Judith	Fai 226	Dorris, James	Abb 28
Saml.	Fai 227	Dorrity, see Douharty	
Doig, Thomas	Spa 188	Dorset, Joseph	Pen 126
Doizlea, Ann Rebecca	Csn 144	Dorsett, William	Bar 52
Dolahite, Sarah	Gvl 246	Dorsey, Cornelius	Chr 83
Dollar, Hanee	Lrs 16	William	Csn 69
Reuben	Spa 192	Wylie	Lan 8
William	Lrs 27	Dorson, Jonas	Gvl 254
Dollard, Ann	Geo 373	Dorton, Wm.	Spa 180
Dolton, James	Gvl 265	Dorum, William	Csn 147
John	Gvl 252	Dosier, John	Bar 56
Randol	Gvl 266	Doss, John	Pen 128
Solomon	Gvl 266	William	Pen 128
Dominic, Henry	Nby 73	Dosset, James	Pen 125
John	Nby 73	Philip	Cfd 111
Dominick, John	Lex 569	Doster, William	Yrk 623
Don(?), John	Edg 156	Dothwaite, Robert	Bft 86
Don, Alexander	Csn 101	Dotson, Charles	Gvl 249

Doty, Daniel	Pen 123	John	Nby 73
Doud, William	Edg 176	William	Nby 73
Doude, Ann	Fai 226	Dowling, see also	
Doudle, Mary	Lex 578	Dooling	
Douglas, James	Csn 151	Dowling, Cageby	Ora 507
James	Ker 429	Jabez	Ora 505
Jesse	Dtn 113	Downen, Thomas	Nby 73
Jesse	Yrk 619	Downey, Joseph	Abb 11
John	Bar 61	Martha	Abb 2
John	Mbo 52	Downing, John	Chr 92
Thomas	Lan 6	Joseph	Abb 5
Douglass, Alexr.	Fai 238	Joseph	Lrs 19
James	Csn 125	Downs, David	Nby 73
John	Fai 232	Ezekiel	Pen 137
John	Fai 239	James	Nby 73
John	Sum 607	John	Nby 73
Molley	Edg 177	Jonathan Esq.	Lrs 45
Nathl.	Csn 133	Joseph Esq.	Lrs 45
Robert	Fai 207	Thomas	Nby 73
Robt.	Fai 206	Dowthet, Solomon	Gvl 250
Saml.	Wil 472	Doyle,	
William	Wil 473	see also Dyall	
Dougless, James	Chr 74	Doyle, Edward	Pen 132
Dougharty, John	Dtn 122	Edward	Pen 133
Doughaty, John	Yrk 623	Simon	Pen 132
Dougharty, Mary	Ora 513	Dozer, Abraham G.	Edg 137
Thomas	Dtn 121	John	Geo 371
Wm.	Dtn 121	John, Senr.	Geo 392
Dougherty, Jeremiah	Pen 124	John, Senr.	Mrn 434
Doughlas, Alexander	Lan 4	Jolly	Mrn 436
George	Lan 6	Richard M.	Edg 137
James	Lan 4	Thomas	Edg 136
Doughty, slaves of	Geo 374	William	Edg 176
Doughty, Benjn.	Dtn 117	Draffan, Joseph	Lan 6
George	Cfd 109	William	Lan 6
Joseph	Pen 123	Drafts, Michael	Lex 573
Levi	Dtn 122	Drage, Eason	Edg 151
Randolph	Dtn 117	Drake, Benjamin	Lrs 29
Thomas	Cfd 109	Chas. Estate	Csn 195
Thomas	Csn 149	James	Abb 33
William	Csn 69	John	Csn 90
William Jur.	Sum 606	Mary	Abb 16
Willm.	Csn 104	Micajah	Edg 165
Douharty, James	Dtn 119	Milla	Edg 140
Douthard, John	Pen 109	Richd.	Uni 222
Douthat, John	Gvl 250	Drakeford, John	Ker 417
Dove, ---ha	Edg 144	Richard	Ker 421
Archibald	Dtn 127	Drakford, Sarah	Ker 417
Benjn.	Fai 229	Draper, John	Lrs 34
Jacob	Edg 145	Jonathan	Lex 497
John	Dtn 128	Thomas	Ora 505
Dover, John	Pen 108	Thomas	Uni 242
Elijah	Yrk 628	Travis	Uni 242
Zepheniah	Yrk 628	Drawdey, Daniel	Ora 513
Dow, Robert	Ker 396	Drayton, slaves of	Geo 374
Dowdall, Sarah	Gvl 273	Chas.	Csn 167
Dowden, John	Sum 601	Jacob	Csn 126
Dowdle, Allen	Yrk 624	John Excelle	Csn 139
James	Pen 158	Thos.	Bft 128
John	Pen 158	Thos.	Csn 167
Robert (2)	Pen 158	Dreher, George	Lex 579
Dowdy, George	Cfd 102	Henry	Lex 567
Thomas	Cfd 102	John	Lex 576
Will	Lan 3	Drehr, John	Lex 483
Dowes, Jesse	Nby 73	Rachel	Lex 497

Drennan, Hugh	Pen 155		Duberry, Wm.	Spa 207
Tobitha	Geo 363		Dubert, Philip	Lex 483
Drennen, John	Nby 73		Dubois, Ann	Csn 175
Drennes, George	Csn 140		Lewis	Csn 124
Drennon, David	Pen 158		Peter	Csn 102
Hugh	Yrk 620		Saml.	Geo 364
James	Pen 158		Dubose,	
John	Fai 213		see also Debose	
John	Nby 72		Dubose, Andrew	Dtn 119
John	Pen 158		Andrew Jr.	Dtn 121
John Esqr.	Yrk 621		Benjamin	Dtn 128
Rachell	Pen 158		Benjn.	Dtn 119
Robert, Junr.	Nby 72		Daniel	Dtn 118
Robert, Senr.	Nby 72		Dolitha	Dtn 119
Thomas	Pen 158		Elias	Dtn 118
Thomas, Junr.	Yrk 621		Eliehu	Ora 525
Thomas, Senr.	Yrk 621		Ezekiel	Sum 591
William	Nby 72		Isaac	Ker 397
William	Pen 157		Isaac	Ora 525
Drew, Langston	Pen 157		Jeremiah	Dtn 118
Lewis	Mrn 447		Jeremiah	Dtn 127
Drewitt, Nicholas	Yrk 630		Jesse	Dtn 113
Drewprey, Drewry	Gvl 279		Joseph	Csn 151
Drexler, John	Csn 122		Lydia	Dtn 118
Driggers, Elija	Csn 61		Peter, Jr.	Dtn 121
Elisha	Csn 61		Samuel	Csn 195
Drigars, Ephraim	Mrn 454		William	Dtn 118
Thomas	Mrn 444		William	Sum 591
Driggers, John	Mbo 52		Ducart, Jonothan	Gvl 269
John	Mbo 59		Duceshill, Leroy	Abb 31
Jordan	Mbo 60		Duck, Joseph	Pen 160
Mark	Mbo 59		Timothy	Dtn 117
Mathew	Mbo 59		Ducker, William	Edg 141
Naomi	Mbo 59		Duckett, Jacob	Nby 72
Thomas	Mbo 59		James	Lrs 26
William	Sum 601		Joseph	Nby 73
Drinkard, Francis	Abb 10		Josiah	Nby 72
Drinkwater, John	Abb 33		Lydda	Nby 72
Driskill, John	Gvl 249		Richard	Lrs 26
Driver, Christopher	Pen 163		Thomas	Nby 72
Elizabeth	Dtn 121		Duckworth, Benjamin	Pen 119
Leonard	Lex 563		Charity	Pen 119
Drouillard, Js(?)	Csn 147		Duddell, James	Csn 123
Droze, Isaac	Sum 605		Duddly, Elizabeth	Edg 154
Drue, Else	Mrn 437		Dudley, Ambrose	Pen 118
John	Mrn 437		Thomas	Bft 108
Newit	Mrn 437		Samuel	Ker 425
Drumman, Benjamin	Abb 39		William	Pen 118
Drummon, David	Spa 210		Dudney, Arthur	Yrk 626
Epheraim	Spa 183		Wm.	Chr. 90
Polley	Spa 174		Due, Abraham	Mrn 452
Drummond, Daniel	Lrs 31		Absolum	Mrn 458
Daniel	Yrk 625		Christopher	Mrn 445
James	Csn 152		James	Dtn 126
James	Pen 142		John	Mrn 444
John	Csn 133		Reuben	Mrn 455
Nathaniel	Lrs 31		Duen(?), Will	Lan 5
Drumon, James	Bar 44A		Duff, Abram	Pen 106
John	Bar 44A		Dennis	Gvl 248
Duan(?), Charles	Gvl 260		James	Pen 105
Duan, Elisha	Gvl 245		James	Pen 118
Duanes, Thos.	Gvl 281		James	Yrk 631
Dubar, Peter F.	Csn 120		James, Capt.	Yrk 631
Dubel, Joseph	Csn 85		John	Pen 114
Duber, Philip	Lex 575		Joseph	Pen 112

John	Spa	183	Thomas	Geo	373
John	Spa	184	Dunne, Mary	Ker	396
Joseph	Gvl	272	Dunnevant, Wm.	Fai	228
Joseph	Lrs	25	Dunning(?), Miles B.	Col	369
Sarah	Chr	91	Dunning, James	Dtn	116
Wm.	Spa	181	Dunnlap, Jane	Ker	407
Wm.	Spa	182	Dunston, Richard	Mbo	52
Dunkley, Sarah	Fai	196	Duntze, Gerard	Fai	199
Dunklin, James	Lrs	42	Dupies, James, Junr.	Bft	116
William	Gvl	270	James, Senr.	Bft	102
Dunlap, ---	Csn	133	Dupoister, James	Uni	240
Dunlap, Benjamin	Yrk	619	Dupont, Abrm.	Bft	104
David	Lrs	43	Chrs.	Bft	132
David	Pen	137	Corn. Est	Bft	104
David	Yrk	619	John	Csn	61
George	Lan	3	Dupre, Cornelius	Geo	365
Henry	Lan	3	James	Wil	477
James	Abb	8	Lewis	Csn	108
James	Ker	407	DuPre, Mary	Csn	175
James	Lrs	18	Dupre, Saml.	Geo	374
John	Fai	218	Estate of		
John	Yrk	619	Dupree, Benjamin	Csn	80
John Esqr.	Abb	39	Mary	Wil	477
Oliver	Geo	369	Duprie, John	Uni	250
Robert	Ker	407	Durant, Ben	Wil	472
Robert	Lan	2	George	Geo	377
Saml.	Lan	3	George	Wil	473
Samuel	Lan	2	Henry	Geo	385
Samuel	Lan	8	Henry	Sum	611
Samuel	Lrs	18	Thos.	Geo	380
Sam. C.	Lan	2	Durborough, John	Uni	240
Will.	Lan	7	Duren, George	Ker	413
William	Abb	35	Jesse	Ker	423
William	Csn	151	John	Ker	415
William	Yrk	619	John, Senr.	Ker	415
William, Maj.	Lrs	28	Durham, see also		
Dunman, Daniel	Nby	72	Kerrum, Durrum		
William	Pen	146	Durham, Charles	Pen	113
Dunn, Andrew	Chr	73	Daniel	Pen	113
Andrew	Chr	74	David	Pen	104
Burwell	Sum	610	John	Spa	167
Francis	Pen	127	James	Edg	148
Henry	Sum	608	William	Pen	104
Isham	Ker	401	Durley, Horatio	Pen	156
Isham	Sum	611	Durr, J.	Col	363
James	Chr	79	M.	Col	363
Joel	Fai	225	Durragh, James	Pen	160
John	Cfd	109	Durram, Jos:	Col	383
John	Csn	134	Durrum, Arthur	Abb	36
John	Ker	423	Stephen	Abb	36
John	Sum	604	Dursse, Luesia	Csn	146
Lemuel	Bft	104	Dusk, Peter	Edg	165
Roger	Sum	595	Dutart, John	Csn	195
Simeon	Chr	85	Dutch, Stephen	Csn	117
Sylvester	Sum	595	Dutton, John	Abb	33
Sylvester, Junr.	Sum	607	Duty, Richard	Lrs	35
Sylvester, Senr.	Sum	608	Duvall, Alexr.	Gvl	282
Thomas	Cfd	109	Benjn.	Gvl	281
Thomas	Ker	409	Lewis	Lrs	17
William	Fai	225	Dwight, Oriden Daniel	Csn	153
Dunnagan, Olly	Sum	609	Rebecca	Geo	379
Dunnagin, Thomas	Gvl	245	Dyal, Michael	Edg	186
Isaac	Gvl	245	Thomas	Dtn	117
Dunnam, John	Geo	373	William	Fai	231
Robt.	Mrn	458	Dye, Elisha	Fai	240

George	Fai 201	John B.	Pen 135
John	Fai 201	Samuel	Gvl 246
Martin	Gvl 259	Thos. P.	Gvl 244
Phillip	Fai 218	Earley, Enoch	Pen 151
Dyer, Elisha	Pen 112	Early, Andrew	Wil 463
Hezekiah	Lrs 42	Earnest, Henry	Spa 191
John	Mbo 52	Thomas	Pen 103
Joshua	Pen 111	Wm.	Spa 188
Dykes, Abel	Ora 517	Earwood, H. Andrew	Pen 124
Benjamin	Ora 519	Robert	Pen 124
Burden	Ora 519	Easley, John	Gvl 255
Daniel	Ora 519	John	Pen 116
Darcas	Ora 523	John, Junr.	Gvl 257
David	Ora 527	Milington	Gvl 264
George	Ora 517	Pleasant	Gvl 263
George	Ora 527	Robert	Pen 105
George, Junr.	Ora 529	Thos.	Gvl 263
Isaac	Ora 517	William Junr.	Gvl 257
Isaac	Ora 527	Wm.	Gvl 256
James	Ora 531	Eason, Abraham	Ora 507
William	Ora 517	George	Ora 507
Dyson, Abraham	Lrs 18	James	Pen 160
Aquilla	Yrk 632	William	Ora 507
James	Nby 73	East, Benjn.	Gvl 272
Maddox	Yrk 632	Josiah	Lrs 28
Dyzell, Jas. Est.	Col 395	Tarlton	Lrs 28
		Thomas	Lrs 24
		Thomas, Senr.	Lrs 24
E		William	Lrs 28
		William, Junr.	Lrs 29
		Eaterling, Enoch	Ora 547
Eady, Danl.	Csn 69	James	Mrn 455
George	Csn 69	Jesse	Mrn 453
James	Csn 69	Jonathan	Ora 509
John	Csn 69	Saml.	Mrn 461
Jonathan	Csn 69	Shadrach	Mbo 52
Judith	Mrn 460	William	Mbo 52
Molly	Mrn 461	Eastes, Benjamin	Lrs 18
Nancy	Mrn 461	Eastirling, H.	Col 363
Wm.	Csn 69	Eastis, Elisha	Lrs 42
Eagle, Barbara	Ora 551	Eastland, Thomas	Nby 74
John	Bar 48	Eastlind, Hezekiah	Nby 74
Eakin,	Yrk 622	Eastlinger, George	Spa 178
Alexander, Junr.		Eastmead, Richard	Bft 132
John	Yrk 621	Easton, Susanna	Csn 103
Thomas	Yrk 622	Eastres, Charles	Gvl 269
William	Yrk 618	Josiah	Gvl 269
William	Yrk 622	Eastridge, Ephraim	Nby 74
William, Senr.	Yrk 622	Garlant	Gvl 257
Eakins,	Yrk 621	Eastris, Charles Jr.	Gvl 270
Alexander, Senr.		Obediah	Gvl 270
Eals, John	Abb 28	Eastwood, Iserael	Spa 177
Earbey, Wm.	Gvl 274	John	Bar 51
Earhart, Catharine	Lex 567	Eaton, Henry	Pen 111
Godfrey	Lex 579	Joseph	Edg 139
Jacob	Lex 570	Joseph	Pen 135
Jacob	Spa 169	Lewis	Pen 116
Leonard	Lex 559	Reuben	Pen 136
Eargle, see Arighel,		William	Pen 112
Erigle, Ergal		Eaves, Mark	Chr 91
Earle, Bayless	Gvl 264	Eazell, John	Ker 407
Bayles	Spa 180	Ebherard, Elizabeth	Ora 549
Elias	Gvl 243	Eberly, John	Col 385
George W.	Gvl 244	Eccles, Robert	Nby 74
John	Gvl 244	Echols, Davison	Pen 149

John	Pen 128	John	Pen 103
Eckhard, Jacob	Csn 117	Margarett	Pen 157
Eckells, John	Csn 61	Thomas	Pen 103
John Junr.	Csn 61	William	Pen 157
William	Csn 61	Edmonson, James	Pen 119
Wm.	Col 375	Marget	Nby 74
Eckles, Mathew	Fai 222	Edmunds, Alexander	Edg 142
Edavis(?), John	Chr 82	Wm.	Fai 240
Eddinfield, David	Bar 55	Edninson, A.	Col 363
Eddings, Joseph Senr.	Col 375	T.	Col 363
William	Cfd 102	Edson, Timothy A.	Csn 82
William	Csn 183	Edward, John	Lan 9
Wm.	Col 375	Mary	Mrn 444
Eddins, Abram	Nby 74	Richd.	Mrn 439
Benjn.	Edg 159	Saml.	Mrn 439
Christopher	Edg 149	Thomas	Lan 3
James	Edg 159	Edwards, Alexr.	Csn 125
Silvia	Lex 572	Ambros	Abb 31
Eddy, James	Wil 465	Ann	Bft 116
John	Csn 115	Benjn.	Edg 158
Patience	Wil 464	Catharine	Csn 151
Samuel	Csn 61	David	Bar 51
Samuel	Wil 465	David	Pen 107
Eden, James (2)	Csn 151	David	Yrk 630
John	Csn 151	David	Cfd 102
Jonah	Csn 151	Edward	Csn 69
Joshua	Csn 83	Edward	Nby 74
Mary	Csn 151	Edward	Abb 20
Thomas	Bft 140	Elizabeth	Sum 609
Edenfield, Mary	Bar 55	Elizabeth	Chr 92
Thomas	Bar 56	Enoch	Abb 4
Edinfield, William	Bar 55	George	Bft 126
Edens, John	Cfd 108	George	Bft 140
John	Mbo 52	George	Dtn 114
Richard	Mbo 52	Henry	Csn 94
Edenton, James	Spa 168	Isaac	Uni 218
James	Uni 233	Isaac	Uni 246
John	Spa 172	Isaac	Mbo 52
John	Uni 233	Isabella	Abb 20
Ederington, Francis	Fai 202	James	Cfd 102
George	Fai 201	James	Csn 97
Henry	Fai 201	James	Uni 231
Jeremiah	Fai 201	James	Chr 80
Jno.	Fai 201	Jarrot	Pen 144
Edes, Agness	Fai 233	Jesse	Bft 118
Edge, Daniel	Geo 378	John	Cfd 102
Major	Fai 203	John	Chr 80
Thomas	Fai 203	John	Csn 69
Edgey, James	Spa 196	John	Gvl 261
Edings, Joseph	Bft 140	John	Gvl 262
William	Lrs 38	John	Lex 495
Edins, Alexander	Pen 110	John	Pen 113
Jacob	Pen 110	John	Spa 186
John	Cfd 108	John	Sum 584
Samuel	Pen 110	John, Jr.	Cfd 102
William	Pen 115	Joseph	Abb 17
William	Pen 141	Joseph	Cfd 107
Edminson, William	Pen 103	Joseph	Chr 79
Edminston, John	Abb 4	Joseph	Gvl 260
Edmiston, Andrew	Abb 21	Joshua	Spa 191
John	Abb 5	Lewis	Pen 138
David	Abb 4	Margaret	Ora 543
Edmonds, Ann	Mrn 450	Mary	Cfd 102
Edmondson, James	Pen 103	Mary	Mbo 52
James	Pen 150	Mary	Nby 74

Robert	Chr 90	William	Ker 405	
Stephen	Bft 138	Ellot, Joshua	Uni 238	
Thomas	Edg 163	Ellum, William	Sum 608	
Thomas	Lrs 41	Elmore, Allen	Nby 74	
William	Edg 169	Charles	Lrs 41	
William	Lrs 23	Isaac	Nby 74	
Wm.	Bft 138	Jacob	Sum 584	
Ellire, Jeremiah	Pen 114	James	Yrk 627	
Ellis, Abigail	Gvl 268	Jesse	Csn 131	
Archibald	Cfd 108	John A., Maj.	Lrs 25	
Benja.	Geo 374	Matthias	Nby 74	
Charles	Yrk 630	Randolph	Mrn 453	
Edmon	Uni 239	Ridgeway	Nby 74	
Ellison	Edg 182	Stephen	Nby 74	
James	Abb 8	Thomas	Nby 74	
James	Abb 15	William	Dtn 122	
Jesse	Pen 117	Elot, Robert	Bar 46	
John	Cfd 102	Elott, John	Csn 82	
John	Chr 81	Elrod, James	Pen 109	
John	Edg 180	Abraham	Pen 103	
John	Nby 74	Adam	Gvl 260	
John, Senr.	Yrk 628	Isaac	Pen 103	
Joseph	Abb 15	Jeremiah	Pen 120	
Peter	Uni 239	Peter	Pen 160	
Richard	Bft 138	Samuel	Pen 133	
Robert	Abb 15	William	Pen 154	
Sam: Junr.	Csn 175	Elsey, George	Csn 61	
Samuel	Csn 111	John	Fai 195	
Samuel	Csn 175	John	Fai 234	
Thomas	Csn 97	Elishaw, John	Lex 487	
Thomas	Edg 138	Elstob, Symon	Csn 81	
Thomas	Edg 182	Elsy, Lewis	Fai 195	
Underhill	Sum 610	Eltom, Anthony M.	Abb 10	
Will	Lan 5	Elton, Samuel	Nby 74	
William	Abb 15	Elvis, George	Geo 390	
William	Edg 148	Susannah	Geo 391	
William	Edg 165	Ely, John	Fai 205	
William	Edg 181	Elzey, Berry	Ora 523	
William	Yrk 627	Jesse	Ora 521	
Wm.	Chr 88	Mary	Ora 517	
Wm.	Uni 239	William	Ora 523	
Elliser, Jacob	Lex 574	Elziph, Jonathan	Mrn 436	
Ellison,	Yrk 626	Emberson, Henry	Spa 210	
Alexander Senr.		James	Pen 148	
George	Fai 235	William	Ker 399	
Henry	Csn 111	Embery, Zach	Spa 200	
Henry	Csn 142	Embray, Wm.	Chr 82	
Hugh	Yrk 626	Embrey, Abraham	Spa 198	
James	Chr 86	James	Spa 197	
James	Gvl 269	Emerson, James	Abb 37	
James	Yrk 626	Thomas	Abb 37	
John	Csn 148	William	Abb 37	
Oran	Edg 172	Emlong, Jas.	Csn 151	
Robert	Fai 203	Endsley, Abraham	Lrs 22	
Robert	Dtn 126	Andrew Junr. (2)	Lrs 22	
Robert	Pen 118	James	Lrs 23	
Robert, Capt.	Yrk 626	England, Alexander	Csn 154	
William	Csn 137	Charles	Pen 142	
William	Edg 178	English, Alexander	Chr 88	
William	Fai 227	Andrew	Abb 2	
William	Lex 562	Andrew	Abb 37	
Ellisson, Charles	Ora 511	Edward	Sum 595	
Ellit, Archibald	Gvl 250	James	Abb 37	
Elkins, John	Ker 403	James	Ker 399	
Robert	Ker 405	James	Ker 401	

Falconer, Alexander	Yrk 620	Farnandez, Henry	Uni 243
William	Cfd 102	Farr, ---	Csn 179
William	Lan 7	Elizath.	Col 377
Falkinder, James	Lan 6	Frederick	Lex 569
Fallow,		Joseph	Col 377
see also Felaw		Michael	Lex 569
Fallows, Elisabeth	Yrk 626	Richd.	Uni 229
Fann(?), Barney	Pen 119	Robert	Pen 123
Fannan, Jacob	Abb 39	Samuel	Abb 5
Fannin, Jacob	Edg 135	Thos. Senr.	Col 377
Fanning, Abraham	Ora 527	Thos. D.	Col 375
John	Ora 527	Thos. J.	Bft 102
Fant, Abner	Fai 202	W. B.	Csn 167
Samuel	Fai 202	Wm. B.	Uni 229
William	Fai 196	Farrah, George	Edg 162
Faquier, Henry	Yrk 620	Peter	Edg 162
Farah, Chesley	Edg 172	Farrar, Andrew	Lex 570
Fare, James	Chr 93	Thomas	Pen 121
Fares, Thomas	Edg 186	Farrington, Jehu	Yrk 621
Faries, Alexander	Yrk 618	Farrol, James	Csn 119
Alexander	Yrk 619	Farrow, John	Lrs 18
Alexander	Yrk 629	John	Spa 194
Arthur	Yrk 631	Rachel	Spa 194
Isaac	Yrk 621	Thomas	Csn 116
James	Yrk 621	Thomas	Nby 75
James	Yrk 631	Thomas	Spa 194
James Junr.	Yrk 631	William	Nby 75
John	Yrk 629	Wm.	Spa 194
Margaret	Yrk 617	Faugourson, James	Gvl 260
Robert Esqr.	Yrk 631	Nicholas	Gvl 261
William	Yrk 619	Thos.	Gvl 260
William	Yrk 623	Wm.	Gvl 260
Faris, Absalom	Pen 115	Faukner, Sarah	Edg 175
Absalom	Pen 116	Faulk, Wm.	Uni 229
Dorcas	Uni 243	Faulkinburg, Henry	Lan 10
James	Pen 120	Isaac	Lan 10
John	Chr 79	Jacob	Lan 10
Levy	Gvl 275	John	Lan 10
Matthew	Chr 75	John	Lrs 30
Peggy	Pen 104	Faures, Laurence	Csn 100
Thomas	Chr 79	Faust, James	Edg 157
William	Pen 104	Faunter, James	Edg 158
William	Pen 115	Fawling, William	Csn 62
Farley, James	Csn 124	Fawn(?), Alexander	Bft 84
Owin.	Csn 135	Fawn, Will	Lan 8
Farmer, Absalom	Pen 160	Fay, Charles	Geo 371
Benjn.	Gvl 262	Faysoux, Ann	Csn 69
Berry	Gvl 274	Fayzaux, Ann	Csn 113
Ezekiel	Spa 209	Feagin, Benjamin	Mbo 60
Federick	Gvl 273	Edward	Mbo 53
Francis	Abb 17	James	Mbo 53
Frenus	Pen 143	Fearies, Thomas	Fai 240
James	Dtn 124	Joseph	Fai 231
John	Gvl 258	William	Fai 220
Joseph	Fai 222	Feaster, Andrew	Fai 229
Luke	Ker 423	John	Fai 229
Michl.	Col 383	Fearwell, Thos.	Geo 383
Nathan	Spa 208	Federick, Thomas	Bar 53
Robert	Sum 609	Fee, Robert	Chr 78
Shederick	Spa 209	Feemster, James	Yrk 624
Thomas	Dtn 124	Joseph	Yrk 624
Thomas	Lan 10	John	Yrk 622
Thomas	Sum 613	John	Yrk 624
Wm.	Spa 199	Saml.	Chr 76
Zachariah	Ker 427	Fegle, Laurence	Nby 75

Felaw, Henry	Edg 156	Ferrile, Will.	Lan	3
Felben, Charles	Csn 61	Will	Lan	5
Felder, Daniel	Uni 235	Ferrill, Thomas	Fai	218
Frederick	Ora 549	Will.	Lan	10
Henery	Ora 543	Ferry, Champion	Wil	475
Peter	Ora 503	Fervox(?), Joshua	Bft	86
Samuel	Ora 541	Fetherston, Jacob	Chr	81
Felker, Peter	Mrn 453	John	Chr	73
Fell, ---	Csn 159	Few, Wm.	Gvl	258
Thomas Jr.	Csn 124	Fewell, John, Junr.	Yrk	620
Thomas Senr.	Csn 124	John, Senr.	Yrk	620
Feller, George	Nby 75	Fewkway, Thomas	Bft	92
Fellon, William	Pen 130	Fickling, Francis	Csn	187
Felps, Enock	Edg 186	Henry	Csn	187
William	Wil 468	James	Bft	132
Feltman, George	Nby 75	Jeremiah	Csn	183
Felton, Emeriah	Pen 157	Jeremiah	Csn	187
Harred	Pen 153	Joseph	Col	375
Felts, Andrew	Nby 75	Mary	Bft	120
Frederick	Cfd 102	Saml.	Bft	140
Fenden, Peter F.	Csn 61	Saml.	Col	375
Thos.	Col 385	Samuel	Csn	183
Fendley, James	Lrs 38	Thomas	Csn	187
Fenley, Thomas	Chr 93	Wm.	Bft	140
Fenly, John	Chr 81	Fiddy, William	Csn	79
Fennel, Dempsy	Bar 46	Field, Jeremiah	Pen	112
Henry	Bar 46	John C.	Col	393
Isham	Bar 44	Fielder, Barthow.	Uni	227
Fennil, Arthur	Bar 46	George	Spa	192
Fenwick, Edwd. Est.	Col 377	Fields, Andrew	Edg	143
John R.	Geo 372	Bartholomew	Dtn	122
Fergeson, Hugh	Pen 141	Batholomew	Dtn	127
William	Pen 140	Ephraim	Dtn	119
Ferguson, see also		Fielder, Francis	Spa	185
Faugourson		Fields, James	Pen	139
Ferguson, Aaron	Ker 401	John	Bft	81
Ann	Csn 102	John	Lrs	35
Benjamin	Sum 597	John	Pen	112
Berkley	Bft 84	Obediah	Abb	15
Charles	Bft 94	Rebecca	Bft	110
Daniel	Sum 595	Rebecca	Csn	118
Isaac	Fai 223	Redden	Bft	90
James	Lan 5	Samuel	Bar	45
James	Lan 9	Thomas	Pen	139
James	Pen 115	William	Mbo	53
James	Pen 127	Willm. B.	Csn	86
James	Pen 164	Fife, David	Abb	7
James F.	Bft 140	David, Sr.	Abb	11
John	Abb 22	James	Csn	134
John	Csn 113	William	Abb	11
John	Lan 9	Fifer, John	Nby	74
John	Pen 164	Fike, Abel	Pen	163
Richard	Lrs 25	Fikes, George	Nby	75
Robert	Yrk 625	Filby, Absolom	Lrs	25
Ward	Lrs 24	Files, Abner	Pen	140
William	Yrk 625	Adam	Pen	163
William H.	Bft 126	Jeremiah	Pen	140
Wm.	Fai 223	John	Pen	163
Ferington, Absolom	Abb 21	Manly	Pen	140
Ferraud, Alexander	Csn 99	Filing, see Phelan		
Ferrell, Charity	Bft 88	Fillpot, Daniel	Bar	58
David	Sum 597	John	Pen	154
Ephraim	Edg 150	Filpeck, George	Uni	248
Mary	Bft 88	Peter	Uni	249
Ferrer, Parron	Pen 146	Phillip	Uni	249

Thomas	Abb	8	Moses	Geo	381
William	Lrs	32	Nathaniel	Gvl	255
Flemming, Elijah	Yrk	623	Osten	Geo	392
Samuel	Lex	487	Richd.	Gvl	272
Flemmon, James	Spa	200	Richd.	Uni	247
Flemons, Bailey	Lan	4	Robert	Nby	75
Fletchal, Thomas	Chr	85	Saml.	Spa	184
Fletcher, John	Gvl	247	Saml. Junr.	Geo	388
Flewelling, Thomas	Lrs	26	Saml. Senr.	Geo	388
Flewett, Samuel	Csn	137	Stephen	Sum	613
Fley, Samuel	Sum	585	Thomas	Spa	205
Flin, James	Lan	9	Thomas Junr.	Sum	613
James	Nby	75	Thomas Senr.	Sum	612
William	Edg	161	William	Bft	90
Judith	Lrs	30	William	Nby	75
Flinn, Charles Estate	Csn	183	William	Pen	156
Margaret	Ker	396	Floyed, Garland	Gvl	273
Flint, Joseph	Csn	75	William	Pen	136
Thomas	Mrn	461	Fludd, Danl.	Col	377
Flinter, James	Lex	497	Hiram	Col	381
Floid, John	Chr	84	Fluker, George	Edg	177
Flood, Daniel	Csn	117	Fogal, George	Ora	541
John	Fai	217	Fogartie, Francis	Csn	155
Florance, Zachariah	Csn	100	James	Csn	97
Florin, Lucas	Csn	85	Lewis	Csn	155
Floto, J. H.	Csn	110	Fogarties, Miss	Csn	82
Flowed, Granbery	Edg	145	Foley, Flood	Geo	388
Flowers, Andrew	Pen	162	John	Geo	388
Bennet	Mrn	437	Mason	Spa	192
Bright	Dtn	126	Folk,		
Drury	Dtn	119	see also Fulk		
Harmon	Mrn	459	Folk, Francis	Mbo	53
Jacob	Dtn	120	Jacob	Bar	68
Jesse	Dtn	120	Jonathan	Mbo	53
John	Dtn	115	Roberson	Bar	64
John	Fai	216	William	Sum	587
John	Mrn	437	Folker, John C.	Csn	144
Rachel	Mrn	437	Folkner, David	Gvl	273
Rachell	Geo	385	Folly, Badre	Wil	467
William	Dtn	119	Charles	Wil	468
Floyd,			Folmed, Jnas	Csn	138
see also Flowed			Foltz, J. F.	Csn	129
Floyd, Alexr.	Pen	136	William	Csn	69
Allen	Dtn	117	Fondren, Richd.	Spa	169
Andrew	Yrk	626	Wm.	Spa	170
Aron	Spa	184	Fontayson, John	Csn	175
Baxter	Sum	609	Foost, Christian	Bar	64
Buckner	Sum	609	Foot, George	Chr	83
David	Uni	236	John	Fai	199
Ebenezar	Spa	189	Newton	Fai	205
Edward	Csn	175	Wm.	Chr	76
Elisha	Pen	140	Footman, John W.	Csn	98
Enoch	Spa	188	Forbes, George	Pen	120
Enoch	Uni	236	John	Yrk	618
Francis	Geo	388	Joseph	Yrk	618
Frederick	Geo	388	William	Pen	132
George	Spa	184	Forbis, Edward	Abb	27
Grono	Dtn	117	Rachel	Abb	27
James	Geo	390	William	Abb	27
James	Yrk	626	Forbush, Jesse	Nby	75
Jesse	Sum	613	Ford, Barrett	Abb	37
John	Gvl	260	Blakely	Yrk	632
John	Nby	75	Daniel(?)	Gvl	273
Mary	Bft	130	Edward	Gvl	280
Maurice	Dtn	117	Elias	Bar	65

Frances	Yrk 632	William	Abb	23
Gardner	Fai 228	Forgy, Jonathan	Lrs	38
George	Geo 369	Forman, Isaac	Yrk 622
George	Mrn 439	James	Yrk 622
Hannah	Col 379	Samuel	Yrk 622
Henry	Bar 61	Forniss, James	Mbo	53
Hezekiah	Fai 222	William	Mbo	53
Isaac	Col 375	Forrans, William H.	Csn 102
Isaac	Lan 5	Forrest, James	Abb	24
J---	Edg 144	Jesse	Edg 133
Jacob	Csn 122	Thos. H.	Csn 119
James	Col 375	Forrester, Chrisn. C.	Bft	81
James	Mrn 447	David	Gvl 253
James Junr.	Mrn 447	Isham	Gvl 253
Jesse	Fai 233	Hardy	Gvl 253
Jesse	Gvl 273	Richd.	Gvl 253
John	Chr 80	Forrister, Alexr.	Spa 196
John	Mrn 458	Hutchens	Spa 176
John	Nby 74	Mark	Spa 177
Joseph Junr.	Mrn 458	Owen	Spa 195
Malacai	Col 379	Solomon	Spa 176
Manley	Spa 181	Thos.	Spa 195
Margarett	Geo 372	Forshaw, Edward	Csn 191
Mary Est.	Col 379	Jas C.	Col 393
Mary	Sum 585	Forshner, Joseph	Ora 553
Nathaniel	Mrn 438	Forsythe, John	Bft 118
Nathl.	Fai 222	Fort, Albert	Dtn 113
Preserved	Mrn 439	Burwell	Sum 595
Ralph	Yrk 632	Elizabeth	Dtn 125
Richard	Abb 37	Jesse	Fai 199
Richard	Bar 65	John	Csn 175
Robert	Ker 423	Wiley	Sum 610
Robt. Est.	Col 379	Forten, Richard	Bar 51
Samuel	Abb 37	Fortenberry, Mary	Spa 205
Stephen	Mrn 447	Fortner, John	Edg 183
Stephen	Gvl 272	Nathan	Edg 184
Susan	Col 379	Thomas	Edg 184
Thomas	Lrs 37	Fortune, William	Pen 122
Thos. Est.	Col 379	Foshee, Benjamin	Lrs 34
Timothy	Csn 126	Fosset, Richd.	Uni 224
William	Geo 363	Rolley	Spa 203
Wm.	Chr 81	Wm.	Spa 178
Wm.	Spa 180	Foster, Ambrose	Edg 154
Wm.	Spa 181	Ambrose	Pen 124
Zadock (2)	Spa 191	Andrew	Lan 7
Fordham, Richard	Csn 83	Anthony	Spa 193
Fords, Elijah	Ora 505	Benjamin	Csn 175
Fordum, Jered	Sum 604	David	Bar 61
Forehands, James	Sum 600	Elizabeth	Wil 475
Foreman, Benjamin	Bar 49	Frances	Geo 375
Charity	Edg 142	Francis	Uni 248
Isaac	Edg 142	Gabriel	Pen 105
Jacob	Bar 60	George	Pen 108
Susanna	Bar 65	George	Uni 246
Fores, Abraham	Csn 142	Henry	Abb 23
Richd.	Mrn 461	Henry	Spa 210
Forest, Charity	Csn 90	Henry	Uni 244
Forester, John	Lrs 17	Isham (2)	Spa 204
Forgason, David (2)	Nby 75	Jacob	Pen 137
Johnson	Nby 75	James	Abb 6
Forgett, M.	Col 387	James	Abb 7
Forgey, William	Abb 7	James	Abb 11
Forguson, Daniel	Abb 23	James	Bft 108
Daniel	Abb 38	James	Gvl 248
James	Abb 40	James	Lan 7

James	Uni 249		David	Uni 246
James	Pen 103		Edmond	Spa 177
James Senr.	Abb 7		Elijah	Nby 75
Jean	Spa 210		Eliza	Uni 216
Jeremiah	Pen 103		Ellis	Uni 245
Joel	Nby 75		Ellis	Uni 246
John	Abb 12		Enoch	Pen 149
John	Abb 13		Epheraim	Uni 246
John	Lan 2		Francis	Spa 211
John	Fai 240		Godferry	Uni 246
John	Spa 193		Isaac	Gvl 279
John	Spa 202		Isereal	Uni 245
John (2)	Spa 204		James	Edg 156
John	Uni 245		James	Lrs 19
John	Uni 247		James	Spa 180
John, Revd.	Sum 607		James	Spa 189
John Senr.	Spa 211		James, Revd.	Yrk 623
John R.	Csn 81		Jeremiah	Pen 142
Joseph	Abb 13		Jesse	Lrs 15
Josiah	Pen 126		Joel	Lrs 15
Moses	Spa 200		John	Csn 129
Richard	Bar 65		John	Gvl 262
Richard	Yrk 629		John	Lan 4
Robert	Abb 8		John	Pen 149
Robert	Abb 9		John	Uni 245
Robert	Csn 132		John	Uni 246
Robert	Edg 157		John	Yrk 628
Robert	Spa 182		Joseph	Lrs 36
Robert	Spa 202		Joshua (2)	Pen 115
Robert	Uni 248		Josiah	Lrs 19
Robert Junr.	Abb 24		Josiah	Nby 75
Robert Senr.	Abb 24		Levi	Nby 75
Samuel	Abb 18		Maria	Csn 143
Samuel	Abb 24		Mary	Lrs 15
Samuel, Senr.	Abb 13		Michael	Csn 155
Thomas	Csn 118		Moses	Spa 190
Thomas	Spa 167		Obadiah	Pen 142
Thomas	Spa 182		Peter	Geo 392
Thomas	Spa 204		Reuben	Spa 211
Thony	Spa 205		Richard	Csn 155
Will.	Lan 3		Richd.	Geo 392
William	Abb 12		Stephen	Yrk 623
William	Bft 108		William	Lrs 14
William	Csn 133		William	Pen 149
Wm.	Spa 183		Wm.	Chr 77
Wm.	Spa 202		Wm.	Spa 198
Foulke, Mary	Col 377		Fowlker(?), Edwd.	Csn 167
Fountain, Alexr.	Dtn 115		Fox, Jacob	Yrk 617
Dempsy	Dtn 116		Molly	Abb 36
Henry	Dtn 115		Noah	Pen 107
Henry	Mbo 60		Philip	Chr 94
John	Col 381		Titus	Pen 108
John	Pen 123		Foxworth, Abel	Mrn 443
Phebe	Nby 75		Absolum	Mrn 436
Stephen	Bar 49		Elizth.	Mrn 443
Thomas	Dtn 113		Job	Mrn 443
William	Dtn 115		John	Mrn 443
William	Dtn 127		Saml.	Geo 386
Four, Archibel	Uni 245		Thos.	Wil 474
Joicy	Cfd 110		Foy, James	Edg 182
Fowler, Abner	Spa 180		John	Yrk 621
America	Spa 190		Fraizer, Andw.	Fai 211
Archabel	Gvl 262		Frampton, John	Bft 84
Aron	Spa 191		Wilkins	Bft 98
Coleman	Uni 245		Frances, David	Csn 130

Fulmer, Abrahart	Lex 569	Futhey, Hartley	Geo 365
Jacob	Lex 568	Fyall, Peter	Csn 119
John	Lex 569		
John, Junr.	Lex 569		
William	Lex 569	G	
Fulton, Ann	Abb 7		
James B., Capt.	Yrk 621		
Gershom	Pen 152	G---n, John	Edg 185
John	Wil 469	G---n, James	Edg 183
Thomas	Lrs 27	Gabbie, Jonathan	Pen 139
William	Lrs 31	Gabby, John	Yrk 621
Fulwood, Charles	Geo 378	Joseph	Yrk 621
Funches, Daniel	Ora 541	Babeau, Anthony	Csn 150
Sebastian	Ora 541	Gable, Valentine	Lex 566
Fundenburgh, Mary	Fai 203	Gabriel, Mary	Csn 105
Funderburg, Anthony	Edg 154	Gaddy, Thomas	Dtn 115
Isaac	Edg 155	Gadsden, James	Csn 62
Funderburgh,	Edg 156	Christopher	Csn 95
Anthony Junr.		Christopher	Geo 374
Funderburk, David	Lan 9	Martha	Csn 96
Devalt	Lan 9	Philip	Csn 95
Jacob	Lan 9	Gaffney, John	Fai 240
Joseph	Ora 539	Gafford, Michal	Gvl 249
Fuqua, William	Edg 150	Thomas	Lrs 40
Joseph	Edg 151	Gafkin, Henry	Csn 105
Fuquay,		William	Csn 89
see Fewkway		Gage, John	Uni 219
Furgason, Abraham	Chr 88	Gailiard, John	Wil 476
Adam	Chr 89	Gaillard,	
J.	Col 363	see also Gilyard	
James	Chr 80	Gaillard,	Csn 94
John	Chr 88	Bartholomew	
John	Chr 89	Chas. Junr.	Csn 177
Mary	Chr 78	John	Csn 195
Plesent	Chr 79	Jno	Csn 177
Stephen	Chr 85	Jno Estate	Csn 177
Furguson, Jas. E.	Col 395	Peter	Csn 69
Pasience(?)	Chr 77	Peter	Csn 195
Paul	Chr 86	Peyre	Csn 177
Samuel	Chr 73	Theo.	Csn 138
W. C.	Col 373	Theo	Csn 177
Furlow, Alexander	Nby 75	Theodore	Csn 69
Furman, Henry	Csn 167	Theodore Jr.	Csn 81
Josia	Csn 62	Gaily, James	Abb 36
Richd. Revd.	Csn 126	Gain, Jacob	Ker 417
Furnace, Joseph	Nby 75	Gainer, John	Dtn 125
Robert	Uni 227	Samuel	Ker 417
Thomas W.	Nby 75	Gaines, Humphrey	Lrs 41
William	Nby 75	Richard	Lrs 41
Furnece, John	Nby 75	Robert	Lrs 41
Furner, Edward	Pen 139	Thomas	Lrs 40
Furnney, Darby	Mrn 454	Gainey, Etheldred	Cfd 109
Furse, James	Bar 53	John	Cfd 102
Fuse, Jeremiah	Bft 118	Lewis	Cfd 108
Fushee, Charles	Abb 23	William	Cfd 102
Charles	Edg 182	Gainley, Cornelius	Ker 415
Davis	Edg 146	Gains, David	Abb 23
Joseph	Edg 181	Edmond	Nby 75
Nathaniel	Edg 181	Henry	Abb 19
Futch, Jacob B.	Bar 57	John	Abb 23
James	Bar 57	Jonadab	Abb 19
Margaret	Bar 58	Larkin	Abb 20
Zilpah	Bar 58	William	Abb 23
Futheree, Mary	Geo 388	Gairdner, Edwin	Csn 78
Futheree, Willm.	Geo 388	Galagly, Joseph Capt.	Lrs 22

Henry	Pen	136
Gaston, Alexander	Abb	30
Hugh	Chr	78
James	Chr	81
James L.	Chr	76
John	Abb	28
John	Chr	89
Joseph	Abb	5
Joseph	Chr	73
Joseph	Chr	78
Robert	Chr	79
Thomas	Lan	5
Wm.	Chr	81
Wm.	Chr	88
Wm.	Chr	91
Wm.	Gvl	275
Gatch, John Junr.	Bft	81
John Senr.	Bft	88
Gates, Charles	Pen	107
Jacob	Csn	106
James	Nby	77
John	Lrs	34
Josiah	Nby	77
T.	Col	363
Gatewood, Thomas	Edg	169
Gather, Deal	Fai	218
Richard	Fai	238
Gatland(?), Elenor	Pen	162
Gatland(?), Isaac	Pen	162
Gattor, Nicholas	Gvl	277
Gaulding, James	Sum	584
Gault, Robert	Uni	245
William	Uni	247
Gaunt, Almond	Lrs	18
Nebo	Nby	76
Samuel	Nby	76
Gus, Holly	Bar	58
Gause, Benjn.	Geo	382
Gavin, Charles	Ora	545
Robert Junr.	Ora	527
Robert Senr.	Ora	527
Thomas	Ora	543
Gaw, Thos.	Gvl	251
Gay, William	Dtn	122
Gayden, George	Ker	421
Gayle,	Sum	604
Christopher Senr.		
Gayles,	Sum	601
Christopher Jur.		
Gazaway, James	Pen	134
Gazzaway, James	Uni	225
Nicholas	Uni	226
Gear, John	Cfd	102
Geddes, Henry	Csn	101
John	Csn	151
Robert	Csn	99
Gedieze, Esvoir	Csn	106
Gee, Abegel	Pen	163
John	Dtn	117
John H.	Uni	248
Nevil	Abb	4
William	Dtn	126
Geiger,		
see also Guiger		
Geiger, Abraham	Lex	483

Henry	Lex	561
Jacob	Lex	558
John	Lex	483
John	Lex	559
John	Lex	573
Mary	Lex	561
Randal	Lex	561
Gelzer, Francis	Col	377
Gelder, Isaac	Nby	75
Gelaspy, John	Chr	75
Thomas	Chr	91
Gelzer, Thos.	Col	377
Gennerick, John F.	Csn	98
Gennings, Henry	Sum	603
John	Sum	603
Martha	Sum	603
William	Sum	603
Geno, Fousan	Ker	423
Francis	Ker	423
Gentry,		
see also Jentry		
Gentry, Allin	Spa	184
Jerrey	Spa	185
Joel	Lrs	15
Nicholas	Spa	185
Reuben	Spa	184
Saml.	Spa	184
Saml.	Spa	185
Gensel, John	Csn	94
George, Alexander	Lrs	24
Ambrose	Lrs	31
Andrew	Uni	236
Benjamin	Pen	150
Betsy	Uni	250
Britain	Spa	172
David	Ker	405
Dennis	Bar	60
Isaac	Lrs	31
James	Csn	91
Jennet	Abb	36
Jessee	Bar	50
John	Bar	50
John	Pen	158
John	Uni	246
Luddowick	Lex	483
Ludwick	Lex	573
Mark	Csn	83
Mary	Csn	147
Rebecca	Uni	230
Richard	Abb	36
Thomas	Uni	247
William	Lrs	31
Gerald(?), Eliza	Sum	585
Gerald,		
see also Garrell		
Gerald, Bennt	Mbo	61
Thomas	Fai	204
Gerard(?), Eliza	Sum	585
Gerard, Philip	Csn	132
Gerkey, Fredk.	Csn	138
Gerley, John	Csn	139
German, William	Mbo	53
Gerrey, John	Sum	593
Gervais, Mary	Csn	69
Mary	Csn	136

Gespiuses, John B.	Csn 108	Jacob		Fai 220
Geton, Abraham	Uni 240	James		Csn 62
Jacob	Uni 238	James		Csn 115
Joseph	Uni 240	James		Gvl 248
Gettys, John	Lan 9	James		Lrs 26
Getzinger, Benjamin	Lex 491	James		Pen 142
Geurey, George	Wil 478	James		Mbo 53
free black		James		Pen 113
Geuroud, Lewis	Bft 106	James		Wil 471
Gewin, Jeremiah	Cfd 110	James		Yrk 617
Kader	Cfd 102	James Jur.		Sum 603
Geyer, Elizabeth	Csn 140	James Sr.		Sum 600
John	Csn 116	Jarvis		Fai 218
Gibbes(?), Robert	Csn 167	John		Abb 24
Gibbes, Benjamin	Csn 191	John		Lex 561
John	Csn 187	John		Mrn 446
Lewis	Csn 62	John		Pen 119
Robt(?) R.	Col 385	John		Pen 128
William	Csn 167	John		Uni 242
William	Csn 191	Joseph		Pen 113
Willm. H.	Csn 138	Joseph		Fai 192
Gibbins, Michael	Sum 613	Joseph		Fai 235
Gibbons, Andrew	Abb 30	Joseph		Uni 242
Hugh	Bft 140	Josiah		Ora 531
Thomas	Bft 116	Levi		Mrn 444
Gibbs, Anna	Uni 217	Luke		Ker 403
George	Csn 132	Malachi		Mrn 446
Henry	Cfd 102	Mary		Pen 114
Herman	Mbo 60	Matthew		Yrk 626
John	Csn 123	Nancy		Pen 153
John	Spa 207	Nathan		Mrn 450
John	Yrk 632	Nathan		Spa 207
Jonathan	Pen 164	Patrick		Edg 139
Lewis	Csn 122	Reuben		Yrk 632
Robert	Csn 122	Robert		Abb 25
Shadrack	Pen 109	Robert		Csn 136
Stafford	Cfd 102	Robert		Csn 148
Zach	Uni 218	Robert		Fai 231
Gibert, Jonathan	Lex 564	Richard		Pen 111
Peter	Abb 12	Robert (2)		Uni 242
Peter Junior	Abb 32	Royal		Sum 603
Gibhart, Adam	Sum 601	Samuel		Pen 157
Gibson, Abel	Fai 220	Solomon		Edg 157
Abel	Fai 233	Stafford		Cfd 109
Abraham	Fai 237	Stephen		Fai 211
Ambrose	Col 395	Stephen		Mrn 444
Andrew	Fai 213	Teleous		Pen 125
Benjamin	Lex 566	Thomas		Cfd 102
Daniel	Sum 605	Thomas		Lex 497
David	Bar 49	Thomas		Lex 579
Dennis	Lex 578	Thomas		Nby 76
Devinity	Mbo 53	Thomas		Pen 142
Ebenr.	Wil 471	Thomas		Wil 465
Ebenr. Senr.	Wil 474	William		Fai 213
Elias	Abb 30	William		Gvl 260
Ellenor	Pen 139	William		Lan 4
Erasmus	Ora 531	William		Ora 527
Finias	Sum 603	William		Pen 110
George	Spa 208	William		Pen 125
Gideon	Uni 239	William		Pen 142
Harmon	Gvl 251	William		Yrk 617
Henry	Spa 207	Wm.		Spa 169
Humphrey	Fai 236	Wm.		Uni 243
Hutt	Ker 409	Giddings, Isaac Junr.		Sum 605
Isaac	Fai 199	Isaac Senr.		Sum 605

Gillon, Ann	Csn 96	Gitsinger, A.	Col 381
Gillum, Jemima	Nby 77	Gitton, John	Edg 152
Joshua	Nby 77	Given, Mary	Csn 99
Robert	Nby 77	Robert	Ora 503
William	Nby 76	Givens, Daniel	Yrk 624
Gilmor, Archd.	Abb 8	James	Gvl 256
James	Abb 8	James	Yrk 625
Robert	Abb 16	John Senr.	Yrk 625
William	Abb 39	Phillip	Bft 90
Gilmore, Dennis	Csn 62	Saml.	Chr 77
Dolly	Bft 108	Samuel	Yrk 617
Elizabeth	Yrk 619	Samuel	Yrk 625
Enoch	Yrk 627	William	Yrk 623
James	Spa 178	Givham, P.	Col 363
James	Spa 211	Thos. Senr.	Col 377
James	Yrk 625	Givins, Mary	Bft 82
James, Senr.	Yrk 625	Philip (2)	Bft 82
Jany	Ora 509	Gizler, Henry	Nby 76
John	Abb 28	Gladden, Elizabeth	Fai 215
John	Yrk 628	John	Fai 216
Wm.	Spa 177	Littleton	Fai 217
Gilpin, Enoch	Lrs 22	Gladding, Joseph	Csn 88
Gilreath, George	Gvl 258	Gladen, Jesse	Fai 216
Gilyard, Maryann	Bar 58	Gladney, Jane	Fai 206
Ginkins, Arthur	Bar 56	Nancy	Fai 193
Ashford	Bar 64	Paddy	Fai 193
Elias	Bar 46	Thomas	Fai 209
Thomas	Chr 84	Thos. Junr.	Fai 241
Ginn, Elizabeth	Wil 465	Glaeton, Joseph	Ora 523
Jacob	Ker 411	Glaizer, John	Fai 197
Jeptha	Lan 10	Glan, James	Yrk 631
Jesse	Fai 216	Glanton, John	Edg 140
Jourdan	Fai 198	John	Edg 183
Mererick	Bft 112	Glase, Sarah	Chr 80
Meshack	Mbo 59	Glascock, Madin	Nby 75
Moses	Bft 110	Glasgow, Archibald	Nby 75
Priss	Csn 62	John	Pen 155
William	Mbo 59	Mary	Abb 14
Ginnins, Bettey	Spa 184	Robert	Nby 75
Elisha	Spa 185	Wilson	Nby 75
Roland	Spa 184	Glass, Ebenezer	Lex 493
Sukey	Spa 184	Elizabeth	Edg 156
Wm.	Spa 184	Francis	Yrk 620
Gippin, William	Csn 102	Jesse	Bft 90
Gipson, George	Nby 76	John	Edg 156
Girardon, John	Csn 81	Levi	Bft 100
Girerdeau, John	Col 377	Mary	Wil 477
John	Col 381	Glaughon, Elizth.	Mrn 449
Gissendanner, see		Glaze, Daniel	Lan 4
also Kisentaner		Jacob	Lrs 17
Gissentana, David	Ora 537	John	Col 363
David	Ora 555	Thomas	Lan 3
Gissentaner, Daniel	Ora 533	Glazebrook, Mary	Lrs 20
Henery	Ora 533	Glen, David	Lrs 28
Gissentanner,	Csn 103	John	Csn 62
Lucretia		John	Csn 113
Gissentanor,	Ora 533	John	Csn 155
Elizabeth		John	Wil 475
Gissom, John	Pen 153	Rosanna	Nby 75
Gist, M. Est.	Csn 167	Rosanna	Nby 76
William	Csn 62	Glenn, Alexander	Pen 125
William	Csn 99	Alexr.	Uni 231
Giton, Isaac	Uni 241	Blagrove	Lrs 31
Joseph	Uni 241	Barnett	Uni 231
Moses	Uni 241	Daniel	Uni 230

91

David	Nby	76	Gobel, Harmen	Abb 29
George	Lan	6	Godard, Rene	Csn 148
Glen, James	Nby	76	Godbold, Abm.	Mrn 459
Glenn, James	Yrk	632	John	Mrn 436
Jeremiah	Lrs	30	Stephen	Mrn 443
John	Chr	81	Thomas Junr.	Mrn 438
John	Lrs	21	Thos. Senr.	Mrn 436
John	Pen	141	Zachariah	Mrn 437
John	Pen	145	Godbolt, Sarah	Fai 227
Joseph	Pen	134	Godet, John	Csn 93
Joseph	Pen	138	Godfrey, Ansel	Lrs 31
Reuben	Lrs	13	Eliza	Csn 118
Robert	Pen	117	Eliza	Csn 167
Robert	Pen	125	Elizath.	Csn 191
Samuel Senr.	Pen	144	George	Fai 202
Spilsbay	Uni	229	James	Lrs 32
Tyra	Gvl	277	Jesse	Edg 179
William	Pen	111	John	Csn 69
Wm.	Uni	226	John	Csn 117
Glidewell, William	Lrs	21	John	Lrs 46
Robert	Lrs	21	Richard	Geo 392
Glover, Abner	Ora	503	Richard	Mrn 434
Allen	Abb	11	Thomas	Lrs 35
Benjamin	Abb	11	Thomas	Mbo 53
Charles	Csn	100	Wm.	Col 395
David	Edg	151	Godfry, Jesse	Nby 75
Drury	Abb	11	Godley, Benjamin	Bft 116
Editha	Edg	153	Nathl.	Bft 118
James	Yrk	630	Godwin, Henry	Csn 177
Jesse	Ora	501	Simon	Geo 390
John	Abb	3	Goen, Jeremiah	Sum 602
John	Abb	10	Goff, Hannah	Geo 365
John	Abb	38	William	Ker 413
John	Nby	76	Goggins, Baily	Nby 77
Joseph	Bft	118	Daniel	Nby 75
Jos.	Col	381	George	Nby 77
Martha	Nby	77	James	Nby 76
Peter	Ora	503	James	Nby 77
Richard	Edg	184	Thomas	Nby 77
Richard	Sum	595	William	Nby 76
Robert	Edg	149	William	Nby 77
Robert	Pen	114	William	Pen 156
Rubin	Abb	3	Gohagan, Joshua	Bft 118
Sanders	Csn	62	Goings, Daniel	Fai 228
Wiley	Edg	188	Henry	Fai 218
William	Abb	18	Goin, Elijah	Chr 94
William	Edg	149	Isaac	Chr 90
William	Edg	164	Job	Chr 90
William	Ora	503	Golagher, John	Yrk 624
Wilson	Bft	130	Gold, Michael	Uni 233
Wilson	Csn	122	Golden, Foster	Spa 194
Zachariah	Edg	184	Susannah	Pen 121
Gluver, William	Pen	162	Goldfinch, Charles	Csn 152
Glymph, John	Nby	77	Goldin, Reuben	Nby 77
Emmanuel	Nby	76	Robert	Nby 77
Gnash, George	Pen	156	Golding, Anthony	Lrs 31
James (2)	Pen	154	James	Lrs 32
Larkin	Pen	155	John	Lrs 40
Goar, Edward	Uni	237	William	Lrs 40
John	Spa	177	Goldsmith, Jessee	Bft 140
Joshua	Uni	236	Wm.	Gvl 276
Thomas	Spa	176	Goleman, Bald	Edg 165
Thomas	Uni	237	Bidy	Edg 165
Goatee, George	Bft	108	Henry	Edg 165
Goates, George	Fai	236		

Golightly,			John	Bar 59
see also Golitly			John	Spa 206
Golightly, Reubin	Bar	64	John	Uni 217
Golitely, David	Spa	201	Richard	Nby 76
Henry	Spa	200	Samson	Uni 222
Wm.	Spa	201	Solomon	Lrs 14
Golitly, Christr.	Spa	201	Theophilus	Edg 133
Emma	Spa	200	Thomas	Lrs 19
Shands	Spa	200	Theophiless	Lrs 15
Gollitely, John	Spa	205	Wm. D.	Mbo 59
Golman, John C.	Edg	187	Goodyear, William	Mrn 458
Golphin, Thomas	Bar	54	Googe, John	Bar 62
Gomer, Stephen	Mbo	53	Robert	Bar 56
Gooch, James	Spa	189	Goram, Harvin	Chr 83
Good, Elizabeth	Uni	241	Gordan, Adam	Lrs 22
Henry	Uni	241	Gowen	Uni 232
John	Yrk	624	John	Uni 231
Sarah	Csn	116	Gorden, ---mes	Edg 147
Goodacre, Thomas	Spa	179	Benjamin (2)	Nby 76
Goodden, Joseph	Gvl	251	Ely	Nby 76
Goode, Anna	Edg	175	James	Nby 76
John	Gvl	247	Patrik	Bar 61
Lue	Edg	174	Thomas	Edg 160
Mike	Edg	166	Thomas	Nby 76
William	Bar	48	William	Nby 77
Goodgine, Robert	Gvl	256	Gordon, Alexdr.	Chr 93
Wm.	Gvl	257	Andrew	Csn 152
Goodlett, David	Gvl	243	Benjn.	Uni 231
James	Spa	202	David	Wil 466
John	Gvl	248	David	Yrk 622
Robert	Gvl	255	Elizabeth	Csn 86
Robert	Spa	202	George	Lrs 28
William	Gvl	247	Hugh	Yrk 631
Goodman, Charles	Lrs	32	James	Cfd 102
Claibon	Lrs	32	James	Chr 76
Joseph	Nby	76	James	Csn 134
Meriah	Lrs	32	Jane	Pen 157
Samuel	Lrs	32	Jesse	Gvl 245
Timothy	Lrs	32	Jesse	Uni 232
Walter	Nby	76	John	Bft 84
William	Abb	40	John	Bft 139
Goodon, Daniel	Ker	417	John	Pen 105
Goodrum, Allen	Fai	217	John	Wil 470
Thomas	Fai	191	John	Yrk 627
Goodson, Arthur	Dtn	116	Margret	Chr 87
James	Dtn	120	Margaret	Sum 608
James	Dtn	123	Melia	Bft 104
George	Dtn	123	Moses	Sum 608
William (2)	Dtn	116	Nat	Uni 242
William	Dtn	123	Palsey	Csn 144
Willm.	Geo	388	Richard	Csn 128
Wm.	Col	363	Robert	Abb 7
Winney	Sum	609	Saml.	Chr 75
Goodtown, Peter	Csn	93	Thomas	Csn 79
Goodwen, Nathan	Edg	165	Thomas	Csn 93
Goodwin, Ann	Geo	365	Thomas	Sum 607
Brittain	Cfd	111	William	Csn 143
Cafford	Pen	112	William	Yrk 627
Charles	Bar	64	Wm.	Bft 104
Ebenezer	Ora	551	Gore, Davis	Chr 83
Elizabeth	Lrs	13	Eleaser	Chr 90
James	Bar	58	James	Chr 84
John	Abb	26	James	Chr 95
John	Ker	409	John N.	Spa 206
John	Pen	112	Joshua	Chr 84

John	Chr 82	Grarrett, Joab	Uni 234
John	Dtn 114	Graser, Conrod J.	Csn 153
John	Fai 230	Grass, John	Bar 62
John	Ker 399	Grastie, John	Uni 222
John	Ker 417	Gravenstine, Fredk.	Csn 143
John	Lan 9	Graves, Capt.	Bft 134
John Junr.	Geo 391	Agnes	Mbo 53
John Senr.	Geo 386	Agnes	Mbo 61
Joseph	Geo 389	Archd.	Mrn 453
Joshua	Ker 409	Charles	Csn 62
Mary	Yrk 631	Charles	Csn 113
Mircor	Geo 388	Hardy	Mrn 461
Morris	Mbo 53	James	Col 395
Narcissus	Sum 604	James	Lan 9
Nelson	Sum 609	John	Mrn 455
Richd.	Csn 84	John	Mrn 459
Sarah	Ker 415	Joseph	Abb 33
Serah	Ora 503	Joseph	Mrn 435
Thomas	Ora 503	Lewis Esq.	Lrs 38
Will.	Lan 6	Massa	Csn 122
Will.	Lan 8	Moses	Bft 84
Willm.	Geo 386	Rachel	Dtn 120
Willm.	Wil 468	Richard	Cfd 102
Wm.	Chr 86	Robert	Cfd 108
Graimes, John	Bft 96	Thomas	Mrn 444
Grainger, Cannon	Geo 389	William	Abb 4
John	Geo 390	Gravitt, Milley	Spa 185
Robt.	Gvl 264	Gravley, John	Gvl 266
Thomas	Geo 389	Gray, Abraham	Gvl 264
Wm.	Gvl 255	Alexander	Csn 100
Grairs(?), Henry	Lan 5	Alexr.	Col 381
Gramling, Christiana	Ora 535	Alexr.	Spa 202
Grand, Lewis	Csn 105	Andrew	Abb 12
Grange, Hugh	Col 377	Benjn.	Csn 62
Granger, John	Geo 387	Caleb	Csn 99
Saml.	Geo 388	Catharine	Lrs 29
Grannerett,	Csn 92	David	Pen 157
Christopher		Daniel	Pen 158
Grant, Alexander	Lrs 37	David	Fai 209
Ann	Csn 87	Federick	Nby 75
Daniel	Spa 198	George	Nby 76
George	Lrs 34	Hampton	Spa 206
Hetty	Csn 93	Henry	Spa 180
Hugh	Csn 195	Henry	Spa 182
Humphrey	Uni 216	Isaac	Gvl 264
Isaac	Nby 77	Isaac	Lrs 24
James	Chr 86	Isaac	Pen 141
James	Gvl 254	Isabella	Lrs 29
John	Dtn 128	Jacob	Lan 7
John	Fai 223	James	Bft 140
John Senr.	Fai 217	James	Mbo 53
Lucy	Ker 405	James	Pen 141
Mary	Mbo 59	Jarret	Nby 75
Randolph	Fai 217	Jesse	Pen 146
Richd.	Gvl 254	John	Bar 58
Robert	Geo 363	John	Bft 130
William	Gvl 247	John	Lrs 23
William	Gvl 254	John	Lrs 25
William	Pen 124	John	Nby 75
Wm.	Spa 198	John	Spa 173
Grantham, James	Mrn 457	John	Spa 191
Jesse	Dtn 121	John	Spa 204
John	Mrn 458	John Junr.	Edg 144
Nathan	Dtn 122	John Senr.	Abb 8
Grarret, Dickison	Pen 162	John Senr.	Edg 144

Thomas	Sum 602	Grininger, John	Csn 195
William	Geo 388	John C.	Csn 69
William	Edg 140	Grinnen, John	Sum 597
William	Nby 76	Grisham, Franky	Chr 83
William (2)	Pen 112	Moses	Chr 84
William	Pen 134	Thomas	Spa 209
William	Sum 602	Wm.	Chr 87
Wm.	Gvl 263	Jeremiah	Chr 75
Young	Gvl 253	Grissell, Joel	Edg 152
Griffith, Benjamin	Gvl 278	Grissham, David	Fai 228
John	Edg 167	Grissit, Lydia	Ora 545
Joseph	Edg 180	William	Ora 545
Lidda	Nby 76	Grissle, George	Edg 172
Nicholas	Edg 167	Grissom, John	Pen 131
S.	Col 363	John	Pen 141
Thomas J.	Csn 81	Grissum, John	Csn 177
William	Cfd 102	William	Edg 148
Wm.	Gvl 279	Grist, Barnet	Edg 186
Griffits, Abraham	Ora 551	Benjn	Spa 197
John	Ora 521	Gristle, John	Spa 197
Thomas	Ora 521	Griswold, John	Spa 193
Griggory, Dempsy	Sum 613	Gritman, John	Abb 8
Griggs, John	Fai 227	Grives, James	Bft 140
John	Wil 465	Groagan, David	Gvl 249
Shadrick	Fai 227	Groce, Thomas	Pen 110
Grigory, Edward	Pen 113	Groceman, Mary	Csn 135
Isaac	Gvl 257	Grogan, Bartholomew	Spa 181
Isaac	Spa 179	Henry	Gvl 249
Jeremiah	Gvl 274	John	Spa 181
Jeremiah	Lex 489	Groom, Joseph	Mbo 60
Wm.	Fai 223	Rachel	Mbo 60
Grigs, Sarah	Col 395	Grooms, James	Sum 605
Grigsby, James	Edg 179	John	Mbo 59
John	Edg 184	John	Sum 589
Rydon	Edg 177	Mildred	Ker 427
Grigson, Dorothea	Csn 97	Nace	Csn 62
Grim, George	Lex 562	Richard Junr.	Sum 605
Grimball, John	Bft 128	Richard Senr.	Sum 605
Paul	Bft 118	Solomon	Mbo 61
Thos.	Bft 118	William	Sum 603
Grimbol, John	Csn 122	Gross, Charles	Csn 109
Grimes, Benjn.	Fai 232	George	Lex 483
Charles	Ora 547	George	Lex 573
David	Pen 104	John	Bar 63
Delilah	Nby 76	William	Bar 63
Edward	Fai 226	Grossman, Henry	Csn 103
Eliza	Sum 585	Grouter, Martha	Mrn 460
George T.	Bar 69	Robert	Mrn 460
Green	Pen 122	Groves, Joseph	Lrs 35
Isaac	Bar 67	Groze(?), John	Geo 363
Isaac	Fai 222	Grubbs, Enoch	Fai 229
James	Ora 545	Eve	Edg 153
James	Pen 133	John	Ora 517
John	Nby 76	Peter	Lex 578
Joshua	Fai 235	Ralph	Ora 517
Nathan	Bar 69	Thomas	Edg 176
Stafford	Fai 226	William	Fai 207
William	Bar 69	Gruber, Charles	Csn 139
William	Fai 222	Christian	Csn 143
Grimkie, Jno F.	Csn 125	John	Col 385
Grimm, Laurence	Lex 562	Philip	Lex 579
Grimsley, Lewis	Ker 417	Philip	Nby 76
Grinage, Aaron	Edg 169	Samuel	Csn 106
Grindle, Benjn	Pen 124	Grubs, Richard	Abb 17
John (2)	Pen 123	William	Abb 19

John Senr.	Edg 185	Joseph	Edg 151
Joseph	Abb 35	Joseph	Lrs 17
Marlborough S.	Csn 118	Peter	Lrs 18
Matthew	Edg 136	Hammontree, John	Abb 28
Matthew	Edg 147	Hampton, Benjamin	Nby 77
Nathan	Cfd 103	John	Lex 495
Nathan	Cfd 110	John	Lex 577
Paul	Csn 100	John	Spa 180
Paul	Col 391	Richard	Edg 154
Robert	Chr 75	Richard	Sum 587
Robert	Chr 82	William	Sum 587
Robt.	Wil 463	Winna	Gvl 262
Robt.	Wil 472	Wm.	Spa 176
Thomas	Pen 119	Hanagan, Barnabas	Mbo 53
William	Ora 509	Hanahan, John	Csn 183
William	Pen 114	Martha	Csn 183
William (2)	Pen 118	William	Csn 183
Wm.	Pen 135	Hance, Mary	Spa 169
Wm.	Fai 239	Hancock,	
Hamiter, Jacob	Lex 484	see also Hencock	
Hamley, Sebenia	Uni 217	Hancock, John	Cfd 103
Hamlin, Hannah	Csn 84	John (2)	Edg 151
Saml.	Csn 155	John	Lan 9
Thos.	Csn 155	John, Jr.	Cfd 103
Wm.	Csn 163	John J.	Cfd 110
Hammel, John	Edg 144	Joseph	Chr 87
Hamell, Joseph	Yrk 621	Joseph	Lan 9
Hammer, David	Nby 79	Josiah	Cfd 103
Hammerick, Nimrod	Lex 484	Josiah	Lan 10
Hammett, Charles	Spa 172	Luis	Chr 87
Hamett, Thomas	Csn 98	Philip	Pen 129
Hammett, Wm.	Geo 367	Robert	Lan 8
Wm.	Spa 173	Thomas	Edg 151
Hammilton, John	Uni 241	Thomas	Geo 364
Thomas	Gvl 270	William	Uni 230
Hamminger, James	Abb 3	William, Junr.	Sum 611
Peter	Abb 3	William Ser.	Sum 611
Hammit, Robert	Pen 135	Willis	Cfd 103
Hammiter, Jacob	Lex 567	Hand, Isaac	Cfd 108
Hammitt, Benjn.	Spa 203	Jonathon	Gvl 249
John	Spa 173	Joseph	Pen 161
John	Spa 183	Obediah	Mrn 454
Hammon, Elijah	Pen 107	Robert	Lrs 19
Job	Uni 224	Samuel	Pen 111
John	Spa 184	Handcock, Lucy	Fai 205
John	Spa 185	Handen, Jacob	Pen 123
Joshua	Uni 224	Handrix, Jesse	Fai 241
Mary	Uni 224	Handy, Thomas	Csn 84
Stephen	Ker 405	Hane, Nicholas	Lex 571
Wm.	Spa 186	Hanel, Edith	Nby 78
Hammond, Ambrose	Gvl 268	Jacob	Nby 79
Charles	Edg 135	Hanes, John	Pen 116
Elijah	Pen 106	Joseph	Bft 108
Hannah	Pen 110	Haney, Charles	Pen 128
John	Edg 182	Charles	Pen 154
John	Edg 187	John	Pen 154
Leroy	Edg 152	John	Pen 156
Leroy	Edg 187	Maximilin	Nby 78
Rawleigh	Ker 419	Stephen	Pen 154
Saml Senr.	Ker 421	Thomas	Pen 150
Samuel	Ker 419	Hanguard, Oliver	Csn 149
Samuel	Ker 421	Hankerson, Richard	Bar 59
William	Lrs 17	Thomas	Bar 59
William	Pen 141	Hankins, John	Pen 109
Hammonds, John	Edg 182	William	Pen 109

Harkeness, John	Pen 150	James	Csn 151
John	Pen 155	Jesse	Pen 122
Robert	Pen 155	John	Col 383
Harkins, Hugh	Pen 146	John	Lrs 42
Harkens, James	Nby 78	John	Mbo 61
Harkins, John	Edg 158	John	Pen 126
John	Pen 108	John	Pen 160
Peter	Nby 79	John	Pen 161
Sarah	Pen 108	John	Pen 162
Thomas	Pen 108	John	Spa 181
Walter	Pen 146	John Revd.	Csn 133
Harkness, James	Bar 54	Jos.	Col 383
James	Sum 602	Malachi	Mbo 53
William	Abb 34	Matthew	Yrk 632
Harland, David	Yrk 620	Peter	Edg 142
Harley, Francis	Ora 543	Robert	Chr 94
Elizabeth	Ora 553	Robert	Lan 2
J.	Col 365	Robert	Spa 180
Jackson	Bar 44A	Samuel	Pen 139
Joseph Junr.	Bar 57	Solomon	Col 383
Joseph Senr.	Bar 70	Solomon	Col 395
Harlin, Aaron	Lrs 27	Widow	Lan 2
Harleston, Ann	Csn 146	William	Fai 196
Edward	Csn 69	William	Pen 162
Nicholas	Csn 69	William	Sum 595
William	Csn 69	Wm. A.	Chr 75
Harlin, Ellice	Pen 138	Williamson	Chr 79
George	Lrs 27	Harrel, Alan	Bar 48
George	Uni 222	Elisha	Dtn 120
John	Edg 166	Isaac	Bar 68
Saml.	Uni 222	John	Dtn 123
Samuel	Lrs 21	Joseph	Geo 371
Harling, Mary	Ora 535	William	Nby 79
Harlock, Jasper	Col 395	Zachariah	Bar 65
Harman, Christopher	Pen 115	Harrell, Elizabeth	Dtn 120
Elizabeth	Csn 95	Elizabeth	Dtn 127
ShoeCraft	Mrn 462	Jacob	Sum 602
Harmon,		Levy	Sum 602
see also Hermon		Lewis	Mrn 455
Harmon, Andrew	Spa 201	Michjah	Ker 427
Christian	Lex 484	Richard	Ker 425
Christian	Lex 567	Harrelson, Benja.	Mrn 447
Harmining, John F.	Spa 194	Josiah	Geo 390
Harmon, John	Pen 118	Lewis	Mrn 447
Mary	Nby 78	Moses	Geo 390
Robert	Chr 81	Harrey, Benjamin	Edg 163
Saml.	Chr 85	Harrington, Elyachim	Ora 543
Stephen	Chr 80	Nathaniel	Yrk 631
Thomas	Nby 79	Harris, Abraham	Lex 559
William	Nby 78	Arthur	Cfd 110
Haron, Henry	Chr 87	Augustin	Pen 154
Harp, Caleb	Gvl 282	Barton	Sum 589
Joshua	Lan 11	Benjn.	Edg 155
Thomas	Yrk 621	Benj.	Gvl 250
William	Edg 171	Braddock	Lrs 18
Harper, Benjamin	Lan 2	Charles	Geo 385
Benjamin	Lan 2	Claburn	Pen 154
David	Edg 181	Coleman	Pen 155
Edwd.	Col 379	Daniel	Dtn 120
Edwd.	Col 395	David	Uni 226
Edward	Pen 145	Edmund	Yrk 631
Fredk.	Bft 81	Edward	Lrs 16
George	Geo 388	Ezekiel	Pen 139
Henry	Lan 3	Fitch	Geo 384
James	Chr 80	George	Edg 173

George	Lan	9	William	Lex	559
Handy	Abb	32	Wm.	Spa	210
Jacob	Csn	101	Wm.	Uni	241
James	Edg	183	William Stoutly	Abb	30
James	Mbo	53	Wilson	Abb	8
James	Uni	245	Harrison, Alvin	Col	365
James	Yrk	630	Amos	Bft	130
James Esqr.	Yrk	630	Benjamin	Chr	74
Jesse	Ora	507	Benjn	Edg	188
Jesse	Yrk	630	Benjn.	Fai	221
John	Abb	6	Benjn.	Pen	128
John	Abb	13	Daniel	Fai	221
John	Abb	27	Francis	Fai	195
John	Abb	30	George	Fai	195
John	Bft	100	George	Ker	413
John	Edg	139	George	Lex	497
John	Edg	159	Hannah	Uni	232
John	Geo	385	Henry	Bar	56
John	Gvl	263	Henry	Bft	94
John	Lrs	15	Isham	Spa	205
John	Lrs	21	James	Col	379
John	Nby	78	James	Edg	136
John	Pen	154	James	Gvl	273
John	Spa	175	James	Spa	201
John	Spa	196	Jane	Yrk	626
John	Uni	225	John	Bft	81
John	Yrk	621	John	Csn	177
John	Yrk	630	John	Fai	198
John Esquire	Pen	125	John	Gvl	274
Johnston	Lrs	16	John	Pen	128
Lud	Edg	153	John H.	Gvl	271
Mark	Uni	244	Jonathan	Fai	194
Nancy	Edg	156	Joshua	Fai	194
Nathaniel	Yrk	630	Joshua Senr.	Fai	192
Nicholas	Uni	243	Mary	Bar	69
Nicholas Junr.	Uni	243	Mrs.	Csn	155
Rhuebin	Gvl	250	Rheuben	Gvl	244
Richard	Abb	2	Robt.	Gvl	244
Richard	Pen	133	Robert	Spa	194
Richard	Pen	157	Robert	Pen	129
Richd.	Uni	232	Rueben	Fai	199
Richd.	Uni	244	Spencer	Pen	106
Richmon	Abb	33	Thomas	Pen	128
Robert	Abb	9	Thomas	Pen	129
Robert	Uni	244	William	Bar	69
Robert	Yrk	629	William	Fai	221
Samuel	Abb	10	William	Ker	397
Samuel	Fai	241	William	Pen	122
Samuel	Nby	78	Willm. P.	Csn	96
Saml.	Uni	220	Harriss, Andrew	Csn	79
Saml.	Uni	227	Archibald	Pen	109
Sarah	Pen	115	Benjamin	Pen	132
Sarah	Uni	220	Daniel	Pen	108
Simon	Cfd	103	Francis	Lrs	38
Stephen	Pen	154	John	Lrs	45
Thomas	Abb	32	John	Pen	106
Thomas	Abb	34	John	Pen	115
Thomas	Edg	171	Micagah	Nby	79
Thomas	Spa	170	Minyard	Lrs	28
Timothy	Geo	384	Moses	Pen	129
Tucker Doctr.	Csn	142	Thomas	Csn	148
Tyre G.	Edg	153	Vines	Gvl	277
West	Spa	175	Harrod, John Junr.	Bft	124
Wm.	Chr	83	John Senr.	Bft	110
William	Lex	559	Joseph	Bft	124

Harrol, Samuel	Csn 69	Elizabeth	Csn 97
Harron, Thomas	Nby 78	Elizabeth	Csn 107
Harry (free black)	Sum 602	Jacob	Edg 148
Harry, David	Mbo 53	Jacob W.	Geo 366
John	Bar 57	James(?)	Geo 366
John	Lrs 36	James	Fai 215
Thomas	Csn 62	John	Fai 192
Harskins, James	Csn 191	John	Geo 363
Harson, George	Fai 219	John	Spa 170
John	Fai 192	John J.	Csn 96
Hart, Aron	Uni 218	Jonathan	Pen 143
Benjn.	Fai 213	Phillip	Lrs 22
Daniel	Csn 78	Samuel	Csn 85
Dorcas	Csn 101	Harvick, Jacob	Pen 120
George	Gvl 253	Harville, Simmons	Sum 611
Henry	Bar 67	Harvy, Andw.	Csn 62
James	Dtn 115	John	Bar 55
James	Edg 182	Thomas	Csn 62
James	Fai 195	Harvin, John	Sum 585
John	Csn 191	Richard	Sum 600
John	Edg 153	Harwood, Joseph	Pen 113
John	Gvl 264	Nathan	Pen 114
John	Ora 525	Turner	Pen 113
John	Yrk 618	Hary, Thomas	Bar 56
Joseph	Uni 219	Hase, John	Chr 91
Joseph	Yrk 618	Haseldon, John	Wil 465
Moses	Ker 423	Saml.	Wil 465
Nelly	Uni 218	Haselet, John	Abb 35
Oliver	Uni 220	Hasford, Jane	Geo 366
Pleasant	Gvl 283	Haslett, John	Csn 122
Sarah	Csn 76	Hase, Frances	Nby 79
Thomas	Lan 6	Hasket, Thomas	Nby 78
Thomas	Uni 218	Haskins, Daniel	Ker 403
William	Lex 565	James	Csn 167
William, Capt.	Yrk 618	Jacob	Nby 79
Wm.	Ora 525	Hasle, Henry	Edg 174
Harter, Jacob	Bar 55	Hasleden, Willm.	Mrn 442
Hartgraves, William	Pen 123	Haslett, John	Csn 136
Harth, John	Csn 139	Hassell, James	Sum 595
Hartin, Joseph	Fai 228	Hatch, Jabez	Geo 385
Hartle, George	Nby 79	Robert	Csn 81
Hartley, Amos	Geo 369	Hatchen, ---hn	Edg 147
Amos, Junr.	Geo 369	Hatcher, ---ey	Edg 147
Daniel	Lex 578	Benjn.	Edg 147
James	Col 377	David	Cfd 103
James	Geo 368	Edward	Pen 105
Ludwick	Lex 578	Fleming	Lrs 18
Priscilla	Dtn 125	Isham	Sum 612
Wm.	Col 365	John	Fai 235
Hartness, James	Bar 57	Moses	Wil 467
Jane	Yrk 626	Nancy	Fai 226
Harton, Hardy	Cfd 109	Reuben	Edg 163
Hartsog, Daniel	Bar 57	Seth	Nby 78
George	Ora 545	Terry	Edg 134
John	Ora 505	Thomas	Edg 141
John	Ora 533	Thos.	Fai 236
Hartsfield, Silas	Mrn 438	Will	Cfd 103
Hartstine, Joachin	Bft 114	William	Fai 200
Hartzog, George	Ora 543	Wilmoth	Edg 163
Harvell, Loudon	Mbo 54	Hatchet, Josiah	Spa 203
Haverly, Jacob	Edg 149	Wm.	Csn 167
Harvey, Alexander	Fai 209	Hatfield, George	Spa 171
Archabald	Csn 117	Matthew	Sum 585
Benjn.	Csn 104	Richard	Sum 587
Charlotte	Geo 367	Richard	Sum 597

Sarah	Csn 93	Hay, Samuel	Bft 126
Hathcock, Barna	Mrn 462	Haycock, Charles	Dtn 116
Mark	Fai 233	Haydon, Mathew	Csn 108
Hathorn, Jennet	Wil 473	Hayes, Alexander	Yrk 624
Hatler(?), Philip	Chr 79	Eldridge	Dtn 123
Hatson, Thomas	Dtn 127	George	Lan 3
Hatten, Gasper	Fai 228	James	Lex 579
Hatter, Benjamin	Abb 23	Jesse	Lan 7
Eliz. B.	Csn 138	Jessey	Lan 7
Richard	Lrs 34	John	Dtn 123
Hatton, Francis	Nby 78	John	Dtn 124
John	Nby 79	Joseph	Dtn 121
Hatture, Henry	Csn 79	Mary	Csn 106
Haugabook, Jacob	Lex 558	Susanna	Bar 43
Hausser, Andrew	Ora 535	Hayess, Thomas	Pen 136
Hauser, Elias	Csn 122	Haygood, Buckner	Chr 81
Hauteux, Peter	Geo 369	Henry	Dtn 118
Haves, Jno Junior	Fai 213	Hayne,---	Yrk 632
Havis, Jesse	Fai 219	Hayne, Henry	Col 395
John	Fai 219	Isaac	Col 381
Haws, Spencer	Edg 139	William	Col 377
Hawes, Oliver	Dtn 125	William E., Esq.	Yrk 632
Hawlcom, Solomon	Gvl 252	Wm.	Bft 139
Hawkins, Allen	Gvl 283	Haynes, Alexander	Yrk 630
Amos	Uni 219	William	Uni 247
Amos	Uni 226	Hayney, James	Spa 177
Amos	Uni 230	James	Uni 249
Benjamin	Abb 9	Iseiah	Uni 249
Benjn.	Uni 226	Hayns, Abraham	Pen 139
Danl.	Dtn 115	Hays,
Danl. Jr.	Dtn 115	see also Hase
David	Pen 138	Hays, Beletha	Mbo 53
Eaton	Gvl 244	Benjn.	Mrn 438
Edward	Pen 138	Edward	Pen 139
Federick	Gvl 285	Elijah	Mbo 53
Hannah	Pen 109	Gibert	Pen 147
Isaa	Uni 219	Gideon	Mrn 456
James	Abb 16	Gilbort	Dtn 123
James	Nby 78	Hannah	Mrn 445
James	Uni 228	Henry (2)	Pen 130
Jesse	Gvl 262	James	Edg 182
John	Uni 225	James	Mrn 452
John	Uni 228	James	Pen 130
Joseph	Abb 15	James	Pen 161
Joshua	Gvl 244	Hay, John	Edg 173
Josiah	Gvl 250	Hays, John	Gvl 280
Nathan	Uni 226	John	Mrn 452
Nathan	Uni 228	John	Pen 130
Peter	Spa 203	John	Pen 154
Pinkney	Gvl 244	John	Pen 147
Pinckney	Gvl 285	John	Yrk 624
Robert	Sum 605	Joseph	Spa 171
Thomas	Dtn 123	Peter	Pen 147
William	Dtn 114	Reuben	Mrn 452
Wm.	Gvl 285	Richd.	Uni 234
Wm.	Uni 227	Robert	Abb 33
Wm.	Uni 230	Robert	Mbo 60
Hawks, James	Gvl 277	Robert	Nby 78
John	Pen 109	Saml.	Spa 210
William	Gvl 249	Samson	Uni 216
Hawthorn, Adam	Fai 196	Samuel	Uni 216
Adam	Fai 212	Sarah	Cfd 109
David	Abb 9	Solomon	Uni 216
James	Abb 8	Thomas	Pen 130
Hawthorne, James	Abb 28	Thomas	Pen 147

Thomas	Uni 215	Benjamin	Bar 65
William	Abb 33	James	Csn 90
William	Mrn 452	Jeremiah	Dtn 126
William	Pen 105	Jesse	Lan 3
William	Pen 137	John	Bar 61
William	Pen 147	John	Ker 411
William, Junr.	Mrn 452	Jurdin	Bar 61
Hayward, Saml. Captn	Csn 135	Moses	Lan 8
Haywood, Gideon	Pen 108	Susanna	Dtn 126
Hazell, Sarah	Csn 155	Willm. Estate of	Wil 464
Thos.	Geo 378	Heathcoat, Valentine	Dtn 115
Hazle, Harry	Lrs 38	Heathcock, John	Ker 427
Henry	Pen 152	John Senr.	Ker 427
Richard	Bft 100	Saml.	Ker 427
Thomas	Bft 94	Heaton, Benjamin	Pen 147
Hazlehurst, Robt.	Csn 129	James	Pen 147
Hazelton, Mary	Ker 411	Selathiel	Uni 233
Hazlett, Robert	Lrs 45	Smith	Pen 144
Hazlewood, Joseph	Csn 87	Thomas	Pen 147
Hazzard, William	Bft 130	William	Uni 232
Head, Dannil	Pen 128	Heaver, John	Ora 537
George	Pen 104	Heavy, Dennis	Csn 142
James (2)	Pen 105	Heckleman, Abram	Abb 16
James	Pen 138	Jacob	Abb 16
John	Pen 105	Michal	Abb 17
Oliver	Ker 409	Hedden, David	Spa 183
Peter	Pen 105	Elias	Spa 183
Richard	Pen 104	Elisha	Spa 183
William	Pen 128	James	Spa 190
Wm.	Chr 93	Thomas	Spa 183
Headen, John	Uni 247	Hedgebeth, Peter	Abb 31
Headilston, David	Gvl 255	Hedgecock, David	Mbo 54
Headwright, James	Csn 115	Moses	Mbo 60
Heames, Charles	Uni 247	Hedgepeth, John	Fai 230
John	Uni 247	Hedleston, John	Geo 370
Thomas	Uni 245	Willm.	Wil 470
Heaney, Hiram	Uni 248	Hedson, Peter	Gvl 252
Richd.	Spa 176	Heedly, Peter	Dtn 119
Timothy	Uni 248	Hefling, Jonathan	Spa 207
Wm.	Uni 247	Hegin, John	Gvl 267
Heape, Benjamin	Bft 84	Hegler, Abraham	Lan 10
George	Bft 134	Jacob	Lan 10
Henry	Col 377	Paul	Lan 2
Sarah	Bft 92	Paul	Lan 9
Heard, William	Gvl 244	Heister, James	Gvl 246
Hearn, Drury	Edg 158	Heistor, Guideon	Gvl 257
Edmund	Sum 589	Heith, Sarahann	Mrn 450
George	Pen 121	Heller, Catharine	Nby 78
Hearndon, William Jr.	Cfd 108	Jacob	Nby 78
Harne, Margaret	Csn 191	John	Nby 78
Hearns, Faithful	Uni 242	Hellums, David	Lrs 44
John	Uni 242	William	Lrs 18
Hearon, James	Dtn 121	Helmes, Jonathan	Gvl 274
James	Dtn 127	Heloms, Jonathan	Wil 475
Samuel	Dtn 114	Helsey, John	Csn 97
Hearst, George	Abb 11	Hembre, Edward	Pen 132
John	Abb 11	John	Pen 132
Joseph	Abb 28	William	Pen 132
Robert	Abb 25	Hembree, David	Pen 157
Thomas	Abb 28	James	Pen 157
William	Abb 30	Hembrey, Joel	Spa 199
Heart, Morgan	Lrs 40	Joel	Spa 207
Thomas	Edg 172	Wm.	Spa 199
Hearth, M.	Csn 167	Hemeter, Mary	Bft 94
Heath, Adam	Lan 3	Nicholas	Bft 94

Nathaniel	Dtn 117	Elizabeth	Csn 59
Nathaniel	Dtn 126	James	Pen 136
Nathaniel	Lrs 44	John	Lan 10
Paul	Csn 141	Joseph	Csn 122
Rachel	Ora 541	Lovice	Mbo 54
Reuben	Yrk 628	William	Pen 135
Richard	Cfd 110	Hinton, John	Lrs 38
Richard	Fai 194	Joseph	Uni 232
Richard	Pen 129	Phillip	Uni 226
Richd Junr.	Fai 201	Hiot, James	Gvl 281
Robert	Lrs 25	Hip, Andrew	Nby 77
Samuel	Nby 77	Ann	Nby 77
Soloman	Spa 168	George	Nby 77
Starky	Chr 85	Jacob	Nby 77
Stephen	Lrs 40	John	Nby 77
Thomas	Edg 166	John	Nby 79
Thomas	Nby 78	Joseph	Nby 77
Thomas	Spa 172	Hippers, Peter	Csn 89
Uil	Abb 32	Willm.	Csn 131
William	Abb 13	Hire, Henry	Csn 111
William	Nby 78	John	Col 395
William	Ora 547	Hires, George	Bar 69
William	Yrk 617	Hislop, John	Csn 83
Wm. (2)	Chr 84	Robert	Csn 80
Wm.	Spa 171	Robert B.	Csn 83
William Junr.	Edg 136	Hitchborn, Isaac B.	Csn 153
William Senr.	Edg 136	Hitchburn, John	Csn 126
Hillard, James	Bft 92	Hite, Christian	Lex 577
Peter	Edg 151	Susannah	Abb 4
Hillhouse, James	Pen 147	Hitt, Abner	Lrs 33
John	Pen 144	Henry	Lrs 33
John	Pen 153	Lazarus	Lrs 33
William	Abb 35	Peter	Lrs 33
William	Pen 147	Thomas	Lrs 33
William	Pen 153	Hix, Drury	Wil 468
Hilliard, Armstead	Ker 421	Jeremiah	Wil 468
Philimon	Ker 419	Hixon, John	Ker 409
Hilligas, Philip	Csn 104	Hixt, James	Fai 224
Hillman, Ann	Ker 405	John	Bar 46
Hilton, Guhial	Lan 10	Ho---, Arth(?)	Geo 369
James	Lan 10	Hoagain, John	Bft 88
Jesse	Sum 601	Hoaker, John	Ora 537
John	Bft 98	Hobbs, Bartholomew	Bft 114
John	Pen 118	William	Pen 104
Rebecca	Sum 601	Hobby, John	Spa 192
Samuel	Lan 5	Hobert, William	Pen 119
Himely, John James	Csn 154	Widow	Pen 119
Hinchey, Ezekiel	Lrs 16	Hobgood, John	Mrn 456
Hindman, James	Fai 193	Hobson, James	Pen 130
Hinds, David	Sum 613	Thomas	Pen 131
Dawson	Dtn 125	Hoddson, William	Ker 421
James	Dtn 128	Hodge, Able	Pen 115
Orison	Dtn 116	Abraham	Sum 600
Stephen	Dtn 123	Benjamin	Sum 600
Hineman, John	Spa 186	Benjn.	Fai 225
John	Spa 199	Francis	Abb 36
Saml.	Spa 197	James	Fai 199
Hines, John	Nby 78	John	Lrs 39
Thomas	Chr 89	John	Pen 140
Thomas	Fai 224	John	Sum 600
Hinkler, John	Pen 115	John	Uni 242
Hinkle, Joseph	Chr 94	Joseph	Lrs 34
Philip	Ora 549	Joseph	Sum 610
Hinnant, John	Mrn 438	Martha	Sum 600
Hinson, Charles	Cfd 109	Miles Senr.	Sum 603

Richard	Lrs	39	Hogmires, Benjamin	Lrs	37
Samuel	Uni	242	Hogsden, Thomas	Ora	515
Thomas	Fai	211	Hoke, Michael	Lex	574
Wm.	Uni	242	Stephen	Lex	570
Hodges, Charles	Abb	7	Holaday, William	Lrs	44
Benjamin	Mbo	61	Holamon, Jesse	Bar	63
Dewry	Gvl	270	Holand, Solomon	Gvl	279
Dinah	Mbo	54	Holbeck, P. Est.	Col	363
Edmond	Mbo	53	William	Bft	108
George	Dtn	116	Holbert,		
George	Mbo	53	see also Halbert		
Henry	Mbo	53	Arthur	Pen	143
James	Abb	11	Enos	Pen	160
James	Dtn	122	John	Pen	159
James	Mrn	458	William	Pen	143
John	Abb	5	Holcom, Anna	Spa	207
John	Dtn	113	James	Spa	201
John	Gvl	269	Holcomb(e), see also		
John	Gvl	270	Halcom, Hawlcom		
Joseph	Bft	98	Holcomb, Elisha	Lrs	19
Mary	Mbo	53	James	Lrs	20
Richard	Abb	4	Joseph	Lrs	19
Robt.	Mrn	457	Joshua	Lrs	19
Sion	Mbo	53	Obadiah	Lrs	19
Thomas	Mbo	53	Zachariah	Pen	138
Welcome	Mbo	53	Holden, Richard	Pen	140
William	Abb	7	Richard	Pen	140
William	Mbo	59	Sarah	Mrn	437
Willis	Ker	415	Hol[der], Daniel	Uni	223
Hodgg, Elizabeth	Csn	62	Holder, Alston	Spa	189
Hoff, Gideon	Pen	124	Daivd	Pen	143
Hoffom, Thos.	Col	395	Dempsey	Pen	110
John	Lex	491	James	Gvl	261
Hoffstitler, Jacob	Yrk	628	John	Bar	51
Hoffman, Christina	Lex	483	John	Gvl	247
Hofstitler, Henry	Yrk	628	Joseph	Pen	109
Hog, James	Lan	2	Joshua	Pen	138
John	Lex	487	Lewis	Gvl	248
Hogan, Isaac	Spa	208	Mary	Lrs	27
Millington	Cfd	108	Solomon	Lrs	27
Hog, Rachel	Chr	90	Solomon	Pen	109
Hogan, Nancy	Fai	220	Solomon	Pen	110
Wm.	Uni	229	Thomas	Gvl	248
Hogans, Wm.	Uni	236	Holdridge, William	Lrs	32
Hogarth, William Jr.	Csn	96	Holenback, Maten	Nby	78
William Senr.	Csn	74	Holenhead, Benjamin	Nby	79
Hogarty, Charles	Csn	114	Holiday, John	Sum	601
Hoger, George	Lrs	28	Holigim, William	Pen	128
Hogg, Frederic	Nby	78	Holingsby, Thomas	Csn	191
George	Pen	153	Eliza	Csn	167
James	Abb	23	Holingsworth, David	Lrs	33
James	Yrk	623	George	Lrs	32
James Junr.	Bft	130	George	Lrs	46
James Senr.	Bft	132	James	Lrs	46
John	Bft	130	John	Lrs	46
John	Nby	77	Joseph	Lrs	33
John	Pen	153	Levy	Lrs	33
Joseph	Lex	570	Margaret	Lrs	32
Lewis	Nby	77	Nathan	Lrs	45
Thomas	Yrk	624	Richard	Lrs	33
William	Bft	132	Robert	Lrs	33
Zachariah	Nby	78	Holkman, David	Lex	563
Hoggin, William	Ker	403	George	Lex	563
Hogin, John	Nby	78	Solomon	Lex	563
Hoglin(?), John	Sum	602	Holland, Andrew	Abb	37

Ambrose	Nby 78	John	Bar 68	
Hudnal, Willis	Sum 602	John	Dtn 119	
Hudnel, J---ey	Edg 144	John	Pen 107	
Hudnell, Ezekiel	Edg 170	John	Pen 119	
John	Edg 170	John	Pen 134	
Hudson,		Levi	Mrn 448	
see also Hutson		Mark	Abb 24	
Hudson, Abraham	Gvl 261	Mathew	Cfd 103	
Burrel	Gvl 280	Nathan	Geo 373	
Hardy	Col 395	Natn.	Csn 155	
Isaac	Chr 78	Patsey	Abb 39	
Isaac	Chr 89	Robert	Abb 28	
James	Bft 81	Saml.	Dtn 119	
John	Bft 102	William	Pen 119	
John	Col 395	Hugh, William	Ker 405	
John	Csn 59	Hughe, James	Nby 78	
Joseph	Mrn 454	Hughes,		
Lumford	Gvl 261	see also Hews		
Obediah	Gvl 267	Hughes, Aaron	Lrs 16	
Pleasant	Gvl 261	Arthur	Col 395	
Rush	Ker 403	Benjmain	Lex 578	
Shared	Col 395	Caleb	Lrs 20	
William T.	Edg 152	D.	Col 365	
Huestiss, John	Cfd 103	Edward	Abb 19	
Hueston, Samuel	Csn 84	Edward	Csn 121	
Huet(?), William	Edg 157	Edwd	Col 363	
Hackey	Lan 9	Elijah	Mrn 447	
James	Lan 6	Ezekiel	Lex 578	
Huff,		George	Fai 238	
see also Hoof		George	Lrs 17	
Huff, Daniel	Edg 138	Goodman	Fai 225	
Henry	Pen 106	Henery	Ora 521	
Jacob	Col 387	Isaac	Ora 503	
John	Edg 138	J.	Col 363	
Philip	Pen 104	James	Abb 17	
Sampson	Bar 52	James	Abb 27	
Samuel	Csn 62	James	Csn 82	
Stephen	Bft 120	James	Dtn 120	
Stephen	Pen 105	James	Lex 561	
Wm.	Col 385	James	Lrs 16	
Huffen, Sarah	Bft 90	James	Ora 521	
Huffman, Adam	Abb 11	James	Pen 112	
Daniel	Fai 194	Joel	Lrs 36	
Peter	Ora 539	John	Abb 18	
Stuffle	Fai 208	John	Dtn 114	
Tener	Lex 576	John	Lrs 36	
Hufham, Sillas	Ora 509	John	Lrs 44	
Solomon	Ora 509	John	Ora 521	
Hufman, Peter	Lex 562	John	Ora 535	
Huger, Benjamin	Geo 379	John	Spa 211	
Daniel E.	Csn 114	John Junr.	Geo 381	
Francis Junr.	Geo 379	John Junr.	Ora 523	
Francis Senr.	Geo 373	John Senr.	Geo 380	
Francis Est.	Csn 155	Joseph	Uni 225	
John	Csn 136	M. Junr.	Col 365	
John	Csn 149	Mary	Csn 92	
Mary C.	Sum 587	Moses	Abb 17	
Huges, Thomas	Fai 208	Richd.	Uni 223	
Huggins, Benja.	Dtn 124	Robert	Fai 208	
Burwell	Mbo 53	Stephen	Lex 578	
David	Abb 29	Thomas	Fai 218	
Eli	Csn 155	Thomas	Geo 375	
George	Dtn 119	Thomas	Lrs 37	
Hannah	Mrn 448	Thomas	Uni 224	
James	Lrs 38	William (2)	Abb 16	

William	Lrs	36	Charles	Uni	245
William	Ora	519	Nath	Mbo	54
Willm.	Geo	386	Thomas	Chr	76
Hughey, James	Chr	90	Bennet	Chr	82
James	Pen	135	John	Chr	83
Mason	Chr	90	Hunnel, William	Yrk	627
Hughs, Andrew	Chr	83	Hunt, Charles (2)	Pen	124
Andrew	Pen	105	Elisha	Uni	220
David	Pen	106	Esley	Gvl	246
Isaac	Chr	83	Fanny	Mbo	60
James	Spa	182	Hezekiah	Fai	196
Jesse	Edg	170	Isaiah	Lrs	16
John	Edg	170	Iseiah	Uni	233
Joseph	Spa	191	James	Lan	3
Samuel	Csn	59	James	Lex	491
Thomas	Bar	67	James	Lex	573
Thomas	Chr	84	John	Abb	15
Wm.	Chr	83	John	Ker	409
Hughston, John	Dtn	125	John	Lex	491
Huguenin, Abm	Bft	126	John	Pen	114
David	Bft	128	John	Uni	233
Huit, Eliphalot	Wil	472	Lewis	Lrs	19
George	Lex	497	Marthy	Pen	162
Huiter, Francis	Gvl	246	Mary	Uni	232
Huland, Chas.	Mrn	462	Milley	Fai	212
Huland, Thomas	Mrn	462	Moses	Pen	114
Hulin, George	Bft	106	Richard	Dtn	118
Hull, Daniel	Pen	124	Richard	Dtn	127
David	Bft	96	Saml.	Spa	180
Edmond	Lan	7	Saml.	Uni	232
John	Dtn	124	Saul	Lan	5
John	Lan	6	Thomas B.	Uni	216
John	Pen	120	William	Gvl	247
John Senr.	Pen	120	William	Pen	108
Joseph	Pen	124	Wm.	Uni	236
Philip	Pen	120	Hunter, Agness	Chr	91
Nathaniel	Bar	64	Alexander	Abb	36
William	Lrs	21	Allen	Lex	560
Hulling, John	Yrk	628	Andrew	Dtn	113
Hullum, Willm.	Geo	391	David	Bft	92
Hulsey, Charles	Gvl	270	Henry	Sum	606
Dona	Lrs	42	James	Csn	79
Jennings	Gvl	270	James	Csn	92
Samuel	Gvl	270	James	Dtn	119
Humback, Jacob	Csn	109	James (2)	Edg	157
Humbart, David	Bft	106	James	Lrs	14
John	Bft	106	James	Spa	206
Melchor Est.	Bft	106	Jane	Chr	93
Humbert, Godfrey	Csn	128	Jane	Csn	134
Hume, John	Geo	374	John	Abb	27
Humes, David	Fai	204	John	Cfd	103
Humphrees, George	Pen	104	John	Cfd	110
Humphres, Thos.	Mrn	446	John	Chr	77
Humphress, David	Pen	142	John	Lrs	14
William	Pen	140	John	Nby	77
Humphrey, William	Sum	603	John	Pen	120
Humphreys, Benjamin	Csn	187	John	Pen	135
James (?)	Edg	183	John Esq.	Lrs	28
James	Sum	609	Kesiah	Ora	511
Samuel	Edg	183	Laughlin	Lrs	29
Humperies, John	Spa	168	Matthew	Lrs	22
Humpheris, Charles	Uni	218	Matthew	Lrs	23
Humphries, see also			Moses	Nby	77
Humperies			Nathan	Lrs	31
Humphries, Absolem	Chr	76	Nathen	Nby	79

Patsey	Pen 112	David	Yrk 619	
Robert	Lrs 22	Gilbert	Geo 366	
Starke	Ker 401	Haxtell	Bft 139	
Thomas	Csn 141	Hugh	Csn 134	
Thomas	Pen 135	James	Abb 2	
Widow	Edg 154	Jeremiah	Csn 144	
William	Csn 134	Jno	Fai 206	
William	Nby 78	John, Esq.	Yrk 619	
William	Ora 511	M.	Col 363	
William Esq.	Lrs 23	Samuel	Abb 3	
Huntington, Mary	Csn 129	Samuel	Yrk 619	
Hurd, Sarah	Csn 93	Thomas	Csn 177	
Hurger, Henery	Ora 549	Thos.	Col 377	
John	Ora 551	Thos.	Geo 367	
Hurlong, Hubbard	Abb 38	William	Abb 7	
Hursk, Philip	Cfd 103	William (2)	Nby 78	
Hurst, Charles	Ker 397	Hutchison, Elijah	Edg 182	
Isaac	Sum 607	Stephen	Edg 171	
Jacob	Sum 607	James	Abb 12	
James	Csn 69	James	Lan 7	
James	Sum 607	Hutchisson,	Lrs 14	
Hurt, James	Spa 205	William Junr.	Lrs 14	
Joel	Spa 205	William Senr.	Lrs 14	
John	Spa 168	Hutchusson,	Lrs 21	
Joseph	Fai 231	Robt. Capt.		
Joseph	Spa 208	Hute, George	Lex 580	
Wm.	Spa 168	Hutherly, John	Gvl 252	
Wm.	Spa 183	Hutson, Mrs.	Bft 98	
Huse, James	Bar 48	Benjamin	Dtn 119	
Husk, Harmon	Yrk 622	Benjn.	Edg 149	
Hermon	Yrk 624	David	Uni 230	
John	Dtn 117	Dolly	Lrs 44	
Priscilla	Dtn 122	Drury	Pen 114	
Huskerson, Mary	Lrs 41	Elijah	Dtn 122	
Huskeson, Nancey	Uni 232	Elizabeth	Csn 62	
Huskey, Isaac	Edg 171	Esther	Bft 100	
John	Edg 143	George	Pen 110	
Jonathan	Edg 171	Henry	Lan 4	
Hussay(?), Milly	Mrn 459	Isaac	Pen 114	
Hussey, Bryan	Csn 128	James	Dtn 124	
Isaac	Fai 219	James	Edg 183	
John	Fai 220	Jesse	Dtn 123	
Huston, Andrew	Csn 149	Jesse	Pen 114	
David	Yrk 620	John	Bft 84	
Hugh	Abb 27	John	Lrs 40	
Hughey	Abb 34	John	Pen 110	
James	Abb 23	John	Pen 114	
Jane	Abb 2	Littleberry	Bft 88	
John	Spa 186	Margt.	Col 385	
Will	Lan 2	Mary	Csn 116	
Hutchens, Thomas	Spa 198	Richard	Lrs 36	
Hutcherson, James	Nby 79	Richard	Yrk 623	
Hutcheson, Drury	Spa 178	Thomas	Dtn 119	
Jas	Fai 212	Thomas	Yrk 630	
John	Bft 108	William	Bft 84	
Mary	Bft 128	William	Csn 101	
Sylla	Spa 178	Hutt, Susannah	Ker 409	
Hutchings, Hilman	Col 385	Hutten, William	Abb 11	
Hutchins, Arter	Spa 197	Hutto, Benjamin	Ora 529	
Michael	Pen 122	Charles	Lex 563	
Thomas	Ora 501	Charles	Ora 531	
Hutchinson, Aaron	Mrn 449	Charles	Ora 547	
Alexander	Nby 78	George	Ora 547	
Ann	Csn 167	Gideon	Ora 531	
Arthur	Mrn 449	Henery	Ora 507	

William	Mrn 452	Saml.	Wil 466	
William	Nby 80	Saml. W.	Wil 466	
William	Pen 161	Samuel	Sum 585	
William	Yrk 630	Sarah	Mbo 54	
Wm.	Uni 236	Shad.	Geo 369	
Willis	Sum 613	Shered	Uni 246	
Jaco, John	Uni 226	Sherod	Sum 585	
John Junr.	Uni 226	Shearod	Yrk 627	
Jacobs, Elisha	Lrs 42	Stephen	Gvl 269	
George	Uni 230	Telefaro	Sum 589	
John	Lex 491	Thomas	Pen 153	
John	Nby 80	Thomas	Spa 201	
Joseph (2)	Nby 80	William	Abb 11	
Moses	Nby 80	William	Dtn 113	
Nat	Spa 191	William	Sum 585	
Shadrick	Fai 198	William	Sum 587	
Shadrick	Fai 234	Willis	Geo 391	
Walter	Gvl 260	Willm.	Wil 464	
Wm.	Uni 229	Jameson, Henry	Spa 182	
Zachariah	Fai 238	Joseph	Yrk 624	
Jacqne, Victine	Csn 78	Robert	Chr 75	
Jaggers, Daniel	Chr 82	Robert	Spa 208	
John	Chr 83	Saml.	Spa 167	
Nathan	Chr 84	Jamiesson,	Ora 533	
Jahern, Joseph	Csn 111	Van De Vestine		
Jakes, John	Col 387	Jamison, Alexr.	Fai 209	
James, Aaron	Pen 153	James, Capt.	Yrk 624	
Absalom	Dtn 125	Gardner	Chr 73	
Ann	Bft 96	Thomas	Chr 79	
Anne	Yrk 621	January, Isaac	Pen 116	
Charles (2)	Spa 201	Joel	Pen 106	
Darling	Mrn 454	William	Pen 106	
Deborah	Cfd 110	Jardon, Garrett	Ora 527	
Drury	Uni 245	Jarrod, Hancel	Pen 154	
Edmund	Yrk 627	James	Pen 154	
Elizabeth	Lrs 27	James	Pen 161	
Elizabeth	Mrn 450	William	Pen 154	
Elizabeth	Sum 601	Jarvis, John	Fai 225	
Enoch	Fai 197	Jason, Robert	Lrs 31	
Enos	Dtn 118	Jasper,		
Gavin	Wil 466	see also Jesper		
George	Dtn 128	Jaudon, Elias	Bft 102	
George T.	Bft 81	Elias G.	Bft 102	
James	Dtn 128	James	Csn 177	
John	Csn 103	James Jur.	Csn 177	
John	Geo 391	Isaac	Geo 369	
John	Gvl 246	John	Csn 177	
John	Nby 81	Martha	Bft 98	
John	Pen 105	Paul	Geo 369	
John	Pen 162	Jay, David	Nby 80	
John	Spa 182	David	Nby 81	
John	Sum 601	James	Nby 81	
John	Wil 464	Jesse	Nby 80	
John	Yrk 627	Jesse	Edg 176	
John E.	Sum 608	John	Nby 80	
Joseph	Fai 199	Laden(?)	Nby 80	
Joseph	Gvl 260	Marget	Nby 80	
Joshua	Dtn 118	Thomas	Nby 80	
Joshua	Dtn 127	Jayroe, George	Geo 392	
Isaac (2)	Pen 116	Jean, Burrel	Spa 173	
M.	Sum 587	Phillip	Spa 171	
Matthew	Sum 600	Jeannerett,	Csn 177	
Philip	Cfd 103	Catharine		
Richd	Spa 201	Jeans, Joseph	Lrs 26	
Robert	Csn 177	Jearden, Lewis	Csn 100	

Jeter, Burrel	Edg 156	Daniel	Edg 170
Cornelius	Edg 160	Daniel Senr.	Nby 81
Eliazar	Edg 160	Daniel Junr.	Nby 81
Joseph	Edg 173	David	Edg 166
William	Edg 152	David	Ker 401
Jett, James	Pen 115	David	Lan 10
Jewel, Benjamin	Csn 79	David	Nby 80
Jurden	Bar 47	David	Nby 81
Moses	Bar 55	Dorcas free black	Bft 118
Jimmerson, John	Bft 110	Duglas	Lrs 18
Jimmy (Free Negroe)	Sum 605	Edmund	Edg 156
Jimmy (Free Negroe)	Sum 611	Edward	Csn 82
Jinkins, Catrin	Uni 231	Edward	Edg 155
Charles	Uni 231	Elijah	Spa 168
Frances	Pen 128	Elizabeth	Nby 80
Jesse	Uni 232	Esther	Csn 141
John	Pen 141	Ezekiel	Spa 176
Randle	Uni 231	Federick	Pen 118
Richard	Pen 106	Gannaway	Spa 201
Roll	Uni 231	George	Col 397
Samuel	Uni 232	George	Nby 80
Simeon	Uni 231	Gilbert	Geo 387
William	Pen 127	Haley	Edg 142
Wm.	Uni 232	Henry	Col 383
Jinnings, James	Uni 248	Henry	Lrs 23
Jinnins, Joseph	Edg 139	Hezekiah	Mrn 444
Robert	Edg 139	Isaac	Nby 80
Joe, Thomas	Csn 157	Jabez W.	Csn 154
John, Arthur	Pen 153	Jacob	Bft 112
Ephraim	Mbo 54	Jacob	Csn 146
Jesse	Mbo 54	Jacob Senr.	Wil 475
Roger	Cfd 103	Jacob	Wil 475
Johns, Isaac	Col 397	James	Chr 76
Iseiah	Uni 223	James	Chr 84
Jacob	Col 397	James	Edg 173
John	Col 397	James	Edg 175
John	Nby 81	James	Geo 389
Nancy	Nby 80	James	Lan 3
Johnsey, Aaron	Chr 83	James	Lan 7
John	Chr 84	James	Lrs 22
Wm.	Chr 76	James	Lrs 45
Johnson, Abel	Spa 168	James	Nby 80
Abraham	Ker 401	James	Pen 145
Abraham	Lrs 29	James	Sum 595
Aerick	Ora 511	James	Sum 600
Alexander	Csn 90	James	Uni 246
Ambrose	Lrs 23	James	Wil 475
Andrew	Lan 8	Jehu	Nby 80
Andrew	Nby 80	Jephatha	Pen 105
Barbary	Mrn 448	Jesse	Edg 157
Ben.	Lan 9	John	Bft 110
Benjamin	Chr 94	John	Bft 139
Benjamin	Lrs 28	John	Chr 78
Benjamin	Nby 80	John	Chr 91
Benjamin	Nby 81	John	Chr 95
Benjamin	Sum 606	John	Csn 99
Burrel	Edg 162	John	Edg 173
Burrell	Edg 160	John	Ker 427
Charles	Abb 9	John	Lan 8
Charles	Csn 62	John	Lrs 22
Charles	Csn 69	John	Lrs 32
Charles	Nby 80	John	Nby 80
Clark	Bft 112	John	Nby 80
Clayburn	Spa 202	John	Nby 81
Collins	Uni 226	John	Pen 105

John	Spa 182	William		Csn 62
John	Sum 595	William		Csn 187
John	Sum 606	William		Geo 373
John	Wil 477	William		Mrn 446
Jonas	Bft 118	William		Nby 81
Jonathan	Lrs 34	William		Nby 81
Joseph	Bft 90	William		Sum 610
Joseph	Geo 392	William		Wil 473
Joseph	Lan 5	Willm.		Csn 88
Joseph	Nby 80	Willm.		Geo 386
Joshua	Edg 180	Wm.		Chr 83
Lewis	Edg 177	Wm. Est.		Col 375
Margaret	Ora 511	Wm.		Col 397
Mathew	Lrs 45	Wm. B.		Geo 367
Micajah	Lex 565	Wm.		Spa 203
Moore	Edg 186	Johnston, ---		Csn 133
Morris	Edg 180	Aaron		Fai 226
Nathan	Bft 122	Abraham		Gvl 273
Nenleson(?)	Pen 151	Andrew		Ker 405
Nowel	Spa 176	Ann		Bar 64
Penelope	Geo 387	Arthur		Bar 60
Peter	Edg 157	Benjamin		Gvl 248
Peter	Lrs 19	Beldon		Ker 396
Pheba	Pen 161	Charles		Csn 115
Philip	Edg 149	Charles		Fai 214
Phillip	Spa 209	Christ.		Uni 243
Randolp	Spa 182	David		Spa 177
Reubin	Pen 160	David		Uni 228
Richard	Csn 187	David		Uni 233
Richard Senr.	Edg 186	Elexander		Nby 80
Richard	Edg 142	Francis		Abb 15
Richard	Nby 81	Francis		Gvl 245
Richd.	Col 375	Fanny		Ker 403
Robert Senr.	Nby 80	George		Abb 39
Robert Junr.	Nby 80	George		Abb 39
Robert	Nby 80	George		Bft 139
Robert	Nby 80	Guillam		Mbo 59
Robert	Nby 80	Hannah		Gvl 277
Robert	Nby 80	Henry		Abb 23
Robert	Nby 81	Henry		Lex 571
Robert	Sum 606	Henry		Uni 221
Roland	Spa 204	Hugh		Bar 48
Ruthy	Sum 603	Hugh		Csn 137
Saml.	Mrn 448	James		Abb 9
Samuel	Edg 180	James		Abb 11
Samuel	Lan 6	James		Abb 12
Samuel	Lan 10	James		Abb 29
Samuel	Nby 80	James		Bar 61
Samuel	Nby 80	James		Mbo 54
Simon	Wil 477	James		Spa 176
Soloman	Edg 145	James		Uni 232
Solomon	Edg 164	James		Uni 234
Soloman	Sum 606	Jane		Bar 48
Stephen	Nby 80	John		Abb 10
Stephen	Nby 81	John (2)		Abb 10
Thomas	Lrs 44	John		Abb 36
Thomas	Nby 80	John		Bft 139
Thomas	Nby 80	John		Csn 130
Thomas	Nby 80	John		Dtn 124
Thomas	Ora 509	Jonathan		Lan 5
Thomas	Pen 119	Joseph		Yrk 618
Thomas N.	Sum 604	Josiah		Dtn 120
Timothy	Edg 188	Mary		Bar 48
Tom	Bft 100	Mary		Dtn 117
Will.	Lan 3	Mary		Dtn 123
Will	Lan 5			

Mathew	Fai	203
Mary	Fai	210
Mary	Fai	224
Nathaniel	Abb	9
Nehemiah	Bar	62
Neil	Lan	5
Pheby	Gvl	250
Philip	Yrk	630
Robert	Yrk	632
Rueben	Fai	210
Saml.	Uni	227
Samuel	Lex	571
Samuel	Yrk	617
Sarah	Csn	102
Sarah	Uni	234
Sarah	Yrk	632
Shadrack	Dtn	122
Shederick	Uni	222
Thomas	Fai	192
William	Abb	8
William	Fai	218
William	Nby	80
William	Yrk	617
Wm.	Bft	139
Wm.	Fai	203
Wm.	Gvl	257
Wm.	Gvl	276
Wm.	Uni	217
Wm.	Uni	225
Wm.	Uni	245
Zilpha	Abb	34
Joice, Thomas	Nby	80
Joiner, Benjn.	Edg	159
David	Bar	57
Fred.	Lan	4
Sarah	Bar	57
Jolley, John	Uni	224
Joseph	Edg	159
Jolly, Benjn.	Uni	220
James	Pen	133
John	Sum	593
Joseph	Mrn	456
Joseph (2)	Pen	132
Joseph	Pen	133
Martha	Wil	464
William	Mrn	439
William	Pen	133
Willson	Pen	132
Jon,	Csn	177
Jacob B. Estate		
J'on,	Csn	155
Jacbot B. Est.		
Jonahan, Will	Lan	11
Jonakin, Benjn Senr.	Edg	147
Jonas, Isaac	Bar	61
Jones, ---	Csn	125
A., Mrs.	Csn	70
Aaron	Lrs	19
Abigail	Edg	186
Abner	Csn	136
Abraham	Dtn	115
Abraham	Fai	229
Abraham	Uni	222
Adam Cr. Senr.	Abb	13
Adam Cr. Jr.	Abb	27

Alexander	Csn	116
Alexr. S.	Csn	127
Ammon	Mbo	54
Andrew	Abb	27
Andrew	Col	365
Andrew	Lrs	43
Aron	Abb	10
Benjamin	Abb	13
Benjamin	Dtn	122
Benjn.	Gvl	281
Britton	Edg	152
Britton	Sum	593
Burwell	Cfd	102
Charles	Bft	124
Charles	Col	397
Charles	Lrs	26
Charles	Ora	517
Charles	Uni	237
Clary	Edg	152
Darling	Fai	191
Daniel	Csn	151
Daniel	Sum	604
David	Geo	388
David	Gvl	267
David	Lrs	27
David	Mrn	443
David	Spa	206
Dempsy	Sum	612
Dick	Bft	104
Doctor	Csn	169
Dudley	Abb	37
Edward	Lrs	32
Edwd. Dr.	Csn	115
Elias	Ker	401
Elijah	Fai	225
Elizabeth	Lrs	23
Enoch	Lrs	17
Evan	Col	379
Evan	Geo	391
Evin	Bar	68
Francis	Csn	177
Francis	Pen	114
Frederick	Mrn	442
Fredk.	Dtn	126
Gabriel	Edg	174
Gabriel	Spa	189
Gidion	Dtn	124
Hardy	Mrn	457
Harris	Abb	33
Henery	Ora	525
Henry	Csn	80
Henry	Fai	199
Henry	Lrs	19
Hunter	Spa	173
Isaac	Geo	391
Isham	Edg	140
Isham	Mbo	54
Isiah	Abb	21
Isom	Lrs	37
Jacob	Pen	127
Jacob	Yrk	619
James	Abb	21
James	Bft	108
James	Col	381
James	Csn	155

James	Edg 136	Josiah	Bar 51
James	Edg 148	Josiah	Gvl 264
James	Edg 152	Lewis	Ker 403
James	Gvl 249	Lewis	Pen 132
James	Lrs 18	Lewis	Spa 208
James	Lrs 26	Marmeduke	Lrs 31
James	Lrs 26	Mary	Chr 80
James	Mbo 54	Mary	Gvl 280
James	Mrn 437	Mary	Lrs 18
James	Pen 152	Mary	Sum 601
Jeremiah	Dtn 124	Mate	Edg 145
Jesse	Csn 117	Matthew	Lrs 28
Jesse	Pen 133	Matthew	Sum 602
J. H.	Sum 587	Moses	Abb 12
John	Abb 17	Moses	Pen 143
John	Abb 26	Nacy	Pen 132
John Senior	Abb 32	Nathan	Edg 155
John Junr.	Abb 32	Nathaniel	Bar 51
John	Bar 51	Nathaniel	Csn 129
John	Bft 139	Nathaniel	Ker 413
John	Cfd 103	Obadiah	Edg 156
John	Cfd 110	Patience	Uni 217
John	Csn 157	Perrin	Edg 163
John	Edg 146	Peter	Mrn 450
John	Fai 233	Ralph	Fai 220
John (?)	Geo 366	Richard	Bft 120
John	Gvl 246	Richard	Edg 150
John Senr.	Gvl 263	Richard	Edg 187
John Junr.	Gvl 263	Richard	Sum 609
John	Gvl 266	Richd.	Gvl 276
John Senr.	Gvl 277	Robert	Abb 28
John	Gvl 276	Robert	Abb 8
John	Ker 427	Robert	Dtn 117
John	Lrs 18	Robert	Dtn 125
John	Lrs 20	Robert	Ker 403
John	Lrs 34	Robert	Lrs 20
John	Lrs 43	Robert	Lrs 23
John	Mrn 445	Robert	Ora 505
John	Mrn 450	Robert	Pen 153
John	Nby 80	Robt.	Gvl 264
John	Pen 132	Sam E.	Ora 539
John	Pen 153	Saml.	Bft 139
John	Sum 603	Saml.	Spa 190
John	Sum 612	Saml.	Wil 469
John	Uni 245	Samuel	Abb 15
John Alexr.	Csn 155	Samuel	Csn 137
John B.	Bft 104	Samuel	Gvl 276
John Capt.	Cfd 103	Samuel	Ker 417
John J.	Ker 425	Sarah	Csn 151
John L.	Csn 69	Sarah	Gvl 280
Jonathan	Chr 78	Sarah	Lrs 25
Jonathan	Chr 93	Shepherd	Sum 613
Jordon	Gvl 257	Solomon	Gvl 277
Joseph	Abb 34	Stephen	Abb 21
Joseph est	Bar 68	Stephen	Lrs 35
Joseph	Csn 129	Stephen	Sum 612
Joseph	Edg 146	Stephen	Uni 243
Joseph	Mbo 54	Thomas	Csn 85
Joseph	Nby 80	Thomas	Csn 152
Joseph	Nby 80	Thomas	Csn 177
Joseph	Uni 221	Thomas	Edg 138
Joseph	Uni 222	Thomas	Edg 146
Joshua	Mbo 54	Thomas	Fai 217
Joshua	Pen 127	Thomas	Lrs 19
Joshua	Sum 608	Thomas	Lrs 23

Thomas	Lrs 32	Willm Junr.	Geo 382
Thomas	Lrs 44	Nathan	Bar 68
Thomas	Mbo 54	Jordon, Bickey	Edg 171
Thomas	Ora 505	Henry	Chr 91
Thomas	Pen 149	Levy	Gvl 271
Thos.	Gvl 265	Joseph, Isarael	Csn 120
Travis	Dtn 117	Lizer	Geo 362
Vincian	Bar 50	Samuel	Csn 150
Wallace	Gvl 279	Josephs, Joseph	Csn 144
Wallace Junr.	Gvl 279	Jossin, Esther	Csn 120
Wallis	Nby 80	Jouler, Daniel	Geo 369
Welles	Pen 132	Jourdan, Abner	Yrk 631
Whitmon	Lrs 24	John	Yrk 626
William	Abb 13	Moses	Sum 587
William	Bar 43	Robert	Yrk 626
William	Bar 51	William	Edg 149
William	Bft 106	Jourden, Isaac	Sum 589
William	Col 397	Jourdon, G.	Sum 597
William	Ker 405	Jovancia(?), Andrew	Geo 376
William	Ker 409	Jowell, Gabriel	Lrs 36
William Senr.	Ker 413	John	Lrs 36
William	Ker 413	Jowers, John	Cfd 103
William	Lex 578	Joy, Abraham	Csn 90
William	Lrs 21	Benjn.	Csn 157
William	Mbo 54	Daniel	Csn 108
William	Sum 587	James	Csn 177
William	Sum 597	John	Csn 177
William	Wil 469	Joyner, Absalom	Dtn 128
Wm.	Bft 139	Ann	Bft 139
Wm.	Chr 92	Jesse	Csn 63
Wm.	Col 383	John	Csn 63
Wm.	Gvl 270	William	Fai 232
Wm. Senr.	Gvl 276	Wm.	Bft 139
Wm. Junr.	Gvl 276	Judge, Thomas	Bft 139
Wm.	Uni 221	Judon, Herod	Sum 609
Zachariah	Sum 602	Judith, Dorothy	Ora 539
Jonnakin,	Edg 146	John	Ora 547
Benjn. Junr.		Henery Senr.	Ora 547
Jonston, William	Bar 59	Henery Junr.	Ora 547
William	Bar 63	Henery	Ora 529
Jordan, Abner	Cfd 108	Isaac	Csn 106
Adam Senr.	Geo 392	Julian, John	Pen 109
Adam Junr.	Geo 383	William	Pen 109
Alexr.	Gvl 257	Julon, Azariah	Nby 80
Ann	Dtn 120	Eli	Nby 80
Baxter	Dtn 117	Julun, Jesse	Nby 81
Garnet	Lex 563	Julon, Peter	Nby 80
Jacob	Dtn 123	Julun, William	Nby 81
James	Csn 69	Jumper, Gun Rod	Lex 562
James	Spa 181	Peter	Lex 562
Jean	Spa 168	Samuel	Lex 562
John	Gvl 254	Jurden, Isham	Bar 69
John	Mrn 435	Jurguson, Elijah	Geo 388
John	Spa 176	Jurnigan, Jesse	Geo 388
John M.	Spa 209	Justice, Ely	Sum 587
Joshua	Lan 7	John	Pen 110
Joseph	Cfd 103	Mary	Nby 81
Joshua	Dtn 124	Moses	Dtn 124
Joshua Jr.	Dtn 124		
Over	Mbo 54		
Peter	Dtn 117	K	
Robt. Junr.	Geo 383		
Thomas	Abb 2		
Thos.	Geo 383	K---, Wm.	Geo 372
Willm Senr.	Geo 383	Kaddle, Josiah	Ora 529

William	Csn 110		Richd.	Gvl 261
William	Gvl 247		Solomon	Gvl 261
Wm.	Gvl 280		Thos.	Pen 134
Kelly, Abraham	Fai 223		Warden	Gvl 245
Adam	Nby 81		Wiley	Edg 136
Andrew	Lex 484		William	Yrk 628
Ann	Nby 81		Kempton, Ann	Csn 120
Daniel	Csn 59		George	Csn 121
Daniel	Pen 125		John	Yrk 620
David	Dtn 121		Kenan, Stephen	Chr 78
Edmund	Nby 81		Kendley, Mary	Edg 143
Elizabeth	Lex 572		Kendricks, Anthony	Yrk 631
George	Lex 484		Nancy	Yrk 631
George	Nby 81		Thomas	Yrk 631
George	Ora 529		William	Yrk 631
Jacob	Dtn 113		Keneday, Henry	Bar 48
Jacob	Lex 483		William	Lrs 19
James	Dtn 114		William	Lrs 43
James(2)	Nby 81		Kenedy, Daivd	Abb 14
James	Sum 609		Edward	Abb 35
James Senr.	Nby 81		Francis	Abb 37
James Senr.	Sum 611		Hugh	Abb 9
John	Col 397		Jessey	Abb 35
John	Edg 142		John	Edg 162
John	Nby 82		Kenely, Christopher	Edg 174
John	Pen 137		Kenington, Edward	Lan 9
Joseph	Edg 141		Kenline,	Lex 567
Joseph	Gvl 279		Christopher Jr.	
Martin	Nby 81		Christopher Sr.	Lex 567
Mary	Nby 81		John	Lex 567
Rebecca	Csn 169		Kenmore, James	Yrk 619
Reubin	Lrs 16		John	Yrk 619
Sabrah	Mrn 439		Kennady, Jesse	Geo 390
Samuel	Lex 572		Kenneday, Thomas	Dtn 128
Samuel	Nby 81		Kennard, John	Nby 82
Samuel Senr.	Nby 81		Kennedy, Alexr.	Fai 219
Timothy	Col 385		Andrew	Csn 70
William	Mrn 452		Andrew	Yrk 617
William	Ora 513		Archalus	Uni 237
William	Sum 608		Charles	Pen 141
William	Sum 611		David	Fai 191
William	Yrk 618		James	Col 375
Kelpatrick, Alexander	Pen 125		James	Csn 139
Catherine	Pen 125		James	Fai 206
Kelsey, George	Yrk 620		James	Uni 241
William	Ker 419		Jane	Yrk 619
Kelso, Hugh	Chr 91		John	Csn 59
John	Spa 210		John	Ker 427
Joseph	Spa 211		John	Uni 231
Robert	Chr 87		Joseph	Pen 156
Saml.	Spa 210		Mousefield	Pen 149
Samuel	Chr 93		Nelson	Lan 9
Thomas	Spa 210		Peter	Csn 146
Wm.	Spa 180		Robert	Yrk 625
Kelty, John	Csn 59		Silas	Col 365
Kemp, Aaron	Gvl 262		Susanna	Csn 129
Abisha	Yrk 628		Thomas	Uni 225
Abnor	Gvl 271		William	Uni 240
Alexander	Csn 129		William	Yrk 625
Alse	Gvl 261		William	Ker 397
Asa	Pen 121		Wm.	Uni 225
Hannah	Edg 163		Kennemer, Noah	Pen 108
Hoseah	Spa 181		Kennemore, John	Pen 108
John, Junr.	Gvl 271		Kenner, Samuel	Nby 81
Moses	Gvl 261		Kennerly, Joseph	Lex 483

Joseph	Lex 570	Rhoda	Bar 64
Kenney, John	Edg 184	William	Bar 68
Kennon, Henry	Csn 94	Kershaw, Charles	Csn 143
Kenny, Patrick	Lan 8	Eli	Ker 399
Kent, ---n	Edg 147	George	Ker 399
Henry	Ker 417	James	Ker 399
Henry Senr.	Ker 417	Joseph	Ker 399
James	Sum 602	Mary	Ker 399
John	Uni 249	Saml. Geoffrey	Ker 399
Martha	Uni 249	Sarah	Ker 399
William	Sum 604	Kersk, Andrew	Ora 547
Kenworthy, David	Uni 228	Kerton, Phillip	Mrn 436
Jesse	Uni 227	Kesler, John	Lex 570
Joshua	Uni 228	Ketsinger, Benjamin	Lex 574
Kenzie, Thomas	Yrk 627	Kettle, Jacob	Pen 153
Keown, James	Abb 33	Kettles, Elizth.	Bft 124
Robert	Abb 26	Jacob	Bar 45
Rowland	Abb 9	Kevan, Alex H.	Csn 100
Thomas	Abb 2	Willm.	Csn 130
Ker, John	Csn 78	Key, Elizabeth	Csn 59
Kerbey, Francis	Uni 242	Henry	Edg 134
Richd.	Spa 171	James	Bar 65
William	Uni 242	William	Bar 63
Kerbo, John	Edg 163	William	Edg 168
Solomon	Edg 163	Keys, Peabody	Geo 378
Kerbow, Henry	Bar 49	Peter	Pen 143
Kerby, Archd.	Mrn 445	Keziah(?), Winney	Edg 171
Boland	Uni 242	Kezler, Catharine	Lex 565
Jesse	Gvl 268	Kibler, John	Nby 82
John	Pen 125	Michael	Nby 82
John	Uni 242	Kicklighter, John	Bft 139
Moses	Bar 64	Thos.	Bft 96
Kerk, Tinea	Spa 189	Kidd, Andrew	Yrk 618
Kerly, Jesse	Sum 601	George	Yrk 617
Joseph	Sum 601	James	Chr 93
Josiah	Sum 602	John	Yrk 618
Kern, Daniel	Ora 547	Kids, George	Abb 2
Frederick	Ora 551	Kieth, Cornelius	Dtn 124
John D.	Lrs 26	Danl Junr.	Pen 147
John F.	Csn 146	Danl. Senr.	Pen 147
Kerney, Jessee	Bar 60	Elisha	Dtn 123
Kerr, Andrew	Csn 90	Jehu	Mbo 54
Andrew	Yrk 633	John	Mbo 54
Benjamin	Yrk 621	John Jr.	Dtn 123
Chrst.	Col 365	John Sr.	Dtn 123
Daniel	Yrk 621	Kigar, John	Uni 246
Danl.	Pen 149	Kilbay, Adam	Spa 179
Eliza	Csn 124	Wm.	Spa 178
George	Pen 109	Kilbreath, Edward	Edg 181
Henry	Yrk 633	George	Yrk 621
Hugh	Yrk 628	Kilburn, Eisbella	Pen 117
John	Yrk 623	William	Pen 117
John	Yrk 633	Kilcrease, John	Edg 142
John Junr.	Yrk 633	Lewis	Edg 140
Joseph	Yrk 626	Margaret	Edg 160
Mary	Abb 40	Minor	Edg 140
Robert	Yrk 617	Sarah	Edg 167
Samuel	Csn 138	Thomas	Edg 160
Samuel	Yrk 631	William	Edg 143
William	Abb 5	Kile, Benjn	Uni 248
William	Pen 140	Henry	Uni 248
William	Yrk 626	John	Edg 154
Kerring, Jesse	Csn 63	Kilgore, James	Dtn 123
Kersey, Abraham	Mrn 441	James	Gvl 278
Kersh, John	Bar 64	Killebrew, Kinchen	Lan 9

Killingsworth,	Mbo 54	Harmon	Ker 415
Anderson		Henry	Edg 133
Jesse	Mbo 54	Henry	Edg 185
John	Mbo 54	Henry	Pen 153
Mark	Bar 47	Hickeson	Bft 120
Killion, Wm.	Gvl 271	Jacob	Nby 81
Killough, James	Abb 33	James	Bft 88
Kilpartrick, William	Pen 156	James	Col 375
Kilpatrick, Adam	Uni 219	James	Dtn 120
Andrew	Abb 14	James	Edg 139
Easlar	Dtn 128	James	Lrs 41
James	Pen 123	James	Uni 238
James	Pen 156	John	Dtn 114
John	Chr 75	John	Edg 170
John	Dtn 119	John	Edg 178
Robert	Yrk 624	John	Geo 375
Robt.	Fai 232	John	Ker 403
Thos.	Fai 208	John	Ker 415
William	Abb 38	John	Lan 4
Kimbel, Charles	Spa 175	John	Nby 81
Kimble, Spell	Yrk 630	John	Ora 549
Kimbol, Franics	Edg 161	John	Yrk 623
Robert	Spa 178	John	Spa 187
Kimbold, Archd.	Lan 3	John	Spa 200
Kimborough, Hannah	Dtn 115	John Junr.	Fai 191
Jno	Dtn 115	John Senr.	Fai 223
Kimbrel, Thomas	Spa 176	Joseph	Geo 375
Kimmels, Robert	Abb 29	Joseph	Gvl 257
Kinard, Andrew	Nby 82	Joseph	Uni 230
Elizabeth	Nby 82	Levin	Lrs 30
Fedric	Nby 82	Martha	Geo 387
George	Nby 81	Mary	Lrs 41
George	Nby 82	Mary	Yrk 623
Martin	Nby 82	Miles	Cfd 103
Martin Jun.	Nby 81	Moses	Fai 223
Matthias	Nby 81	Moses	Lrs 37
Michael	Nby 82	Pennington	Nby 82
Michel Senr.	Nby 81	Richard	Ora 519
Peter	Nby 82	Richd.	Bft 94
William	Nby 81	Robert	Pen 162
Kincaid, James	Fai 212	Samuel	Yrk 623
Kincart, Hugh	Yrk 620	Sarah	Spa 188
William	Yrk 620	Silas	Nby 81
Kinder, Michael	Sum 611	Thomas	Chr 75
Simon	Bft 118	Thomas	Geo 375
Kindrick, Abel	Uni 248	Thomas	Yrk 624
Turner	Uni 248	Thomas Junr.	Geo 375
King, Abraham	Geo 390	Will	Lan 7
Benj.	Lan 3	William	Bft 120
Benjamin	Csn 97	William	Cfd 104
Benjamin	Yrk 624	William	Dtn 120
Berry	Ker 413	William	Geo 381
Christopher	Csn 115	William	Lex 577
David	Cfd 104	William	Lrs 45
Daivd S.	Csn 144	William	Nby 81
Eleonar	Csn 94	William	Pen 127
Elijah	Nby 82	Wm.	Gvl 252
Ephram	Pen 163	Wm.	Gvl 258
Etheldred	Nby 82	Kingsborough,	Csn 187
Francis	Yrk 623	William	
George	Cfd 103	Kingsland, John	Csn 89
George	Csn 59	Kingman, Eliab	Csn 130
George	Dtn 120	Kingswood, Jacob	Sum 601
George	Dtn 124	Kinkaid, James	Yrk 627
George	Edg 178	John	Yrk 632

Kinkle, Christian	Ora 549	Josiah	Chr 90
Kinlock, Francis	Csn 157	Wallis	Chr 90
Kinmon, James	Lrs 42	Kirksey, Christopher	Pen 115
Kinmont, David	Csn 128	Christopher	Pen 117
Kinney, John	Lrs 36	Edward	Edg 159
Margaret	Lrs 36	William	Pen 117
Thomas	Abb 24	Kirkwood, John	Csn 91
Kinny, John	Bft 126	Margaret	Pen 131
Kinzie, Peter	Pen 113	Nathan	Abb 27
William	Pen 116	Robert	Abb 34
Kirbey, Joseph	Ker 407	Kirsh, George	Bar 52
Kirbo, Ezekl	Edg 163	John	Bar 63
Kirby, David	Mbo 54	Kirton, Thos.	Geo 391
James	Dtn 118	Kirven,	
James	Dtn 127	see also Karwon	
Nathaniel	Bft 122	Kisentaner, Susanna	Csn 140
Kirk, Hyrum	Pen 109	Kissick, Frances W.	Csn 74
John	Csn 78	Kitchen, Charley	Chr 81
John	Lan 9	Zacariah	Chr 81
John	Lrs 31	Kitchens, John	Gvl 276
Lewis	Lan 8	Thomas	Yrk 628
Matthew	Lan 9	Wm.	Spa 190
Robert	Lan 8	Kite, Shdrick	Bar 47
Stephen	Chr 84	Smith	Bar 46
Kirkland, --hn Senr.	Edg 147	Kitchart, Saml.	Spa 197
Aaron (2)	Edg 146	Kits, Henry	Bar 47
Aaron	Fai 214	John	Bar 47
Ambrose	Fai 200	Kitsinger, George	Nby 82
Benjamin	Bar 62	Joseph	Bar 55
Benjn.	Edg 146	Kitterell, Joseph	Ker 415
Caleb	Edg 146	Kitterlin, Reuben	Ora 501
Daniel	Ker 409	Kittrell, Krissy	Ora 507
Dianna	Bft 118	Kivill, Thomas	Lrs 19
George	Bar 69	Kizer, George	Edg 182
Isaac	Edg 133	Philip	Edg 182
James	Bar 56	Kizzee, Thomas	Spa 179
James	Ker 417	Kleckley,	
James Junr.	Bar 56	see also Clakely	
John	Gvl 250	Klue, Humphrey	Abb 20
Joseph Dr.	Csn 150	Knahle, John	Csn 98
Levi	Edg 155	Knepping, ---	Csn 117
Mary	Fai 239	Knight,	
Moses	Edg 146	see also Night	
Obed	Fai 231	Knight, Aaron	Mbo 54
Reuben	Bar 68	Achilles	Mbo 54
Richard	Bar 46	Alexr.	Cfd 103
Robert	Ora 517	Allen	Yrk 620
Robin	Ora 517	Ann	Mbo 54
Samuel	Ker 405	David	Lrs 18
Snodon	Edg 155	Ephraim	Nby 82
Spiar	Gvl 250	James	Ora 539
Thomas	Cfd 108	John	Cfd 103
Wille	Ker 409	John	Lan 10
William	Fai 198	Martha	Bft 110
William	Ker 409	Night	Lan 10
William	Lan 4	Richard (2)	Cfd 103
Kirkley, James	Cfd 103	Solomon	Bft 112
Sarah	Cfd 103	Thos.	Mrn 446
Kirklin, John	Gvl 257	Knighton, Isaac	Fai 237
Kirkly, George	Cfd 103	Josiah	Fai 216
John	Cfd 103	Peter	Fai 216
Thomas	Cfd 103	Susannah	Fai 217
Kirkpatric, Robert	Lan 3	Thomas	Fai 222
Kirkpatrick, James	Chr 76	Knits, William	Csn 63
Joseph	Chr 90	Knop, Charles	Abb 28

Joshua	Bar	66
Joshua	Dtn	117
Joshua	Mrn	440
Joshua	Ora	501
Lazarus	Mrn	440
Lazarus Senr.	Mrn	440
Lemuel	Mrn	456
Lewis	Ora	503
Mary	Edg	177
Mary	Sum	593
Michael	Uni	218
Nedham	Mrn	462
Nedham	Wil	467
Needom	Lan	10
Noah	Geo	376
Penelope	Nby	84
Randolph	Pen	127
Ruth	Sum	589
Samuel	Bar	53
Sherwood	Wil	467
Simon	Sum	589
Simon	Wil	468
Solomon	Bft	92
Stephen	Bar	66
Stephen	Chr	75
Stephen	Csn	70
Stephen	Csn	120
Stephen	Fai	211
Stephen	Mrn	440
Stephen	Ora	505
Susannah	Edg	175
Tabitha	Dtn	119
Talton	Gvl	270
Thomas	Abb	31
Thomas	Bar	51
Thomas	Csn	157
Thomas	Edg	176
Thomas	Ker	423
Thomas	Uni	218
Timothy	Sum	612
Uriah	Sum	608
William	Csn	144
William	Sum	587
Wm.	Gvl	270
Wm.	Gvl	281
Willm. Coll.	Csn	137
Wm. Coll.	Csn	153
William Junr.	Lrs	23
Leech, David Junr.	Yrk	624
David, Senr.	Yrk	623
James	Spa	208
John	Yrk	623
Joseph	Yrk	629
Margaret	Yrk	618
Leek, Bryant	Lrs	23
George	Lrs	22
James	Lrs	20
John	Uni	239
Samuel	Lrs	30
William Sr.	Lrs	23
Leeke, Alexander	Lrs	22
Samuel	Lrs	27
Lefan, James	Nby	84
Lefevers, see also		
Lufevers		

Lefevre, Stephen	Csn	84
Lefoy, Daniel	Lrs	30
Mathew	Lrs	31
Legan, John	Spa	184
Robert	Spa	205
Legare, Isaac	Csn	153
James	Csn	189
John	Csn	177
Joseph	Csn	177
Joseph Junr.	Csn	153
Nathan	Csn	153
Solomon	Csn	63
Solomon	Csn	112
Thomas	Csn	189
Thomas Senr.	Csn	187
LeGay, Lewis A.	Csn	153
Lege, John M.	Csn	152
Leger, Daniel	Wil	474
Elizabeth	Csn	98
John	Wil	474
Leget, Elias	Bar	61
Legg, William	Edg	180
Legge, Edward Senr.	Csn	92
Mary	Csn	108
Legget, David	Mrn	436
Jesse	Mrn	436
William Jr.	Mbo	54
Leggett, James	Mbo	54
William	Mbo	54
Leggitt, James	Mrn	436
Leggo, Ann	Fai	210
Legon, Blackmon	Gvl	266
Legran, Oliver	Lex	558
Lehre, Ann	Csn	59
Ann	Csn	144
Mary	Csn	102
Thos.	Col	375
Thos.	Csn	119
Leith, Cathe	Col	385
Lembrick, Thomas	Bar	60
Lemaster, Lucey	Spa	172
Lemley, Geo.	Fai	205
Martha	Fai	234
Milley	Fai	205
Lemly, John	Fai	203
Lemmon, Moses	Chr	92
Lemmons, John	Gvl	268
Lemny, Jacob	Col	365
Lemon, Samuel	Lrs	31
Lemons, Robert	Pen	120
Leneau, Henry Estate	Sum	585
Lenham, Joseph	Spa	211
Lenoiment, Andw.	Csn	139
Lenoir, Isaac	Sum	587
John	Sum	589
Lenox, Chas.	Col	385
William	Csn	83
William	Csn	117
Lenvill, Even	Edg	163
Leonard, Coleman	Nby	84
Davies	Lex	559
Henrey	Csn	128
James	Cfd	104
John	Nby	84
Jonas	Spa	191

Thomas	Lrs 46		Liksy, James	Bar 45
Thos.	Col 405		Lile, Ephraim	Chr 75
Thos.	Gvl 272		John	Uni 242
Thos.	Spa 204		Mahon	Uni 242
William	Csn 177		Thos.	Chr 83
William	Dtn 128		Wm.	Chr 79
William	Edg 149		Wm.	Chr 82
William	Edg 153		Liles,	
William	Fai 191		see also Lisles	
William	Mrn 446		Liles, Agness	Chr 85
William	Mrn 458		Aramanos	Fai 200
William	Pen 130		David	Edg 182
Wm.	Col 383		George	Lan 5
Wm.	Col 405		Jesse	Uni 221
Wm.	Spa 179		John	Uni 232
Wm.	Spa 198		Susanna	Uni 221
Willm. Junr.	Geo 388		Vollentine	Fai 201
Willm. Senr.	Geo 390		Lilley, David	Abb 39
William H.	Geo 376		Thomas	Sum 595
Zachariah	Geo 387		Limbacker, Christian	Edg 162
Lewton, Edward	Csn 63		Jonathan	Edg 150
Leygath, John	Ora 537		Limbeker, M. Estate	Csn 177
Ley, Frances	Csn 106		Limehouse, Robt.	Csn 113
Libby, Nathaniel	Csn 81		Linch, Aaron	Lrs 15
Natl.	Csn 153		Elijah	Nby 84
Robert	Csn 81		Isaiah	Nby 84
Liber, Frances	Csn 101		James	Lrs 15
John	Csn 99		John	Gvl 253
Librand, Henery	Lex 489		Joseph	Lrs 27
John	Lex 489		Solomon	Nby 84
Liddell, John	Wil 464		William	Gvl 253
Liddle, Andrew	Pen 130		Lindar, Rd.	Col 397
John	Pen 130		Linderman, John	Gvl 282
Moses	Pen 145		Peter	Gvl 280
Wm.	Pen 148		Lindler, George	Lex 491
Lide, Elizabeth	Dtn 113		Jacob	Lex 491
Hugh	Dtn 115		Jacob	Lex 570
James	Dtn 115		Lindley, John	Lrs 40
John	Mbo 54		Thomas	Lrs 42
Mehetabel	Mbo 54		Lindsay, Barnard	Col 375
Robert	Dtn 115		Patrick	Csn 63
Robert	Mbo 54		Benjamin	Nby 82
Thomas	Mbo 54		Lindsey, Caleb	Nby 83
Liephart, Casper	Lex 573		Charles	Csn 89
John	Lex 573		Charles	Nby 82
Lifrage, Willm.	Wil 472		David	Nby 83
Light, Ebbin	Pen 112		Elisha	Spa 171
Jacob	Pen 114		Isaac	Yrk 628
Tice	Pen 111		Jacob	Nby 82
Lightfoot, Philip	Edg 169		James	Nby 84
Lightly, David	Col 397		James	Yrk 623
John	Col 397		Jean	Uni 236
Lightner, Daniel	Nby 82		John	Abb 14
John	Fai 211		John	Abb 15
Mary	Lex 493		John	Gvl 278
Lights, Leonard	Lex 484		John	Nby 83
Lightsey,			Mary	Nby 84
see Lutesey			Moses	Nby 82
Lightsy, David	Bar 68		Nehemiah	Edg 160
John	Bar 68		Ruth	Nby 82
Lightwood, E.	Csn 169		Samuel	Abb 6
Edward Estate	Csn 191		Samuel	Nby 82
Elizabeth	Csn 123		Sarah	Yrk 628
Likes, George	Lex 572		Thomas	Nby 82
George	Lex 576		William	Lrs 23

145

Lowden, George	Chr 73	Joseph	Uni 220
Oliver	Abb 10	Randol	Bar 56
Lowder, Charles	Bft 106	Soloman	Edg 140
Thomas	Sum 603	Sylvia	Fai 222
Zachs.	Bft 122	William	Mbo 60
Zilpha	Sum 603	Lucey, Isham	Cfd 104
Lowe, Ann	Edg 161	Lucien, Charles	Csn 144
Anthony	Edg 144	Luck, Joseph, Senr.	Yrk 617
Basdel	Edg 188	Lucker, Polley	Edg 150
Horatio	Edg 161	Lucust, Sarah	Lrs 31
John	Edg 151	Lucy, Cadwallader	Cfd 104
John	Csn 143	Ludlam, Jane	Geo 386
John	Edg 185	Josh.	Geo 386
John T.	Edg 149	LueAllen, John	Fai 240
William	Lrs 36	Luellin, Elizabeth	Sum 610
Lowery(?), Elizabeth	Pen 125	Lufe, Benjn.	Csn 131
Lowery, Charles Junr.	Lrs 45	Lufevers, John	Spa 169
Charles Senr.	Lrs 45	Lucey	Spa 172
George	Pen 125	Luis, David	Chr 89
Gidion	Ker 405	Richard	Chr 87
Henry	Pen 122	Wm.	Chr 85
Isaac	Pen 125	Wm., Sr.	Chr 83
James	Lrs 45	Luke, William	Dtn 113
John	Lrs 45	Lukeroy, John	Spa 200
John	Pen 122	Lukroy, Luke	Spa 201
Lowndes, Rawlins	Col 385	Lumbus, John	Abb 21
Sarah	Csn 136	Robert	Abb 21
Thomas	Csn 114	Lumney, William	Sum 595
Lawramore, Robt.	Mrn 455	Lunday, Abigal	Cfd 104
Lowrey, Henry	Lex 565	Drury	Cfd 104
Lourey, James	Chr 82	James	Cfd 104
Lowrey, John	Abb 6	Simon	Cfd 104
Saml.	Chr 78	Lunn, John	Dtn 120
Lowrie, Robert	Yrk 632	Lunor, John	Lex 569
Lowry, Abner	Cfd 104	Lunsford, Edward	Gvl 283
Edward	Fai 227	Luscomb, George	Csn 144
Elizabith	Cfd 104	Lusk, Henry	Pen 149
Henry	Csn 183	John	Uni 240
Isam	Bft 130	Jane	Yrk 617
John	Cfd 104	Nathan	Pen 153
Manning	Pen 126	Robert	Pen 150
Robert	Cfd 104	Saml.	Chr 92
Robert Junr.	Sum 612	Thomas	Uni 240
Robert Senr.	Sum 611	Lute, Joseph	Chr 88
Rosey	Nby 82	Luteral, Robert	Abb 26
Samuel	Fai 238	Lutesey, Daniel	Lex 560
Lowrey, Widow	Edg 154	Lybran, Barnet	Lex 573
Lowry, William	Fai 209	John	Lex 568
William	Fai 238	John Senr.	Lex 567
William	Sum 614	Lybrand,	
Luallin, Daniel	Spa 206	see Librand	
Shederic	Uni 229	Lygthner, John	Lex 497
Lucas, ---	Edg 149	Lyles, Ephraim	Fai 229
Abraham(?)	Edg 149	Matthew	Ker 411
Arthur	Dtn 116	William	Fai 198
Charles	Mbo 54	Lynah, David	Lan 9
Charles Jr.	Mbo 54	Edwd.	Col 397
Edy	Bar 56	Lynch, slaves of	Geo 374
John	Edg 139	Isaac	Spa 193
Ingram	Uni 223	James	Lex 563
Jeremiah	Uni 246	James Dr.	Csn 149
John	Gvl 258	John	Lrs 28
John	Uni 218	Marget	Spa 193
Johnathan Junr.	Csn 153	Nathl.	Wil 468
Jonathan	Csn 153	William	Geo 364

William	Edg 175		Math.	Dtn 122
McCreary, Adam	Bar 50		Robert	Yrk 627
James	Gvl 278		Samuel	Yrk 618
Robert	Bar 51		Willm.	Wil 474
McCredie, David	Csn 133		Wm.	Ker 421
McCree, William			McCullum, James	Uni 245
McCreight,	Yrk 620		Kenneth	Sum 608
David, Junr.			McCune, Saml.	Csn 106
David, Senr.	Yrk 620		McCurdey, William	Pen 150
Jas.	Fai 214		McCurdy, Anney	Abb 32
Jno.	Fai 221		Robert	Yrk 626
John Sr.	Fai 226		McCurley, John	Lrs 39
Robert	Fai 211		Robert	Lrs 39
Robert Junr.	Fai 211		McCurrey, James	Abb 36
William	Fai 214		William Junr.	Abb 36
William	Yrk 620		William Senr.	Abb 36
McCreless, John	Edg 158		McCurry, William	Abb 17
McCrerey, David	Abb 28		McCutchen, George	Wil 466
McCrery, Andrew	Lrs 24		James	Wil 466
Arthur	Abb 29		James	Wil 473
George	Lrs 24		John	Pen 144
John	Lrs 25		McDade, John	Gvl 259
Robert Colo.	Lrs 25		McDale, Saml.	Wil 469
Thomas	Lrs 25		McDanal, Robert	Abb 14
William	Lrs 35		William	Abb 14
McCrorey, John	Fai 232		Mcdanel, John	Nby 85
Hugh	Fai 204		McDanel, Robert	Abb 14
Thomas	Lan 6		McDaniel, Alexander	Abb 27
McCrory, Jennet	Spa 188		Alexander	Yrk 620
Robert	Spa 188		Alexr.	Mbo 60
McCroskey, John	Pen 105		Andrew	Nby 86
McCuaig, John	Mrn 441		Archabald	Gvl 269
McCuen, Joseph	Gvl 282		Bradock	Pen 144
McCullah, Hugh	Abb 29		Bryant	Dtn 122
James	Abb 9		Charley	Chr 90
James	Abb 29		Charles	Fai 192
John	Abb 14		Daniel	Abb 27
John	Abb 29		Daniel	Geo 363
John (2)	Chr 93		Daniel	Nby 86
Mary	Chr 75		Daniel	Ora 501
Robert	Abb 29		David	Fai 210
Robert	Chr 80		David	Gvl 285
Samuel	Pen 155		Drury	Spa 183
Saml.	Chr 75		Edward	Chr 93
Saml.	Chr 82		Edward	Spa 183
McCuller, Joseph	Geo 368		Elizabeth	Edg 178
McCullers, Eliza	Fai 215		Francis	Uni 229
McCulley, Andrew	Bft 138		George	Mbo 56
Jane	Fai 232		George	Nby 86
Thos.	Fai 214		Hamilton	Nby 86
McCulloch, Hance	Bft 81		Henry	Fai 216
Jas	Ker 421		Henry	Pen 131
John	Uni 219		Henry	Pen 153
Wm.	Uni 241		Hugh	Chr 74
McCullock, Marget	Nby 84		Jacob	Edg 186
Mary	Fai 208		James	Abb 13
McCulloh, John	Pen 149		James	Edg 186
Jonas	Chr 90		James	Uni 223
Mary	Chr 87		Jeremiah	Ora 507
Robert	Pen 149		John	Abb 27
McCullouch, H.	Col 399		John	Bar 67
McCullogh, James	Yrk 631		John	Geo 364
McCullough, James	Bft 83		John	Gvl 269
John	Geo 363		John	Pen 142
Mary	Geo 370		John	Spa 168

John	Sum	595	Will.	Lan	5
John	Sum	611	Willm.	Wil	469
John	Uni	225	McDonnald, Jno	Bft	108
Joseph	Fai	194	Stephen	Bft	108
Joseph	Mbo	55	McDonold, Flora	Mrn	441
Joseph	Mbo	59	John	Chr	75
Joseph Jr.	Mbo	55	McDougle, Jno	Fai	221
Josiah	Edg	146	McDoule, Alexr.	Fai	204
Levi	Edg	167	Jane	Fai	220
Lowry	Spa	183	Jno B.	Fai	214
Mary	Edg	146	McDow, John	Lan	3
Mary	Lex	561	Robert	Csn	102
Milly	Gvl	269	Robt.	Csn	64
Minah	Edg	178	Thomas	Lan	3
Patrick	Ker	409	McDowall, James	Csn	141
Richard	Lex	562	James	Pen	103
Robt.	Geo	368	John	Csn	99
Thomas	Mbo	55	John	Lrs	14
Thomas	Mrn	436	Patrick	Csn	78
Thornton	Spa	183	McDowel, David	Spa	179
William	Abb	27	George	Spa	180
William	Edg	184	James	Spa	179
William	Fai	232	John	Csn	153
Wm.	Chr	74	Robert	Spa	179
Wm.	Chr	78	McDowell, Alexr.	Geo	380
Wm.	Chr	80	Andrew	Fai	238
Wm.	Spa	182	Hugh	Ker	397
Wm.	Spa	210	James	Fai	197
Zach	Spa	183	James (2)	Lrs	37
McDanold, William	Lrs	45	John	Fai	192
McDanold,	Lrs	44	John	Pen	134
Archabald Junr.			John	Uni	244
Archabald Senr.	Lrs	44	Mary	Fai	231
John	Lrs	43	Richd.	Geo	381
McDavid, David	Gvl	280	Robert	Lan	4
James	Abb	19	William	Ker	407
William	Lrs	43	William	Lrs	30
McDavis, Andrew	Gvl	278	Wm.	Spa	177
McDearmid, Donald	Mbo	55	McDuffey, Daniel	Cfd	104
McDill, David	Fai	207	McDugal, Alexander	Uni	222
George	Chr	73	Jean	Edg	179
James	Fai	204	Hezekiah	Uni	223
John	Chr	74	Thos.	Uni	232
John	Chr	75	McEacharn, Neil	Mrn	453
Saml.	Chr	75	McEart, Patrick	Csn	75
Thomas	Chr	74	McEbee, Charles	Spa	173
Thomas	Nby	84	Elijah	Spa	172
McDole, William	Mrn	449	Lacey	Spa	173
M'Donal, James	Wil	464	Mary	Spa	173
McDonell, Alexander	Csn	148	Mathew	Spa	172
McDonald(?), E. S.	Csn	70	McElduff, Thos.	Fai	208
McDonald, Adam	Wil	475	William	Gvl	250
Alexander	Uni	219	McElhany, John	Bar	58
Catharine	Yrk	632	Stephen	Chr	78
Christopher	Csn	119	Thomas	Chr	86
Daniel	Sum	605	McElhenny, James	Col	369
Danl.	Lan	3	McElherron, James	Yrk	627
Duncan	Cfd	104	McElisane, John	Yrk	622
Elizabeth	Lrs	29	McElmoil, John	Yrk	619
John	Lan	5	McElmore, John	Edg	145
Middleton (2)	Lan	4	McElmurry, James	Bar	63
Randolph	Cfd	104	Patrick	Bar	63
S. E.	Csn	130	McElroy, Matthew	Chr	90
Thomas	Lrs	20	McElwee, James	Yrk	627
William (2)	Abb	13	John	Yrk	627

William	Yrk 627	Phillip	Ker 427
William, Senr.	Yrk 627	Solomon	Cfd 108
McErn, John	Mrn 455	Thomas	Cfd 107
McEvoy, Sarah	Bft 100	William	Cfd 105
McEwen, Alexander	Fai 241	William	Wil 465
Danl.	Geo 391	McGeech, Benj.	Lan 7
John	Fai 218	McGehee, Benjamon	Pen 128
McEwene, John	Gvl 275	Carr	Abb 23
McFadden, Isaac	Chr 78	Henry	Pen 122
Robert	Spa 191	John	Abb 23
Willm.	Wil 466	McGenny, James	Geo 363
McFaddien, John	Sum 614	Saml.	Geo 363
Robert	Sum 606	McGill, James	Fai 199
Thomas	Sum 607	James	Wil 473
McFaden, Edward	Chr 89	John	Fai 209
Gui	Chr 92	John	Mbo 55
Palph	Chr 79	Margaret	Fai 199
Robert	Chr 79	Richard	Pen 110
William	Ora 513	Roger	Wil 464
McFail, John	Bar 45	Samuel	Pen 150
McFall, John	Chr 89	Saml.	Fai 199
John	Pen 143	McGinnis, Thomas	Edg 165
McFarlan, Alexr.	Csn 125	McGill, Thomas	Yrk 630
McFarlane, Robt.	Geo 375	William	Abb 9
McFarling, John	Yrk 628	William	Ker 421
McFarson, Stephen	Uni 216	McGinney,	
McFatrick, John	Edg 167	see also McGenny	
McFearson, William	Lrs 39	McGinniss, Patrick	Csn 142
McFeaterick, John	Uni 238	McGirt, James	Dtn 124
McFerlin, Charles	Abb 37	McGiverin, Daniel	Csn 151
George	Abb 13	McGladery, Honora	Lrs 41
Andrew	Abb 27	McGlamery, Andw.	Fai 240
Archy	Abb 26	McGloclen, Joseph	Gvl 259
James Junr.	Abb 13	Mcgomery, Samuel	Nby 86
John	Abb 14	William	Nby 86
James Senr.	Abb 13	McGough, William	Abb 8
McFerson, Burjick	Spa 171	McGouley, Jane	Col 399
Jehu	Uni 217	McGowen, James	Lex 571
McFray, George	Abb 29	John	Lrs 34
McGann, Patrick	Csn 134	William	Sum 606
McGarah, Elisebeth	Chr 80	McGraw, Benjn.	Fai 234
James	Chr 73	David	Fai 220
McGarity, James	Chr 89	Edward	Fai 195
Wm.	Chr 92	Edward Senr.	Fai 240
McGarra, George	Lan 3	Edwd. Junr.	Fai 234
James	Lan 3	James	Fai 240
Will (2)		John	Ker 403
McGaw, William	Abb 3	Mathew	Lex 575
McGeachy, Thomas	Cfd 110	Nathan	Fai 225
McGee, --vid	Edg 147	Reuben	Pen 131
Daniel	Wil 467	Solomon	Fai 237
Elisha	Cfd 105	William	Fai 233
Ferrel	Pen 125	McGraty, Peter	Edg 184
Francis	Ora 511	McGregor, Daniel	Abb 38
George	Pen 117	M'Gregor, Danl.	Csn 179
Henry	Pen 125	Laurens	Csn 179
Jacob	Cfd 109	McGregor, William	Abb 38
James	Mbo 55	William	Pen 144
John	Csn 119	McGrew, Thos.	Gvl 251
John	Dtn 121	McGriff, James	Chr 86
John	Geo 371	McGuffin, William	Pen 134
John	Sum 595	McGuire, Elijah	Spa 179
Lucy	Cfd 107	Jane	Uni 249
Michal	Abb 19	John	Fai 203
Philip	Cfd 109	Mary	Csn 120

Rhebe	Spa 180	McKay, Duncar	Cfd 107	
Solomon	Gvl 263	George	Col 369	
William	Csn 75	John	Mbo 56	
McGuirk, John	Dtn 114	Mackay, Mungo	Csn 185	
M'Gullion, Mary	Nby 87	McKedy, James	Abb 9	
McGunkins, Samuel	Gvl 250	McKee, Adam	Abb 15	
McGurney, William	Sum 591	Agness	Chr 82	
McHenry, Alexr.	Fai 191	Alexander	Ker 423	
McHood, Samuel	Yrk 620	Archabeld	Pen 148	
McHughs, Alexr.	Spa 168	Daniel	Edg 161	
James	Spa 168	Daniel	Edg 162	
McHugo(?), Anthony	Csn 152	Elizth.	Wil 473	
McIlduff, David	Geo 380	Issabalia	Chr 85	
McIlhany, James	Csn 128	James	Chr 81	
McIlroy, Mary	Geo 376	James	Mrn 444	
Willm.	Wil 476	Mackee, James, Mrs.	Csn 101	
McIlvane, Sarah	Sum 585	McKee, John	Csn 114	
McIlveen, John	Sum 613	John	Yrk 628	
William	Sum 614	John	Yrk 631	
Willm.	Wil 465	Martha	Abb 15	
McIver, Evander	Dtn 113	Mary	Ker 419	
John	Dtn 122	Michal	Abb 15	
McIlwain, Andrew	Abb 39	Robert	Nby 86	
Andrew	Lan 10	Samuel	Yrk 632	
Henry	Lan 4	Saml.	Fai 232	
John	Abb 39	Sarah	Ker 417	
Margaret	Lan 8	Thomas	Edg 162	
Robert	Lan 2	William	Abb 8	
William	Abb 12	William	Pen 148	
McInear, Samuel	Abb 36	McKegie(?), Duncan	Pen 129	
McInnes, Daniel	Mrn 453	McKeller, James	Geo 364	
McIntire, Daniel	Abb 19	Peter	Mrn 441	
Francis	Lan 6	McKelvey, James	Abb 3	
John	Abb 13	Robert	Csn 70	
John	Pen 112	McKelvy, Hugh	Chr 75	
Thos.	Csn 132	McKenny, Alexander	Gvl 251	
Wm.	Spa 207	McKensey, Benjn.	Gvl 266	
McIntosh, ---	Csn 153	McKenzia, Joseph Junr	Yrk 632	
Alex.	Dtn 124	Joseph Senr	Yrk 632	
James	Dtn 114	McKenzie, Andrew	Csn 153	
John	Dtn 113	John	Bft 130	
John Jr.	Dtn 114	John	Pen 124	
Lachlan	Col 369	Jno	Bft 116	
Lathland	Geo 370	Kennedy	Csn 109	
Laughlan	Dtn 114	Kenneth	Cfd 104	
Simon	Csn 112	Robert	Csn 64	
Sweny	Cfd 107	Roderick	Cfd 109	
William	Dtn 114	Sanders	Pen 140	
William	Sum 614	Wm.	Bft 104	
McIntyre, Alexr.	Cfd 104	McKerly, James	Gvl 268	
Archd.	Mbo 55	McKetrick Robert	Nby 84	
Charles	Mbo 55	McKewen, Saml.	Fai 198	
Daniel	Mbo 55	McKewn, A.	Col 405	
Duncan	Cfd 104	Archd.	Csn 64	
Duncan Jr.	Cfd 107	John	Csn 64	
Peter	Cfd 104	Sarah	Lan 3	
McJunkin, Daniel	Gvl 247	McKey, John	Cfd 107	
Joseph	Uni 220	Mackey, William	Bar 68	
Mary	Uni 223	John	Csn 121	
Saml.	Uni 220	McKey, Malcom	Csn 116	
McKain, Charles	Lan 7	John	Ker 427	
Mackanier, Margret	Abb 35	McKiddey, James	Abb 3	
McKaskal, Allen	Cfd 108	John	Abb 3	
John	Cfd 108	John	Abb 4	
Mackay, Crafts	Csn 132	Thomas	Abb 2	

John	Lrs	32	McMuller, Saml.	Fai	203
McMakin, see McMekin			McMullin, Dougald	Cfd	108
McMan, James	Nby	85	Duncan	Cfd	105
John	Nby	86	Hugh	Spa	178
McManus, Charles	Lan	10	James	Cfd	104
George	Lan	10	Peter	Abb	5
Hugh	Cfd	104	Samuel	Abb	5
McMaster, James	Nby	85	McMurray, John	Lan	2
McMasters, Jas.	Fai	214	John	Lan	6
John	Lan	5	William, Junr.	Yrk	618
William	Abb	3	William, Senr.	Yrk	618
William	Abb	40	McMurtrey, William	Pen	143
McMean, William	Sum	602	Wm.	Pen	127
McMeans, Anthony	Chr	78	McMurtry, John	Abb	5
McMeen, Will. Senr.	Lan	9	William Junr.	Lrs	28
Will. Junr.	Lan	9	McNair, Danl.	Cfd	104
McMekin, Benjn. P.	Spa	209	Danl.	Cfd	110
McMichal, Robert	Abb	29	Elizabeth	Sum	585
McMichel, George	Ora	533	Mary	Dtn	125
Henery	Ora	533	McNary, Gilbert	Lrs	22
Jacob	Ora	555	McNatt, James	Mbo	55
William	Ora	533	Joel	Mbo	56
McMillan, Bennett	Edg	163	John	Mbo	55
Dougald	Cfd	110	Mackey	Mbo	55
Hugh	Lan	2	McNeal, James	Nby	86
James	Cfd	111	Malcom	Sum	602
James	Edg	143	Ralph	Bft	126
James	Edg	163	McNeale, Archd.	Csn	123
Richard	Csn	106	McNeel, Arch.	Fai	239
Thomas	Abb	14	James	Yrk	617
William	Abb	39	John	Fai	239
William	Bar	55	John	Uni	232
William	Edg	163	Robert	Abb	13
Winney	Edg	173	Thomas Capt.	Yrk	630
McMillen, Abner	Pen	162	McNeely, Joseph	Lrs	18
Archibel	Nby	84	Providence	Bar	54
John	Spa	179	McNees, James	Yrk	629
McMillian, Abner	Pen	161	Wm.	Uni	246
Alexr.	Pen	144	McNeese, Robert	Lrs	17
Daniel	Pen	143	McNeill, Neill	Cfd	104
John	Pen	152	McNelly, James	Wil	466
Rowley	Pen	119	McNeltey, Henry	Wil	466
McMillin, Hugh	Chr	92	McNeil, Catharine	Csn	90
Joseph	Spa	208	McNiel, Archd.	Csn	142
McMillon, Henry	Bar	67	McNerton, William	Lrs	15
McMorries, James	Fai	197	McNiell, Alexander	Cfd	105
Joseph	Fai	199	John	Cfd	104
William	Fai	195	Niel	Mrn	441
Wm. Junr.	Fai	198	McNight, Andrew	Gvl	274
McMorris, John	Edg	135	Andrew	Lrs	42
John	Nby	85	Charles	Spa	178
McMuldrow, Hugh	Dtn	113	James	Lrs	42
Hugh	Dtn	122	John	Lrs	18
James	Dtn	113	John	Spa	178
John	Dtn	124	Thomas	Spa	177
John Jr.	Dtn	122	Wm.	Spa	178
Wm.	Dtn	124	Wm.	Spa	179
McMullen, Alexr.	Fai	219	McNinah(?), John	Chr	88
Alexr.	Geo	374	McNish, Henry	Bft	104
Daniel	Ker	421	Jno Est.	Bft	104
James	Abb	32	McPeak, John	Yrk	620
James	Fai	194	McPherson, Duncan	Csn	142
Samuel	Abb	34	Isaac Est.	Col	369
Thomas	Fai	193	James	Bft	100
William	Fai	193	John	Bft	100

Maddis, John	Uni 224	Jemeson	Edg 162
Maddon, James	Edg 180	Jimmerson	Edg 185
Maddox, Benjamin	Abb 19	John	Lex 574
Benjamin	Abb 22	Lewis	Mbo 55
Charles	Abb 20	Nathl.	Fai 207
Hanley	Abb 11	Robert	Nby 85
John	Abb 22	Robert	Sum 600
Maden, John	Nby 85	Thomas	Fai 193
Madern, James	Csn 80	Thos. Junr.	Fai 207
Madius, Daniel	Edg 161	William	Nby 85
Madkins,		William	Sum 606
see also Wadkins		Malony, Samuel	Pen 127
Madkins, James	Pen 160	Malpus, John	Bft 92
Madray, Starling	Csn 59	Man, Christopher	Bft 112
Maffet, Barbary	Chr 74	Elizabeth	Edg 149
Maffett, Samuel	Nby 87	Gilbert	Edg 156
Magan, William	Ker 417	John	Nby 84
Magbee, Saml.	Geo 380	Manasseh	Nby 84
Magill, Ann	Geo 379	Martha	Edg 156
John	Geo 377	Watts	Edg 156
Mary	Geo 370	Mance, William	Bft 102
Richard	Ker 419	Mancel, William	Mrn 457
William	Geo 377	Mancil, Edward	Sum 608
Magness, Samuel	Gvl 245	Mancill,	
Magood, S.	Csn 169	see Mansfield	
Magway, William	Ker 415	Mancor, James	Bft 114
Magwood, Simon	Csn 84	Maner, John	Bft 114
Mahaffa, Sarah	Gvl 262	Samuel	Bft 114
John	Gvl 276	Mandeville, Cornels	Mbo 55
Mahaffee, Sarah	Gvl 278	David	Mbo 55
Mahaney, Benjn.	Gvl 254	Mangrum, Jacob	Cfd 107
Mahew, William	Yrk 632	William	Nby 86
Mahon, John	Lrs 28	John	Nby 85
Mahoney, Wm.	Col 383	Manigault, Gabriel	Csn 97
Mahonny, Patrick	Mbo 56	Gabl.	Csn 155
Main, John	Geo 383	Joseph	Csn 64
William	Abb 12	Joseph	Csn 177
Maine, Elizabeth	Bft 81	Joseph	Csn 89
John	Csn 128	Manley, Elizabeth	Lrs 45
Mainord(?), Nathaniel	Edg 186	Jeremiah	Lrs 45
Mair, Patrick	Csn 134	Jesse	Lan 9
Maire, James	Csn 154	Richd.	Spa 170
Thomas	Csn 133	William	Gvl 271
Major, John	Nby 85	Ephraim	Gvl 268
Majors, Daniel	Fai 201	James	Lrs 37
Elijah	Pen 159	Jesse	Cfd 105
John	Fai 238	John Junr.	Lrs 37
Nathl.	Fai 209	John Junr.	Lrs 44
Sarah	Mbo 60	John Senr.	Lrs 37
Makemson, Andrew	Uni 240	Mann, Gilbert	Abb 38
John	Uni 240	Henry Wm.	Csn 120
James	Uni 240	James	Fai 233
Malcolm, Thomas	Csn 83	John	Abb 37
Malden, Blake	Gvl 285	Margaret	Csn 89
Malin, Elizabeth	Gvl 253	Robert	Abb 37
Mallard, Adam	Bar 45	Spencer	Csn 145
George	Bar 45	Thomas	Abb 37
James	Csn 64	Mannan, John	Abb 40
Mallet, William	Edg 188	Rebecca	Uni 218
Mallone, John	Lex 495	Manning, Edmond	Pen 126
Malloy, Anguish	Cfd 104	Elizabeth	Nby 85
Malone, Drury	Edg 162	Jacob	Sum 606
Drury	Edg 185	Joel	Ora 543
Henry	Fai 202	John, Junr.	Yrk 627
James	Csn 119	John, Senr.	Yrk 627

Laurance	Sum 604	Stephen	Spa 187
Mark		Will. (2)	Lan 3
Mary	Sum 603	Marley, Richard	Csn 179
Thomas	Pen 128	Marlon, Sarah	Geo 384
Thomas, Senr.	Yrk 629	Marlow, Hannah	Dtn 115
William	Yrk 629	Joseph	Gvl 257
Manor, Jacob	Lrs 18	Joseph	Mbo 60
Mansel, John	Nby 86	Nathaniel	Pen 117
Richd.	Fai 206	Marltiss, Thomas	Edg 137
Mansell, James	Gvl 264	Marpard, John	Nby 84
Mansfield, Elizth.	Geo 386	Marple, Northrup	Fai 199
George	Dtn 119	Marrow, John	Csn 136
George	Dtn 127	Marrs, Joseph	Ker 411
Richd.	Geo 364	Peggy	Edg 149
Manson, George	Csn 96	Mars, Benjamin	Ker 409
Thos	Gvl 283	John	Nby 85
Manuel, Peter	Csn 111	Robert	Nby 86
Manure, Thomas	Nby 85	Samuel	Abb 18
Maon, James	Mrn 461	Marsh, Ann	Ker 425
Maples, Thomas	Sum 602	George	Edg 169
Mar, Ann	Csn 127	James	Csn 85
Christopher	Bft 112	John Senr.	Ker 425
Joseph E.	Csn 150	Joshua	Ker 425
Marbrough, Thomas	Edg 148	John Junr.	Ker 425
Marchbanks, George	Lrs 19	Samuel	Edg 138
Jeremiah	Pen 113	Saml.	Mrn 458
Joel	Lrs 19	William	Edg 138
Stephen	Gvl 276	Marshal, Charley	Yrk 622
William	Pen 113	James	Nby 85
Marchant, Dorcas	Pen 105	Samuel	Nby 85
James	Gvl 285	Thos Doctr	Csn 119
John	Edg 179	William	Abb 9
Richard	Edg 179	Wm.	Uni 235
Marco, Christian	Lrs 31	Marshall, Adam	Dtn 113
Marcus, Jas.	Col 383	Eleanor	Csn 96
Joshua	Edg 161	Eliza	Csn 120
Mares, John	Bar 47	Fras.	Geo 364
Marett, Nathaniel	Pen 118	George	Dtn 121
Margey, Robert	Abb 14	James	Fai 200
Margraves, Jesse	Pen 155	James	Ker 415
Marion, Francis	Csn 70	James	Ker 423
Francis D.	Csn 70	James	Wil 465
Job Est.	Csn 70	Jane	Fai 241
Jos. Est.	Csn 70	John	Csn 105
Margt.	Csn 70	John	Fai 208
Mary E.	Csn 70	John	Ker 425
Nathn.	Csn 70	Mary	Lrs 25
Robert	Csn 59	Thomas	Csn 108
Robert	Csn 70	William	Csn 95
Saml. Theo.	Csn 70	William	Csn 138
Wm.	Chr 74	Willm.	Csn 85
Mark, Conrad	Abb 27	Wm.	Csn 163
Henry	Abb 29	Marstin, Benjamin	Csn 107
Markley, Abraham	Csn 101	Martin, ---p	Edg 149
Andw.	Csn 64	Aaron	Mrn 447
Thos.	Col 405	Abner	Ker 427
Marks, Humphrey	Csn 99	Abraham	Pen 108
Samuel M.	Csn 144	Absalom	Pen 115
Marler, Abm.	Wil 474	Alexander	Yrk 625
Ethemore	Wil 474	Alexr.	Uni 240
George	Lan 4	Amos	Uni 216
Henry	Spa 196	Andrew	Fai 231
James	Wil 475	Andrew	Uni 220
John	Lan 4	Bartley	Edg 134
Michal	Abb 19	Benjamin	Pen 115

John	Uni 236	Mathers, Wm.	Gvl 262	
Joseph	Uni 232	Wm. Senr.	Gvl 263	
Moses	Lrs 25	Mathews, Archible	Bft 92	
Saml.	Uni 221	Benjamin	Csn 189	
Thos.	Uni 238	David	Wil 470	
William	Uni 218	Edmond	Dtn 119	
Wm.	Uni 236	Edmund	Csn 189	
Marton, Daniel	Sum 584	George	Csn 104	
James	Geo 376	Isaac	Abb 2	
Marus(?), James(?)	Col 369	Jesse	Spa 174	
Marvell, Matthew	Yrk 630	John	Abb 5	
Mase, Peter	Bar 48	John	Col 405	
Mash, John	Pen 123	John	Csn 169	
Mashburn, Nicholas	Csn 102	John	Dtn 119	
Samuel	Lex 571	John	Spa 201	
Mashio,	Geo 379	Jordan	Dtn 116	
Dr., Estate of		Joseph	Abb 21	
Mason, Benja.	Mrn 440	Moses	Dtn 119	
Broderic	Spa 185	Philip Rev.	Csn 89	
Charles	Bar 57	Reuben	Spa 173	
Daniel	Pen 121	Samuel	Abb 40	
Francis	Spa 205	Sugar J.	Edg 141	
John	Fai 193	Thomas	Bar 53	
John	Lan 2	Thomas	Csn 189	
John	Spa 175	William (2)	Abb 26	
Mary	Csn 152	William	Csn 177	
Robert	Csn 185	William	Csn 189	
Robt.	Gvl 261	Wm. Senr.	Wil 467	
Susanna	Csn 116	Mathias, John	Lex 483	
Wilbon	Lan 2	Jonas	Lex 483	
William	Csn 85	Mathis, Charles	Mbo 55	
Wm.	Gvl 261	Charles	Mbo 59	
Massa, Avery	Gvl 282	Enos	Dtn 119	
David	Gvl 281	Ezekiel	Lrs 44	
Job	Gvl 264	Hugh	Sum 597	
Warren	Gvl 272	Joel	Mbo 56	
Massay, Ann	Lan 10	John	Fai 213	
Elias	Lan 5	Mary	Ker 415	
James	Lan 7	Phillip	Fai 207	
Leburn	Pen 145	Philip	Ker 415	
Will.	Lan 8	Robert	Lrs 44	
Massey, Alston	Cfd 104	Samuel	Bar 69	
Egnew	Abb 9	Samuel	Ker 397	
George	Yrk 619	Samuel	Lrs 31	
James	Pen 135	Samuel	Lrs 44	
John	Cfd 104	Thomas	Mbo 56	
John	Spa 182	Thomas Jr.	Mbo 56	
John	Uni 226	Thomas Junr.	Lrs 43	
John	Uni 239	Thomas Senr.	Lrs 43	
Joseph	Edg 180	Walter	Lrs 44	
Martha	Spa 171	William	Bar 53	
O Gowen	Ker 417	William	Lrs 40	
Rachel	Lan 3	Zebulon	Lrs 31	
William	Yrk 619	Matlock, Nathaniel	Abb 19	
Wm.	Spa 191	Matthews, Abraham	Wil 470	
Massicot, Venve	Csn 104	Alexr.	Wil 468	
Massingale, Bleak	Spa 172	Cajah	Edg 177	
Masters, James	Fai 197	Daniel	Edg 178	
John	Abb 18	David	Edg 148	
John	Abb 19	Drury	Edg 175	
John	Fai 194	Elizabeth	Pen 123	
Notley	Pen 131	Hardy	Edg 180	
Materson, Nevil	Pen 162	Isaac	Edg 150	
Mathear, Thomas	Dtn 127	Isaac	Sum 600	
Matheny, William	Bar 67	Isaac	Wil 470	

Mayhorn, Dixon	Dtn 121		Mecham, Richard	Nby 85
William	Dtn 121		Mechen, Mark	Lan 9
Mayhou, John	Fai 202		Mecomb, Joseph	Csn 99
Maynard, Henry	Cfd 111		Medes, William	Abb 6
Nicholas	Edg 181		Medley, Isaac	Lrs 32
Mayo, Richd. Geo:	Fai 205		Medlin, Lewis	Pen 142
Richardson	Fai 202		Medlock, Absalom	Pen 111
Mayrant, John	Sum 585		Catherine	Gvl 271
William	Sum 587		Charles	Edg 145
Mays, Abner	Edg 136		Charles	Pen 109
James	Spa 210		Samuel	Edg 146
James	Uni 244		Medly, Joel	Dtn 122
Matt	Edg 185		Meed, Andrew	Abb 7
Mattox	Edg 181		Nathaniel	Abb 13
Richardson	Fai 202		Meek, Adam Major	Yrk 629
Samuel	Edg 184		Basil	Yrk 629
Stephen	Edg 137		James	Chr 74
Thomas	Uni 243		James	Chr 94
William	Edg 186		James, Esqr.	Yrk 625
Mayson, Archibald	Edg 142		John	Lrs 34
David	Lrs 23		Moses	Uni 241
Ezekiel	Pen 121		Meekin, Jonathan	Mbo 55
James	Edg 184		Meeks, Joseph	Csn 75
James	Pen 122		Littleton	Pen 136
James	Pen 131		Massay	Pen 136
Job	Lrs 23		Meeley, Thomas	Abb 12
John	Pen 121		Mege, Francis	Csn 64
Mazingo, Lewis	Dtn 121		Meggot, William	Csn 185
Mazyck, Alexander	Csn 179		Megin, Daniel	Lrs 31
Benjn.	Csn 64		Mehaffee, Hugh	Lrs 44
Daniel	Csn 104		Martin	Lrs 44
Isaac	Geo 371		Mehaffy, Robert	Ker 413
Nathl. B.	Csn 81		Mehasel, Joseph	Ker 397
Stephen	Csn 64		Mehurg, Archibald	Lrs 17
Stephen	Csn 70		Susanah	Lrs 16
William	Csn 139		Meiler, William	Pen 116
Meador, Job	Fai 203		Melett, Mary	Sum 584
John	Fai 203		Melians, Elisabeth	Yrk 629
Meadow, John	Lrs 19		Meling, Henry	Edg 150
Meadows, Enoch	Bar 62		Mellichamp, Sainto	Col 369
Jason	Cfd 104		Melmes, Thomas	Csn 64
Jason Jr.	Cfd 105		Melone, Alsa	Ker 425
Jesse	Spa 186		Cornelius	Ker 425
John	Bar 45		John	Ker 425
John	Lan 9		William	Ker 425
John	Spa 186		William Junr.	Ker 425
Lewis	Cfd 107		Melson, Wm. S.	Spa 204
Lewis	Cfd 108		Melton,	
Obediah	Cfd 105		see also Milton	
Obediah Jr.	Cfd 108		Melton, Archelaus	Cfd 104
Thomas	Fai 194		Benjn.	Edg 183
Thomas	Spa 186		Elijah	Gvl 273
Wm	Spa 186		Elisha	Gvl 244
Meanes, Wm.	Uni 243		James	Dtn 126
Means,			John	Gvl 256
see also Menes			Lucy	Edg 145
Means, Hugh	Spa 202		Matthew	Edg 153
Hugh	Uni 243		Nathan	Edg 179
James	Uni 243		Peter	Dtn 126
James	Uni 244		Quinorey	Edg 145
John	Lex 571		Robert	Bar 63
John	Spa 184		Robert	Edg 153
Joseph	Uni 244		Thomas	Edg 180
Thomas	Fai 203		William	Edg 145
Meares, Isaac	Pen 116		Mendenhall, John	Mbo 55

Meneal, James	Nby 85		Jonathan	Edg 154
Menely, Samuel	Abb 20		William	Ker 425
Menes, Elisabeth	Chr 89		Meyrat, Abraham	Ora 533
Wm.	Chr 84		Miars, Oxner	Edg 154
Mercer, Francis	Ker 427		Miaxon, Michael	Bft 112
Jesse	Dtn 123		Michael, George	Bft 81
Martin	Dtn 124		Michal, Bennet	Abb 15
Nathan	Dtn 123		Michau, Abram	Csn 179
Thomas	Bar 69		Duplessy	Csn 179
Thomas	Dtn 114		Manasseh	Csn 179
Thomas	Dtn 120		Isaac	Csn 179
Merchant, Messor	Edg 179		Noah	Geo 374
Peter	Csn 143		Paul	Wil 471
Mercier, John	Geo 367		Michel, Hesekiah	Bar 60
Meredith, Thomas	Fai 223		Margaret	Csn 103
Meridith, Henry	Lrs 16		Michiau, Paul	Geo 377
Merit, Obadiah	Pen 103		Micke, John	Fai 216
Meriweather, John	Abb 23		Mickle, John	Fai 238
John H.	Abb 23		Mickler, Peter	Lex 483
Joseph	Abb 23		Middle, Jno J.	Bft 94
Mary	Abb 23		Middleton, Ann	Col 405
Nicholas	Abb 21		Ann	Csn 136
Zacheri	Abb 12		Elisabeth	Pen 150
Merrell, Charles	Pen 148		H. Estate	Csn 179
Benjamin	Csn 151		Henry	Mrn 445
Merret, Benjn. Junr.	Gvl 252		Hugh	Edg 138
Merrett, Ephraim	Pen 140		Hugh	Gvl 284
Stephen	Pen 140		Hy.	Bft 90
Merrcer, Samuel	Pen 128		Jane	Lrs 23
Merrick, John	Bar 54		John	Cfd 105
Merrimon, Joshua	Ker 421		John	Gvl 247
Merrit, Benjamin	Pen 128		John	Mrn 442
Benjn.	Gvl 252		John	Pen 150
Mary	Bar 63		John Capt.	Lrs 38
Whiten	Gvl 251		Jno Estate	Csn 179
Merritt, James	Pen 103		Josiah	Cfd 107
Steven	Pen 119		Lowery	Ker 411
Sylvanus	Yrk 620		M.	Col 405
Merry, Patrick H.	Csn 81		Martin	Mrn 442
Mervin, Ann	Bft 120		Mary	Bft 94
Mesh--, Jesse	Lan 5		Mary	Csn 84
Messer, Francis	Ker 425		Mary	Csn 95
Frederick	Ker 425		Mary	Csn 169
Nicey	Ker 425		Richard	Cfd 105
Methene, Daniel	Lrs 35		Richard	Pen 150
Metthing, Daniel	Ora 505		S. Est.	Csn 169
Mettiny, Charles	Ora 505		Sarah	Mrn 462
Metts, Adam	Nby 85		Solomon	Csn 101
Metz, Christopher	Ora 543		Thomas	Lan 4
Cristopher	Ora 545		Thomas	Pen 109
George	Lex 491		Willis	Mrn 442
George	Lex 569		Midleton, Stephen	Bar 46
George	Lex 575		Miers, Abraham	Chr 84
Henery	Lex 491		Abram	Lan 10
Henry	Lex 569		Migel, John	Lrs 40
Mets, Henry	Nby 86		Mikel, Ephraim	Csn 185
Metz, John	Lex 484		Ephraim Junr.	Csn 185
John	Lex 575		Josiah	Csn 185
Mary	Lex 575		William	Csn 185
Yost	Lex 579		Milam, Bartlett	Lrs 30
Meurset, Emelia	Csn 142		John Capt.	Lrs 29
Mew, Sarah	Geo 378		John Junr.	Lrs 29
William	Geo 382		Thomas	Lrs 31
Mey, Florian C.	Csn 91		Milbanks, Wm.	Gvl 264
Meyers, Isaac	Ker 427		Miles, ---am	Lex 563

Lewis	Cfd	104	Saml.	Chr	74
Mechlin	Lrs	43	Moffett, James	Fai	207
Nicholas	Abb	3	Matthew	Yrk	625
Rachel	Edg	161	Molay, Andrew	Abb	37
Sion	Edg	170	Molan, Peter	Csn	115
Stephen	Pen	132	Molden, John	Gvl	269
Stephen	Sum	589	Westley	Gvl	262
Thomas	Geo	372	Mole, George	Bft	96
William	Abb	5	Jacob	Bft	94
William	Csn	136	Sophia	Bft	96
William	Pen	108	Moles, Jacob	Col	397
William Esq.	Lrs	29	James	Csn	91
William Junr.	Lrs	43	Molett, Elizabeth	Bft	88
William Senr.	Lrs	43	Molisee, John	Gvl	265
Wm. (2)	Uin	250	Mollenux, Elisabeth	Yrk	627
Robert	Yrk	617	William	Yrk	627
Mitchum, James	Gvl	266	Molroy, William	Abb	20
Mitler, George	Ora	549	Momson, James	Col	403
Mixen, John Junr.	Bar	47	Mon, George	Edg	162
Adriel	Bar	67	Moncreif, Susanna	Csn	92
Cornelius	Bar	47	Moncrief, John	Csn	91
Francis	Mbo	55	Moncrieffe, John	Csn	129
George	Ora	521	Monford, James	Lrs	26
Jehu	Dtn	121	Hugh	Lrs	26
John	Bar	44	Monge, Thos.	Gvl	267
John	Bft	92	Mongin, Jno D.	Bft	134
John	Bft	86	William	Bft	128
John Jur.	Bar	46	Monglet, George	Lex	483
Meredith	Mbo	60	George	Lex	573
Micah	Dtn	114	Monguis, E. Est.	Col	385
Michael	Bft	92	Monk, James	Csn	133
Reuben	Bft	92	John	Edg	146
Robert	Bft	100	Thomas	Lex	497
Samuel	Dtn	119	Monnohon, John	Sum	593
William	Dtn	121	Monpoy, Henry	Csn	154
William	Dtn	127	Monroe, Amelia	Csn	85
Mobley, Benjn.	Gvl	250	Daniel	Ora	511
Cage	Fai	202	Montague, Charles	Csn	81
Cullen	Fai	202	Montan, Anthony	Csn	124
Edward	Edg	155	Montgomery, see also		
Edward	Edg	159	Mcgomery, Mtgomery		
Edward	Fai	197	Montgomery, Andw.	Fai	208
Isaac	Fai	203	Benjmain	Abb	10
Isaiah	Fai	205	Charles	Fai	213
Isham	Fai	202	Charles	Lan	6
Ishom	Fai	230	David	Bar	50
Jeremiah	Edg	159	David	Lan	6
John	Fai	230	David	Nby	85
Levy	Fai	197	George	Yrk	620
Michael	Edg	182	Hilary	Yrk	633
Samuel	Fai	220	Hugh	Bar	53
Samuel	Fai	230	Hugh	Lan	6
Thomas	Fai	229	James	Lan	6
William	Chr	92	Jennett	Wil	464
William	Edg	177	John	Lan	2
William	Fai	201	John	Lan	4
William	Fai	203	John	Lan	10
William (2)	Fai	205	John	Spa	208
Mobly, Saml.	Chr	82	John Jr.	Lan	10
Mock, Benjn.	Edg	161	Jonathan	Lan	8
Frederick	Lex	580	Jonathan	Pen	133
George	Nby	85	Joseph	Lan	8
Mody, Robert Junr.	Mrn	448	Ninnan (2)	Lan	9
Moer, William	Csn	111	Rebekah	Yrk	633
Moffet, Colo.	Pen	150	Robert	Lan	6

Robert	Lan 9	David	Abb 26
Robert	Lan 11	David	Ker 415
Saml.	Fai 220	David	Mrn 460
William	Pen 105	David	Pen 133
Will	Lan 6	Ebsworth	Spa 138
Monts,		Edward	Yrk 631
see also Muntz		Edwd.	Geo 386
Monts, Stephen	Edg 169	Elener	Nby 86
Mood, Peter	Csn 148	Eliab	Pen 143
Moodee, John	Ora 519	Elijah	Pen 104
Moodey, Asa	Sum 595	Elisha	Pen 121
Robert	Sum 597	Eliza	Fai 228
Solomon	Sum 595	Elizabeth	Fai 191
Moodie, Benjamin	Csn 89	Ephraim	Lrs 15
Moody,		Ezekiel	Mrn 451
see also Mooty		George	Csn 121
Moody, Andrew	Dtn 116	George	Spa 185
Asa	Dtn 115	Henry	Fai 219
Charles Junr.	Mrn 462	Hugh	Pen 111
Charles Senr.	Mrn 448	Hugh	Spa 208
Daniel	Pen 112	Isham	Sum 584
Danl. Senr.	Mrn 448	Isham Junr.	Sum 585
Jacob	Pen 139	James	Abb 32
James	Bar 55	James	Bft 92
James	Mrn 448	James	Bft 96
Jesse	Mrn 448	James	Fai 237
Joel	Pen 113	James	Lan 6
John	Dtn 115	James	Lrs 20
John	Gvl 266	James	Nby 84
Joseph	Sum 602	James	Pen 133
Robt. Senr.	Mrn 448	James	Spa 173
Roderick	Dtn 116	James	Spa 182
Rusha	Bar 56	James	Spa 199
William	Abb 27	James	Wil 468
Moon, John	Edg 159	James	Yrk 632
John	Gvl 277	James family	Wil 478
Jonathan	Pen 104	(free black)	
Patrick	Csn 163	James, Senr.	Yrk 617
William	Fai 228	James W.	Lrs 20
Mooney, John	Bar 60	Jane	Pen 158
Jonathan	Yrk 627	Jeremiah	Spa 186
Joseph	Nby 85	Jeremiah	Sum 612
Valentine	Yrk 628	John	Abb 25
Moonyham, John	Sum 611	John	Abb 32
Thomas	Sum 611	John (2)	Csn 110
Moor, John	Nby 86	John	Csn 150
Robert	Abb 19	John	Csn 153
Stephen W.	Csn 110	John	Fai 207
William	Abb 19	John	Geo 375
Moore, Aaron	Lrs 18	John	Gvl 250
Aaron	Pen 140	John	Ker 423
Abraham	Pen 161	John	Lan 7
Abraham	Spa 199	John	Lan 8
Alexander	Abb 26	John	Lrs 16
[Alexan]der, Esqr.	Yrk 617	John	Lrs 31
Ann	Spa 169	John	Lrs 39
Arbin	Edg 163	John	Lrs 45
Austin	Lrs 17	John	Nby 85
Benjamin	Abb 4	John	Nby 86
Benjamin	Ora 509	John	Ora 519
Benjn.	Mbo 55	John	Pen 104
Burt	Pen 113	John	Pen 143
Charles	Spa 181	John	Spa 205
Charles	Spa 203	John	Spa 209
David	Spa 190	John	Sum 595

Elizabeth	Edg 143	William	Abb 39
Elizabeth	Gvl 277	Morrall, Dempsy	Dtn 125
Elizabeth	Pen 104	Morrel, William	Pen 163
Genl.	Sum 587	Morrell, Jordan	Edg 157
George	Lrs 38	Saml.	Csn 64
Harey	Edg 173	Morris, Benjamin	Bar 69
Henrey	Csn 132	Benjamin	Chr 73
Henry	Lrs 44	Benjn.	Mbo 56
Henry	Spa 177	Burrel	Abb 10
Henry	Spa 209	Charles	Bft 122
Isaac	Dtn 116	Charles	Fai 198
Isbel	Abb 26	Charles	Nby 87
James	Col 399	Drewry	Gvl 269
James	Edg 145	Edetha	Cfd 109
Jeremiah	Pen 154	Edward	Bar 62
Jesse	Gvl 261	Elisha	Bar 56
John	Gvl 251	Elizabeth	Abb 31
John	Nby 85	Ephraim	Mbo 56
John	Pen 133	Hezekiah	Abb 35
John	Pen 156	Isaac	Fai 198
John	Spa 189	Jacob (2)	Dtn 118
John	Uni 230	Jacob	Spa 176
John	Yrk 628	James	Chr 76
Melan	Abb 26	James	Csn 144
Michael	Sum 604	James	Dtn 117
Nancy	Gvl 260	James	Edg 158
Peter	Edg 168	Jefrey	Abb 33
Peter	Yrk 628	Jesse	Cfd 104
Redly	Pen 103	John	Bar 61
Reid	Pen 113	John	Bft 122
Robert	Lrs 30	John	Chr 73
Samuel	Yrk 628	John	Dtn 117
Silas	Uin 235	John	Dtn 118
Solomon	Dtn 116	John	Edg 143
Soloman Jr.	Dtn 116	John	Fai 198
Spencer	Lex 495	John	Fai 200
Spencer	Lex 580	John	Fai 235
Stephen	Gvl 251	John	Ker 405
William	Edg 151	John	Pen 113
William	Edg 187	John	Pen 158
William	Lrs 18	John	Spa 175
Wm.	Gvl 251	John	Spa 178
Wm.	Spa 170	John	Spa 187
Wm.	Spa 181	John	Uni 249
Wm.	Uni 221	John	Yrk 623
Wm. Doctor	Col 405	John	Yrk 624
Zachariah	Pen 133	Jno Junr.	Fai 222
Morgandollar, John	Bft 126	John Senr.	Pen 162
Morgen, Ormond	Pen 128	Joseph	Edg 158
Morgin, Christopher	Chr 88	Joseph	Edg 163
James	Pen 134	Joseph	Edg 178
Jarcott	Chr 81	Joseph	Fai 223
John	Chr 79	Joseph	Mrn 435
Reubin	Bar 44A	Lewis	Col 391
Rubin	Nby 86	Lewis	Csn 123
Wm.	Chr 81	Nimrod	Nby 86
Morints(?), Robert	Nby 86	Richard	Bar 56
Morison,	Lrs 14	Richard	Edg 158
Alexander Capt.		Richard	Ker 401
Morphey, Wiley	Abb 4	Robt.	Wil 472
Don Diego	Csn 119	Samuel	Abb 13
Morrah, Arthur	Abb 12	Spence	Fai 206
Hugh	Abb 38	Stephen	Dtn 117
Mary	Abb 37	Thomas	Bar 48
Thomas	Abb 39	Thomas	Bar 62

Thomas	Chr 91	Alexdr.	Chr 74
Thomas	Fai 217	Ann	Geo 368
Thomas Major	Csn 92	David	Chr 73
William	Abb 34	David	Gvl 274
William	Bar 61	George	Pen 104
William	Edg 158	Joel	Gvl 264
William	Fai 198	John	Chr 75
William	Mbo 55	John	Chr 81
William Jr.	Mbo 55	John	Gvl 275
Wm.	Chr 89	John	Lan 4
Wm. (2)	Spa 175	Marshall	Pen 113
Wm.	Spa 206	William	Chr 73
Wyatt	Edg 143	Moseby, William	Ker 397
Morrison, A. B.	Csn 131	Moseley, Backster	Uni 245
Andrew	Chr 85	Charles	Abb 33
James	Edg 133	David	Spa 181
James	Fai 206	Edward	Edg 140
John	Abb 20	James	Uni 246
John	Csn 153	John	Edg 161
John	Geo 374	John	Edg 188
Jos.	Col 399	John	Uni 245
Margaret	Ker 419	Joseph	Abb 40
Robert	Chr 86	Joseph	Edg 186
Thomas	Chr 89	Natl.	Abb 40
William	Abb 20	Richard	Abb 34
Morriss, George	Csn 140	Robert	Edg 134
Samuel	Nby 87	Samuel	Edg 161
Samuel	Pen 132	William	Edg 167
Morriston, Rebecca	Sum 589	Wm.	Edg 137
Morrow, Arthur Junr.	Abb 29	Mosely, Absalom	Bar 61
Arthur Senr.	Abb 29	Drury	Lrs 38
David	Chr 78	George	Lrs 15
David	Lan 8	Isaac	Lrs 35
George	Chr 82	John	Fai 238
James	Abb 14	John	Lrs 35
James	Chr 86	Richard	Ker 417
James	Lan 2	Samuel	Gvl 265
James	Lan 7	William	Bar 49
James	Pen 153	William	Bar 61
John	Abb 14	William	Fai 238
John	Chr 95	William	Gvl 245
John (2)	Pen 134	Moser, Philip Doctr.	Csn 153
John	Yrk 622	Abraham	Csn 79
John Junr.	Abb 7	Henry	Csn 78
John Junr.	Abb 29	Josiah	Csn 147
John Senr.	Abb 7	Lion	Csn 147
John Senr.	Abb 29	Solomon	Csn 146
John E.	Spa 173	Moss, Abraham	Yrk 627
Joseph	Chr 87	Charity	Yrk 627
Mary	Chr 93	Ebenezar	Spa 194
Mary	Spa 174	Giblert	Yrk 627
Richard	Pen 152	James	Gvl 247
Robert	Gvl 274	Jarred	Spa 194
Saml.	Spa 200	Jesse	Pen 107
Samuel	Gvl 274	John	Pen 107
Thomas	Pen 147	John	Pen 141
Thomas	Pen 157	Joseph	Yrk 627
William	Abb 35	Matthew	Pen 138
William	Nby 85	Obediah	Spa 194
William	Ora 523	Reuben	Yrk 627
Wm.	Spa 174	Samuel	Lan 4
Wm.	Spa 175	Samuel	Pen 141
Mortimer, Edwd.	Csn 133	Samuel	Yrk 627
Mortimore, Willm.	Csn 97	Traves	Lrs 15
Morton, Alexander	Csn 148	Wm.	Spa 194

Willm.	Geo 369	Thomas	Edg 141
Murdon, Edward	Pen 112	Murray, Charlotte	Csn 152
Murfee, Moses	Mrn 450	Hannah	Geo 364
Murfet, Robert	Nby 84	James	Nby 86
Murff, Samuel	Fai 212	James S.	Ker 396
Sophia	Fai 212	John	Csn 80
Murfy, Mary	Nby 85	John	Sum 587
Murph, Henry	Lex 561	Jos: James	Csn 185
Murphey, ---y	Edg 148	Saml.	Col 387
Bird	Uni 238	William	Bft 84
Charles	Abb 22	William	Geo 364
Charles	Fai 219	Murrel, Drury	Uni 237
Charles	Lrs 31	John	Uni 218
David	Ora 523	Jno Estate	Csn 179
Ebenezer	Lrs 38	Thomas	Csn 179
Eliza	Csn 129	Murrell, Jno Jona.	Csn 153
Eliza	Sum 587	John P.	Geo 373
Elizabeth	Sum 612	Rebecca	Geo 374
George	Fai 209	Robert	Csn 153
Humphry	Bft 110	Thomas	Csn 153
James	Edg 142	William	Sum 585
John	Gvl 255	Wm.	Geo 372
John	Lrs 23	Murrer(?), Daniel	Geo 379
John	Lrs 39	Murrey, Andrew	Edg 177
John	Ora 545	Benjamin	Abb 37
Joseph	Gvl 268	James	Abb 36
Mala	Ker 401	John	Pen 149
Mark	Uni 237	Nicholas	Gvl 252
Milley	Edg 150	Nicholas	Spa 171
Moses	Dtn 115	Tidus	Abb 38
Sion	Uni 237	Murry, Wm.	Chr 95
Thomas	Lrs 27	Wm.	Col 405
William	Lrs 27	Muscave,	Csn 110
William	Sum 601	Leonard Henrey	
William	Sum 604	Musclark, John	Nby 85
William	Sum 612	Muse, Daniel	Fai 228
Wm.	Ora 521	Thomas	Fai 196
William Jur.	Sum 602	Musgrove, Robt	Geo 374
Willis	Dtn 127	Salley	Spa 193
Murphree, Aaron	Pen 114	Musslewhite, James	Bft 96
Daniel	Pen 114	Mussenwhite, Joshua	Mrn 443
David	Pen 114	Myer, Andrew	Lex 497
James	Pen 114	Andrew	Lex 579
Mary	Pen 113	Benedick	Lex 569
Moses	Pen 114	Ulrick	Lex 579
Roger	Pen 160	Ulrick Junr.	Lex 497
Solomon	Pen 113	Ulrick Junior	L-x 579
William	Pen 114	Ulrick Senr.	Lex 497
Murphy, Archd.	Wil 473	Myers, Allexander	Ora 523
James	Chr 84	Absalom	Ora 545
James	Edg 134	Benedict	Lex 495
James	Lrs 27	Cath:	Col 405
John	Abb 15	Daniel	Dtn 117
John	Chr 91	Daniel	Mrn 454
John	Lan 6	Daniel	Ora 549
John	Yrk 617	Daniel	Ora 551
Malachi	Mrn 445	David	Cfd 104
Mathew	Mbo 55	Elizabeth	Lrs 41
Robert	Yrk 617	Esther	Geo 362
Roger	Lrs 38	Frances	Csn 145
Stephen	Bar 63	George H.	Csn 90
Wm.	Chr 94	Henry	Pen 124
Willis	Bar 63	Isarael	Csn 143
Murrah, George	Edg 162	Jacob	Ora 535
James	Edg 161	Jacob	Ora 549

James	Lrs 41	Solomon	Csn 150
James	Mrn 454	Nations, Amos	Pen 130
John	Cfd 104	Bayles	Pen 138
John	Csn 59	Cristopher	Gvl 279
John	Mrn 462	John	Gvl 279
Joseph	Col 369	Joseph (2)	Pen 137
Levi	Geo 362	Nathan	Pen 112
Michael	Csn 144	Thos	Gvl 276
Michl.	Col 397	Naugher, John	Uni 224
Samuel	Cfd 104	Mary	Uni 250
Samuel	Csn 147	Neace, Peter	Gvl 268
Serenius	Bft 106	Neal, Benjamin	Nby 87
William	Cfd 104	Briton	Gvl 254
Mylne, James	Csn 76	Elizabeth	Nby 87
Myre, John	Bar 64	Hannah	Yrk 627
Myrick, Henry	Bar 55	James	Edg 178
James	Bar 63	James	Yrk 625
		John	Bft 130
		Jonathon	Abb 35
N		Lewis	Edg 177
		Robt	Gvl 266
		Samuel	Bft 90
Nabours, Abraham	Lrs 13	Stephen	Bft 130
Benjamin	Lrs 42	Thomas	Bft 132
Benjamin	Lrs 45	Thomas	Pen 132
Charles	Lrs 21	William	Nby 87
Jacob	Lrs 13	Nealey, Samuel	Gvl 246
John	Lrs 21	Neally, Robert	Nby 88
John	Lrs 42	Nealy, George	Nby 87
Robert	Lrs 43	James	Nby 87
Saml.	Lrs 13	James	Nby 88
William	Lrs 21	Neasom, Thomas	Dtn 127
Naignear, John	Bft 104	Neale, Doctr.	Csn 113
Nail, see also		Neaves, John	Lrs 32
Neil, Niel		Nebuhr, John D.	Csn 146
Nail, James	Pen 148	Neederman, John	Uni 235
Nancy	Pen 148	Neel, Ann	Fai 217
Samuel	Pen 134	David	Spa 193
Naites, Paul	Lex 574	James	Pen 133
Nall, Nathan	Pen 145	John	Chr 80
Richard	Pen 123	John	Chr 85
Nally, Abraham (2)	Pen 103	Jane	Fai 232
Nance, Elisebeth	Chr 94	Robert	Fai 231
Frederic	Nby 87	Stephen	Uni 240
Sherard	Chr 87	Thomas	Lan 6
Zach	Uni 216	Wm.	Spa 193
Nanns, Mr. Est.	Col 375	Zacheri	Abb 19
Nanson, Elizabeth	Dtn 118	Neeley, Andrew	Yrk 620
Napier, Thomas	Csn 134	David	Yrk 619
Nappier, Absolom	Edg 151	James	Yrk 620
Drury	Edg 149	Jane	Yrk 619
Nathaniel	Edg 151	John	Yrk 620
Naron, Elizabeth	Dtn 118	Mary	Yrk 620
Narrimore, Edward	Lan 10	Samuel	Yrk 621
Edw. Senr.	Lan 10	Samuel	Yrk 622
Naser, Philip	Csn 142	Thomas	Yrk 618
Nash, see also Gnash		William Junr.	Yrk 620
Nash, Abner	Abb 8	Neelins, Abraham	Fai 199
Edward	Lrs 42	Neely, Ann	Fai 213
John	Abb 22	David	Chr 91
Miles	Spa 186	James	Chr 91
Polly H.	Abb 8	James	Fai 196
Reuben	Abb 8	James Junr.	Fai 235
Thomas P.	Bar 57	John	Fai 213
Nathan, David	Csn 83	John	Lan 6

Robert	Chr	93	Leanah	Lrs	38
Robert	Yrk	618	Lewis	Pen	146
Saml.	Chr	91	Nathaniel	Bar	58
Saml.	Spa	183	Richard	Nby	87
Thomas (2)	Chr	89	Robert	Gvl	258
Wm.	Chr	94	Robert	Nby	87
Neesbet, Thomas	Chr	80	Samuel	Fai	228
James	Chr	75	Samuel Junr.	Sum	604
Neese, Battston	Ker	403	Samuel Senr.	Sum	606
Negrin, J. J.	Csn	140	Thomas	Fai	199
Neice, Jacob	Lex	559	Thomas	Lan	9
Neighbours, Francis	Lrs	45	Thos. Junr.	Fai	205
Neighbors, Heat	Gvl	270	William	Bar	46
Jacob	Gvl	271	William	Fai	230
Neighbours, Nathan	Nby	88	William	Gvl	254
Neighbors, Samuel	Gvl	270	William	Lrs	36
Neighbours, Solomon	Cfd	105	William	Nby	87
William (2)	Nby	87	William	Yrk	624
Neil, Daniel Senr.	Edg	153	Willm.	Wil	470
Gasper	Edg	153	Wm.	Chr	78
James	Lrs	22	Wm. Jr.	Gvl	258
Margaret	Lrs	24	Nely, William	Abb	22
Peter	Csn	94	Neroth, Lewis	Csn	100
Philip	Col	379	Nerren, Aquilla	Abb	36
Samuel	Lrs	28	Nesbet, Agness	Chr	75
William Esq.	Lrs	28	Saml., Junr.	Fai	203
Neiley, James	Lrs	33	Nesibt, Alexander	Lan	6
John	Lrs	32	Benjamin	Lan	6
Joseph	Lrs	32	Elisabeth	Yrk	625
Neill, Andrew	Ker	419	Francis	Yrk	632
Benjn.	Mbo	60	John	Lan	6
Lewis	Dtn	116	Joseph	Lan	6
Neilson, John	Ker	396	Saml.	Fai	198
Neisbitt, Samuel	Lrs	43	Will.	Lan	6
Nell, Jesse	Csn	109	Nesibtt, Jeremiah	Gvl	250
Nelson, Abner	Nby	87	Jonathan	Spa	208
Alexander	Bar	57	Robt.	Geo	375
Ambrose	Csn	92	Nesmith, Ann	Wil	477
Andrew	Gvl	279	John	Wil	469
Daniel	Lan	8	Mary	Mrn	460
David	Lrs	36	Saml.	Wil	470
David Junr.	Sum	591	Thomas	Yrk	632
Edward	Gvl	258	William	Yrk	632
Eli	Bar	64	Nettles, Elijah	Ora	537
Elisha	Gvl	275	George	Csn	64
Frances	Csn	92	Isham	Wil	467
George	Pen	120	James	Csn	64
Gideon	Nby	87	Joseph	Csn	64
Hansil	Nby	87	Joseph	Csn	70
Hugh	Uni	224	Josia	Csn	64
Isaac	Csn	109	Malacai	Csn	65
James	Abb	10	Mark	Col	399
James	Chr	78	Mary	Dtn	117
James	Edg	166	Robert	Dtn	126
James	Fai	219	Robt.	Csn	64
James	Sum	606	Samuel	Dtn	126
Jared	Sum	591	Stephen	Col	405
John	Bar	57	William	Bar	51
John	Bar	61	William	Csn	64
John	Gvl	264	William	Ker	403
John	Nby	87	William	Ker	405
John	Spa	176	Zach	Dtn	126
John	Sum	606	Zach.	Fai	222
John (2)	Uni	223	Neufville, Ann	Csn	100
John Senr.	Bar	53	Isaac	Csn	104

Ephraim	Lrs	33	Nolton, Grant	Sum	610
John	Abb	19	NonnyMaker, Jacob	Lex	570
Reuben	Uni	227	Nores, William	Bar	55
Richard	Nby	88	Norman, David	Uni	237
Thomas	Uni	230	George	Gvl	268
Wm.	Uni	230	Isaac	Spa	208
Nighten, Jesse	Sum	597	John	Uni	236
Nights, John	Csn	65	Jonathon	Uni	237
Nimmons, Andrew	Bar	49	Martin	Lrs	40
William	Bar	52	Robert	Uni	237
William	Nby	87	Thomas	Uni	237
Nipper, David Henry	Csn	144	Norred, Saml.	Abb	5
Nisbett, Alexander	Csn	70	Norrel, Hugh	Uni	225
Andrew F.	Spa	209	James	Abb	24
James	Spa	168	Jane	Abb	27
Saml.	Spa	209	Saml.	Spa	180
Nisbit, Robert	Sum	613	Norrell, William	Edg	154
Temperance	Sum	604	Norris, Abnor	Gvl	249
Nish, Archid.	Col	405	Agnis	Edg	170
Nisk, James	Csn	64	Andrew	Pen	121
Niswanger, Jacob	Lrs	40	David	Gvl	249
Nix, Ambrous	Chr	83	Edetha	Cfd	105
Berry	Bar	57	Frederick	Geo	384
Edward	Bar	48	George	Csn	64
George	Bft	90	James	Cfd	105
George	Bft	90	Jane	Pen	154
Henry	Bft	94	Jemimah	Lrs	44
John	Chr	76	Jethru	Edg	138
John	Yrk	620	Joel	Cfd	105
Robert	Chr	83	John	Dtn	115
Nixon, Absolum	Lrs	44	John	Edg	134
Elizabeth	Lrs	14	John	Edg	138
Elizabeth	Sum	593	John	Gvl	246
Henry	Lrs	44	Nathan	Edg	170
John	Ker	415	Nathaniel	Gvl	284
Stephen	Ora	507	Patrick	Pen	153
Tracey	Ker	409	Robert	Gvl	285
William	Ker	397	Samuel	Lrs	41
Nixson, Wm.	Col	383	Stephen	Edg	170
Nobbs, Samuel	Csn	150	Thomas	Lrs	42
Noble, Alexander	Abb	8	Thomas L.	Csn	64
Ezekiel	Csn	99	Thos.	Geo	384
Nobles, Abihu	Bar	54	Thos.	Gvl	249
Bee Lamo	Ora	519	William	Abb	2
Elijah	Edg	171	William	Abb	19
Hezekiah	Edg	133	William	Cfd	105
Joshua	Lrs	23	William	Edg	170
Josiah	Edg	134	William	Lrs	43
Lewis	Edg	138	William Senr.	Abb	19
Mark	Edg	165	Wilson	Abb	19
Mary	Bar	54	Norriss, Patrick	Fai	227
Nicholas	Bar	54	Norroy, John	Csn	105
Solomon	Edg	166	North, Bee	Col	399
Thomas	Lrs	17	Charles	Col	399
Zepheniah	Edg	171	Richd. B.	Csn	127
Noblett, Saml.	Spa	200	Susanna	Csn	121
Noland, Aubury	Nby	87	Thos.	Col	387
George	Nby	87	Northcut, Benjamin	Abb	17
George	Uni	231	William	Dtn	120
John	Spa	175	Northern, Samuel	Gvl	261
Shadrick	Pen	141	Northon, Christian	Ora	511
Sherod	Pen	158	John	Lex	489
Susannah	Pen	130	William	Ora	543
Noles, Richard	Bft	112	Norton, Edward	Pen	118
Nolin, Philip	Chr	94	Fielder	Spa	171

178

Oquinn, John	Ker 423	Overby, Mesheck	Lrs 35
Ormond, William	Csn 90	Nimrod	Lrs 35
William	Yrk 631	Overstreet, James	Bar 47
Orphan house	Csn 110	Jeffery	Bft 120
Orr, Alexander	Pen 157	John	Bft 120
Jehu	Pen 154	Moses	Mbo 56
Mary	Dtn 117	Nathan	Bft 120
Robert	Pen 105	Overturn, Daniel	Csn 191
William	Pen 119	Owen, David	Chr 86
Orrick, William	Pen 127	David	Lrs 33
Ortner, Jacob	Uni 216	George	Gvl 265
Orum, Henry	Lan 4	John	Csn 104
Osborn, Benjamin	Abb 15	John	Chr 94
Daniel	Lrs 30	John	Csn 126
Daniel Junr.	Lrs 37	John	Mrn 444
David	Lrs 28	Samuel	Chr 76
John	Abb 17	Solomon	Chr 85
John	Lrs 37	Thadeus	Spa 208
Matthew	Yrk 630	Walter	Mrn 444
Thomas	Abb 15	William	Mbo 56
Thomas	Csn 114	Owenby, Arthur	Pen 117
William	Lrs 29	James	Edg 171
William	Lrs 36	Owens, Archd.	Ker 421
Osborne, Henry	Csn 139	Archibald	Lrs 18
Thos. Senr.	Col 369	Bailey	Pen 114
Osburn, Reps	Edg 174	Benjamin	Fai 211
OSheilds, Crecey	Spa 199	Bird	Fai 215
OShields, Jethero	Spa 199	Caleb	Cfd 105
John	Spa 197	Charles H.	Yrk 621
Osteen, Thomas Junr.	Sum 602	Daniel	Gvl 268
Thomas Senr.	Sum 602	David	Fai 218
William	Mrn 454	David	Nby 88
Oswald,		Elijah	Pen 106
see also Oswould		Elisha Junr.	Mrn 457
Oswald, Mathew	Lex 565	Eliza	Fai 233
Oswell, Wm.	Col 379	Elthred	Bar 52
Oswold, Martin	Lex 565	Enock	Edg 169
Oswould, Henry	Lex 564	Hardy	Pen 129
Henry Jr.	Lex 564	Henry	Nby 88
Michael	Lex 564	James	Fai 209
Otis, Joseph	Csn 130	James	Fai 241
Ott, Anne	Ora 553	James	Pen 109
Gaspar	Ora 535	James	Spa 208
Jacob	Ora 535	Jesse	Nby 88
Jacob Junr.	Ora 549	Job	Fai 212
Jacob Senr.	Ora 549	John	Abb 38
Peter	Ora 535	John	Cfd 105
Peter	Ora 553	John	Fai 217
Ottery, Alexr.	Spa 185	John	Lrs 24
James	Lex 565	John	Nby 88
Otto, John	Csn 98	John	Spa 182
Otts, John	Spa 185	John	Spa 202
James	Spa 186	John Jur.	Cfd 105
Martin	Spa 184	Jonathan	Edg 156
Saml.	Spa 183	Joshua	Abb 17
Ottwell, Benjamin	Pen 105	Joshua	Gvl 279
Out, Eli	Csn 153	Langsford	Csn 65
Outen, Aaron	Fai 225	Larkin	Fai 233
Moses	Fai 225	Lucy	Wil 464
Nathl.	Gvl 255	Matthew	Ker 427
Outlaw, Bently	Cfd 110	Nancy	Lrs 15
George	Dtn 122	Owen Junr.	Bar 52
William	Cfd 110	Owen Senr.	Bar 51
Outzs, see Ootes		Peter	Wil 465
Ovelton, John	Ker 415	Philemon	Bar 47

Charles Junr.	Bft 114	Hugh		Nby 90
Charles Senr.	Bft 130	James		Chr 73
Daniel	Uni 215	John		Uni 244
David	Mrn 455	Robert		Nby 90
Elisha	Edg 161	Thomas		Dtn 116
Fox	Col 399	Thomas		Uni 243
Hezekiah	Uni 222	Parker, Abel		Gvl 269
Jesse	Mrn 460	Andrew		Abb 3
Jesse	Nby 90	Benjamin		Bar 54
Jesse	Uni 246	Benjamin		Csn 153
Job	Csn 145	Benjamin		Sum 591
John	Csn 59	Burrel		Bar 44A
John	Csn 121	Catharine		Csn 149
John	Nby 90	Charles		Abb 11
John	Pen 136	Charles		Abb 34
John	Pen 138	Daniel		Edg 136
John	Uni 221	David		Pen 147
Jno Junr.	Csn 59	Elijah		Mbo 56
Jonathan	Pen 139	Elisha		Cfd 105
Joseph	Csn 59	Elisha		Mbo 56
Joseph, Esqr.	Yrk 623	Florida		Csn 85
Joshua	Uni 223	George		Cfd 105
Joshua Rev.	Lrs 22	George		Csn 65
Parmenas	Uni 221	George		Csn 81
Peter	Csn 59	Hugh		Gvl 257
Philip	Yrk 627	Isaac		Csn 153
Richd.	Uni 215	Isaac		Edg 154
Robert	Bft 108	Isaac		Uni 241
Robert	Uni 216	Isaiah		Uni 241
Thomas	Csn 59	James		Abb 4
Thomas	Csn 71	James		Abb 21
Thomas	Edg 162	James		Bft 94
Thomas	Uni 215	Jesse		Uni 216
Thomas	Uni 221	John		Abb 35
William	Lrs 21	John		Csn 65
William	Pen 139	John		Csn 107
William	Uni 216	John		Edg 154
William	Uni 222	John		Geo 385
Wm.	Uni 221	John		Lrs 15
Wm.	Uni 248	John		Pen 159
William Senr.	Mrn 456	John		Yrk 629
Palmore, Solomon	Pen 115	Jno		Bft 132
Pane, Isaac	Gvl 263	John Junr.		Csn 65
John	Gvl 263	John Junr.		Csn 146
Richard	Nby 90	John Senr.		Csn 65
Pannel, Wm.	Fai 228	Jonathan		Sum 613
Wm. Junr.	Fai 229	Joseph		Abb 11
Pannell, Andw.	Fai 229	Joseph		Bar 64
Pardue, Gideon	Edg 152	Joseph (2)		Edg 154
Lilliston	Edg 140	Joseph		Yrk 628
Pare, Allen	Yrk 619	Josiah		Ker 425
John	Sum 613	Margarett		Geo 385
Parham, Richard	Yrk 619	Martha		Csn 107
Wm.	Mbo 60	Mathew		Abb 11
Paris, David	Spa 175	Mathew		Abb 36
Henry	Sum 610	Matthew		Edg 151
Nat	Spa 176	Moses		Mbo 59
Parish, Edward	Ker 425	Nathan		Edg 142
Isaac	Yrk 630	Richard		Edg 140
Jeremiah	Ker 423	Samuel		Edg 151
Jeremiah Junr.	Ker 425	Sarah		Csn 113
John	Gvl 275	Serah		Ora 535
Obed	Nby 90	Silus		Wil 468
Wyatt	Mbo 59	Simon		Geo 382
Park, George	Uni 243	Stephen		Mbo 56

James	Spa 190	George	Ker 427
James	Spa 206	George	Pen 119
Jesse	Bft 132	James	Gvl 263
John	Bft 83	John	Geo 370
John	Pen 117	John	Ker 427
John	Pen 125	Joseph	Ker 401
John	Pen 150	Ledford	Pen 135
John	Yrk 632	Moses	Pen 130
Joseph	Lrs 15	Samuel	Ker 399
Littleberry	Yrk 631	William	Ker 403
Matthew	Sum 595	Willm. R.	Csn 120
Peter	Yrk 627	Paysinger, Fedrick	Nby 90
Reuben	Ker 397	Peace, Isaac	Csn 126
Samuel	Ker 399	John	Gvl 256
Thomas	Pen 130	Joseph	Csn 138
Thos.	Col 399	Peach, John	Ker 415
Widow	Lan 4	Peack, James	Gvl 278
William	Abb 7	John	Gvl 277
William	Bft 130	Peacock, Archibald	Mrn 441
William	Csn 189	Henry	Abb 20
Wm.	Col 371	Levy	Bar 56
Wm.	Col 399	Mary	Bar 51
Patteton, John A.	Csn 76	Samuel	Edg 155
Pattey, Charles	Uni 247	Peaden, Alexander	Gvl 275
Pattisson, Charles	Ora 515	David	Gvl 275
John	Ora 513	Samuel	Gvl 275
Patton, Alexr.	Fai 241	Wm.	Gvl 274
Patton, David	Chr 79	Peak, Elizabeth	Bft 122
David	Fai 232	John	Csn 104
David	Yrk 631	John	Col 391
Catharine	Csn 86	Peake, Nathl.	Geo 377
James	Chr 79	Pearce, Abner	Cfd 109
James	Yrk 619	Dickson	Mbo 56
John	Lan 5	Earl	Csn 129
Mathew	Spa 186	Isaac	Col 391
Saml.	Uni 244	John	Mbo 56
Sarah	Spa 183	Sarah	Mbo 56
Thomas	Uni 244	Silas	Mbo 56
Thomas	Yrk 619	Pearse, Steward	Ker 401
William	Uni 244	Pearson, Aaron	Mbo 56
Wm.	Uni 244	Aaron Jr.	Mbo 56
Patty, Tapley	Chr 88	Abel	Uni 235
Paty, Marget	Nby 89	Anthony	Spa 209
Paul, Agness	Fai 206	Charles	Spa 188
Andrew	Abb 40	Charles	Spa 192
Andrew	Mbo 56	Elizabeth	Spa 192
Archibald	Fai 192	Frances	Spa 192
Archd. Senr.	Fai 193	Henry	Mbo 60
William	Abb 40	Henry	Spa 191
William	Fai 192	Isaac	Uni 233
Paulk,		Jacob	Uni 232
see also Polk		James	Fai 226
Paulk, Jacob	Uni 219	James	Sum 605
Jean	Uni 219	John	Fai 210
Joshua	Uni 219	John	Lrs 24
Rachel	Uni 219	John	Lrs 33
Pawley, George	Geo 379	John Genl.	Fai 196
James	Dtn 126	Joseph	Uni 232
John	Geo 378	Joseph	Yrk 625
Persaval	Geo 379	Mahlon	Uni 234
Paxton, John	Ora 503	Marget	Spa 192
Susanna	Yrk 625	Moses	Mbo 56
Payden, John Senr.	Gvl 274	Reuben	Edg 187
Samuel Senr.	Gvl 274	Phebee	Spa 190
Payne, Daniel	Ker 409	Phillip	Fai 200

Wm.	Uni 228	J.	Col 407
Wm.	Uni 237	James	Ora 523
Peaster, Michael	Nby 90	Jas. Est.	Col 369
Peaty, Austin	Fai 237	John	Ora 521
James	Uni 227	Josia	Col 385
Peay, Austin F.	Ker 397	Thos.	Col 407
Nicholas	Fai 217	Wm.	Ora 523
Pebarte, John	Csn 139	Wm. Est.	Col 369
Peckley, Jacob	Lex 484	Pender, Thomas	Mrn 448
Peden, Thomas	Spa 192	Pendergast, Jas.	Col 385
Pedembox, Uriah	Nby 90	P. E.	Csn 150
Pedimbox, Adam	Nby 90	Pendergrass, David	Chr 76
Peebles, Lewis	Ker 425	John	Chr 88
Peek, Benjn.	Spa 197	John	Lan 3
Martha	Uni 219	Samuel	Sum 600
Zachariah	Uni 219	Wm.	Chr 87
Peeke, John	Sum 589	Pendleton, Edwd.	Csn 88
Peeler, Anthony	Yrk 625	Oliver	Csn 128
Peeples, Darling	Bar 67	Pendroey, Henry	Pen 117
John	Bft 81	Pene, Isabella	Csn 149
Josiah	Bft 100	Penn, Abraham	Pen 108
Pegg, Martin	Fai 220	Jeffery	Nby 89
Samuel	Pen 104	Pennel, Burrell	Uni 216
William	Pen 104	Pennell, Jonithan	Gvl 267
Pegues, Claudius	Cfd 105	Penney, Eliza	Fai 231
James	Mbo 56	Henry	Uni 234
Marcey	Mbo 56	Joseph	Fai 230
Malachi	Mbo 56	Thomas	Spa 181
William	Cfd 105	Pennil, Lewis	Uni 216
William Jr.	Mbo 56	Pennington, Abel	Gvl 267
Peigne, Lewis	Csn 150	John	Spa 191
Peirce, Elizabeth	Spa 200	Penny, James	Nby 90
Pelakee, Catharine	Bft 96	John	Csn 59
Pelaskee, John	Bft 96	Peoples, Henery	Ora 503
Pelfray, Joseph	Spa 195	John	Chr 91
Pelham, Gilbert	Lex 571	Sarah	Sum 591
William	Bft 88	Elizabeth	Sum 591
Pellam, John	Bar 55	David	Sum 593
Peller, William	Pen 111	People, George	Dtn 118
Pellins, Ann	Csn 131	Peoples, David	Ker 409
Pellom, Ambres	Bar 63	Isham	Ora 505
Pellot, Onazia	Csn 109	Pepper, Dan P.	Bft 104
John	Csn 109	John	Csn 153
Pellum, Charles	Lex 562	John	Pen 161
Pelmore, John	Uni 221	Peppen, Joseph	Csn 129
Pelott, Charles	Bft 128	Pepper, Saml.	Pen 160
Richard	Bft 104	Perdue, William	Cfd 110
Saml.	Bft 128	Perdriau, Elizabeth	Csn 179
Pemberton, George	Nby 89	Perineau, John	Col 407
(distiller)		Perkins, Benjamin	Ker 397
George Junr.	Nby 89	Charles	Edg 178
George Senr.	Nby 89	David	Cfd 105
Isiah	Nby 90	James	Dtn 118
Jesse B.	Nby 89	James	Dtn 127
John	Bar 62	James	Ker 413
Richard	Nby 90	Jerden	Sum 603
Pence, Charles	Lex 487	Jesse	Mbo 56
Charles	Lex 570	John	Cfd 105
Isaac	Lex 484	John	Pen 141
Isaac	Lex 570	Mary	Nby 90
Isaac	Lex 576	Moses	Pen 125
Jacob	Fai 205	Polley	Nby 90
John	Pen 114	Reece	Dtn 116
Philip	Lex 487	Samuel	Ker 413
Pendarvis, E.	Col 407	Samuel	Lex 559

Ute	Abb	17	Phillip	Lan	2
Permenter, James	Edg	186	Richard	Lan	4
John	Edg	136	Richard	Pen	127
Perminter, James	Edg	184	Simeon	Edg	145
Permon, Dale	Abb	31	Tignal	Lan	4
Peronneu, William	Csn	100	Zadock	Lan	7 ·
Perreneau, Ann	Csn	119	Person, Benjamin	Nby	89
Margaret	Csn	127	Enoch	Nby	89
Perret, Abm.	Wil	475	Enock	Nby	89
slaves of Est.			Febe	Nby	89
Martha	Wil	475	Hannah	Nby	89
Samuel	Dtn	116	John	Nby	89
Perrett, Nedham	Wil	467	Joseph	Nby	89
Perry	Lrs	43	Marget	Nby	89
Perrey, Isaac	Abb	31	Samuel	Nby	89
James	Abb	6	Thomas	Nby	89
Jobe	Sum	589	Pert, Nancy	Abb	38
John	Abb	26	Perts, John	Nby	90
Richard	Abb	6	Michael	Nby	90
Thomas	Abb	26	Peryman, Munford	Edg	133
William	Abb	26	Pester, Casper	Nby	90
Zachariah	Abb	25	John	Nby	89
Perrigin, Henry	Spa	178	Peters(?), A. Est.	Col	369
Job	Spa	177	Peters, Christopher	Ora	521
Perrin, Catharine	Abb	2	John	Yrk	625
George H.	Edg	184	Peterkin, Alexr.	Mbo	56
Robert	Edg	168	Peterson, Benjamin	Lrs	33
Sally	Edg	168	John	Pen	135
Samuel	Edg	173	Peter	Spa	172
William	Abb	2	Peter	Uni	240
Perritt, William	Sum	614	Samuel	Abb	32
Perry, Allen	Ker	403	Thomas	Nby	90
Ann	Bft	83	William	Lrs	45
Benjamin	Lan	7	Petre, Alexr.	Csn	116
Benjn.	Col	371	Petrie, Alexr.	Col	407
Benjn.	Pen	127	Peter	Chr	88
Catharine	Csn	96	Pettet, Benjn.	Spa	198
Crawford	Edg	178	Henry	Spa	211
Edwd Junr. Est.	Col	371	John	Spa	172
Edwd Senr. Est.	Col	371	Joshua	Spa	206
Eleanor	Csn	151	Nathan	Spa	206
Ezekial Junr.	Edg	155	Pettey, Absolom	Uni	240
Frances	Csn	89	Charles	Uni	240
George	Ker	405	George	Ker	423
George	Sum	589	George	Uni	239
Harbert	Bft	106	James (2)	Uni	240
Harget	Nby	89	Jervis	Abb	17
Isaac	Col	371	Joshua	Uni	239
James	Ker	411	Petteygren, John	Ker	405
Jas.	Col	387	Pettigrew, Alexr.	Dtn	117
James Junr.	Ker	411	George	Abb	36
Jesse	Fai	210	James	Abb	4
John	Pen	106	William	Abb	32
John	Sum	607	William	Dtn	117
Joseph	Fai	239	Pettipool, William	Fai	220
Jos:	Bft	83	Pettis, Jeremiah	Bar	58
Jos. Est.	Col	369	John	Bar	59
Josiah	Ker	409	Pettius, James	Abb	10
Kade	Mbo	60	Pettus, George Capt.	Yrk	630
Lamuel	Fai	226	Petty, Gideon	Ker	421
Lewis	Fai	210	Phadias	Dtn	124
Mathew	Bft	130	Thomas	Yrk	629
Nathaniel	Pen	126	William	Dtn	116
Peter	Bft	83	Zachariah	Ker	421
Peter	Lan	4	Pettypoole, Wm.	Gvl	284

Jesse	Ora 521		Moses	Lrs 40
Joel	Lrs 20		Moses	Lrs 45
Joseph	Nby 90		Zeffeniah	Spa 199
Phineas	Bft 90		Pipes, John	Spa 179
Samuel (2)	Nby 90		Pipkin, Arthur	Dtn 120
William	Gvl 260		Danl.	Geo 380
Piester, John	Csn 124		Pipkins, Asa	Sum 584
Piester,			Eleazar	Sum 584
see also Pester			Pippen, John	Dtn 114
Pig, Edward	Cfd 105		Pippin, Benjn.	Dtn 115
Pigg, Edward	Lan 5		John	Dtn 116
Pigot, Charles	Dtn 118		Micajah	Dtn 115
Charles	Dtn 127		William	Dtn 115
Elizabeth	Dtn 127		Pirkins, Samuel	Nby 90
Nathaniel	Sum 614		Pirkle, George	Spa 176
Pigott, Nathaniel	Geo 372		Pishon, Mathias	Csn 119
Pike, James	Edg 156		Pistell, Francis	Abb 5
John	Edg 177		Pitchford, Danl.	Pen 148
Molley	Edg 177		Pitman, Drury	Geo 387
Pikes, Benjamin	Mbo 56		Hardy	Geo 387
Pilcher, Robert	Yrk 626		James	Gvl 256
Pile, Nicholas	Gvl 278		Joel	Geo 389
Pilgrim, Amos	Pen 118		John	Edg 164
Amos	Spa 186		John	Gvl 281
Ezekiel	Pen 118		John	Spa 173
Michael	Gvl 285		Josiah	Edg 164
Thomas	Pen 118		Moses	Mrn 441
Pilkington, Druray	Mrn 449		Moses	Mrn 451
Pilkinton, James	Mbo 56		Philip	Cfd 108
Pillsbury, Amos	Csn 85		William	Ker 415
Samuel	Csn 88		Pittchel, Frankey	Fai 206
Pimble, Elizabeth	Ora 555		Pitteet(?), John	Pen 141
Pinckney, ---	Csn 71		Pittert, Edward	Pen 137
Charles	Csn 123		Pittes, Moses	Mrn 452
Charles	Csn 151		Pittman, James	Sum 585
Charles	Csn 163		Pitts, Aaron	Nby 89
Roger	Csn 113		Caleb	Nby 89
Roger	Csn 153		Charles (2)	Nby 89
Thomas	Csn 121		Charles	Pen 146
Thomas	Csn 179		Daniel	Nby 89
Thos. H.	Col 391		David	Edg 174
Wm. C.	Col 399		Edward	Nby 89
Pindar, John	Yrk 632		Gilbert	Ora 531
Pingston, William	Pen 154		Henry (2)	Nby 89
Pinkerton, James	Pen 124		James	Nby 89
John	Abb 5		James	Sum 597
John	Abb 19		Jehu	Nby 89
Pinkney, slaves of	Geo 374		Jeremiah	Sum 589
Pinks, William	Fai 204		John	Cfd 105
Pinkston, Obadiah	Pen 155		John	Mbo 56
Peter	Pen 154		John	Nby 89
Pinkstone, William	Yrk 626		John	Ora 525
Pinnel, Peter	Uni 218		John	Sum 585
Pinor, John	Mbo 59		Joseph	Nby 89
Pinson, Aron	Spa 199		Levi	Nby 89
David	Gvl 245		Mark	Pen 164
Duke	Lrs 45		Mary	Nby 89
Duke Junr.	Lrs 36		Thomas	Edg 174
Isaac	Lrs 36		Thomas	Nby 89
Howard	Lrs 35		Thomas	Ora 527
John	Lrs 35		William (2)	Nby 89
John	Lrs 36		William	Pen 162
John Junr.	Lrs 36		Placide, Alexander	Csn 136
Joseph	Nby 89		Plant, John	Nby 90
Joseph	Spa 182		Stephen	Lrs 44

William	Nby 89	Nancy	Uni 216
Plat, Thomas	Bar 54	Robert	Dtn 122
Plats, Sophiah	Bar 55	Taylor	Yrk 629
Platt, David	Csn 65	Thomas	Dtn 117
Herman	Yrk 619	Thomas	Dtn 127
John	Col 407	Pollard,	Gvl 282
John	Wil 474	Benjamin Junr.	
Platts, George	Col 399	Benjamin Senr.	Gvl 280
Player, Aaron	Sum 613	George	Ora 511
Joshua	Csn 153	John	Lex 493
Robert	Bar 69	John	Sum 593
William	Sum 613	Joshua	Dtn 123
Pledger, John	Mbo 56	Joshua	Dtn 127
Philip	Mbo 56	Richard	Abb 23
William	Mbo 56	Robert	Abb 39
Wm. H.	Mbo 56	William	Lrs 32
Plexco, George	Yrk 624	Wm.	Gvl 282
Henry	Yrk 624	Wm.	Spa 203
Henry, Senr.	Yrk 626	Pollen, Robt	Gvl 273
James	Yrk 624	Pollock, Ann	Lrs 24
Pliler, Conrad	Lan 9	Solomon	Csn 104
Jacob	Lan 5	Polony, A.	Csn 191
Paul	Lan 5	Jno L. Doctr.	Csn 127
Plomberg, Peter	Csn 80	Polson, Henry	Cfd 105
Plowden, Edward	Sum 606	John	Mbo 59
Pluer, Peter	Csn 108	Polston, Aron	Abb 15
Pluet, Peter A.	Lex 571	Pond, Wil--	Edg 187
Plumb, George	Geo 365	Ponder, Hezekiah	Pen 161
Plumer, Moses	Bar 54	Jesse	Yrk 627
Plumett, free bleck	Csn 116	Margaret	Gvl 257
Plumlee, Denton	Gvl 251	Thos.	Gvl 257
Stephen	Gvl 251	Pons, William	Col 399
Plunket, Charles	Nby 90	Pool, Abraham	Spa 193
James	Nby 90	Abram Junr.	Sum 584
John	Nby 90	Adam	Chr 84
Robert	Nby 90	Benjn.	Uni 242
William	Nby 90	David	Sum 585
Plutt, Mary	Lan 3	David	Sum 597
Poag, John	Yrk 622	Esther	Pen 157
Joseph	Yrk 622	Francis	Nby 89
Samuel	Yrk 622	George	Spa 176
Thomas	Yrk 619	Isaac	Csn 148
Pocher, Peter	Bar 67	James	Lrs 42
Pockras, David	Fai 205	James	Spa 201
Poellnitz, Baron	Mbo 56	Jesse P.	Uni 242
Poge, William	Gvl 265	John	Edg 174
George	Gvl 265	John	Spa 194
Pogue, Elizabeth	Pen 156	Micajah	Abb 21
James	Pen 156	Seth P.	Lrs 16
Mone.	Csn 97	Thomas	Abb 39
Pohl, Elias	Csn 148	Walter	Fai 194
Poinset, Elisha Doctr	Csn 118	Wm.	Spa 174
Polk, Abel	Dtn 126	Wm.	Spa 200
Charles	Yrk 629	Poole, Isaac	Ora 527
Daniel	Dtn 125	Mary	Lex 559
Daniel Jr.	Dtn 125	William	Lex 558
Jesse	Bft 92	Poor, John	Pen 146
John	Bft 100	William	Pen 143
John	Dtn 126	Poore, William	Pen 162
John	Dtn 128	Pooser, Elisha	Col 407
John	Yrk 629	Henry	Col 407
Joseph	Dtn 127	Pope, Charles	Gvl 282
Luke	Bft 92	Elijah	Edg 154
Luke	Dtn 124	Elizabeth	Nby 89
Mary	Yrk 617	George	Edg 180

Pound, Peter	Ors 537	John L.	Csn 85
Pounds, John	Cfd 110	Poyden, John Junr.	Gvl 274
John	Gvl 284	Prach, Lucey	Edg 148
Pow, Elizabet	Ora 541	Pranam, James	Csn 65
Powe, Alexander	Cfd 105	Prater, John	Pen 116
Erasmus	Cfd 105	John	Pen 119
Thomas	Cfd 105	Robert	Pen 119
William	Cfd 105	Susannah	Pen 119
Powel, Dice	Chr 88	Zachary	Edg 178
George	Nby 90	Amos	Nby 89
James	Spa 208	Bazel	Lrs 25
Nathaniel	Bar 50	Holoway	Lrs 24
William	Sum 607	John	Lrs 26
Powell, Abraham	Edg 146	Josiah	Lrs 24
Abraham	Pen 115	Josiah	Lrs 26
Charles	Edg 151	William	Lrs 21
Charles	Mrn 443	Prator, John	Pen 135
Isham	Ker 396	Middleton	Gvl 248
James	Cfd 105	Phillip	Nby 89
James	Lrs 41	Pratt, Elizabeth	Sum 604
James (2)	Pen 113	George	Nby 89
James	Uni 227	James	Pen 135
James	Yrk 626	John	Chr 87
James Jr.	Cfd 110	John Capt.	Csn 131
Jesse	Fai 221	Jonathan	Nby 89
John	Dtn 128	Joseph	Abb 16
John	Edg 157	Saml. H.	Csn 133
John	Fai 240	William	Sum 606
John	Pen 140	Wm.	Chr 87
Joseph	Cfd 105	Preaster, John	Bar 68
Joseph	Ker 413	Nicholas	Bar 55
Richd.	Uni 221	Preoleau, Alice E.	Csn 141
Robert	Nby 89	Ann	Csn 141
Robert	Pen 143	Prentice, James	Csn 104
Samuel	Lrs 29	John	Csn 141
Thomas	Cfd 109	Prescoat, Benjamin	Sum 608
Thomas	Fai 240	John	Bar 51
Thomas	Lrs 29	John	Bar 64
William	Ker 409	M.	Col 399
William	Fai 240	Prescot, John	Ora 523
William	Lrs 41	Prescott, Aprim	Ora 523
William	Pen 108	Presley, Anthony	Ker 411
Power, Holoway	Lrs 19	Charles	Ker 409
Jacob	Lex 493	Charles	Uni 232
Jacob	Lex 570	David	Abb 12
John	Edg 149	David	Abb 28
John	Spa 192	John	Abb 30
Nathaniel	Lrs 19	John	Abb 30
Samuel Junr.	Lrs 30	John	Ker 409
Powers, Alexander	Pen 130	Thomas	Abb 30
Bartley	Uni 236	William	Abb 29
Derby	Mbo 59	Presnal, Jacob	Nby 90
Francis	Spa 209	William	Nby 90
George	Csn 107	Pressley, William	Csn 142
John	Lrs 14	Prester, Adam	Bar 68
John	Mrn 437	Adam	Col 399
John	Mrn 446	Preston, Thomas	Fai 193
Lucey	Spa 210	Prestwood, Jonathan	Cfd 105
Nicholas	Dtn 126	Jonathan	Dtn 122
Rachel	Spa 197	Thomas	Cfd 105
Susanna	Uni 225	William	Cfd 105
William	Lrs 14	Wm. Jr.	Cfd 107
William	Nby 90	Prevost, Mary	Csn 91
Poyas, John E.	Csn 65	Prewett, Alexr.	Spa 198
Jno E. Doctr.	Csn 120	Richd.	Uni 225

Elizabeth	Csn 145	Joseph	Spa 172
Pye, Peter	Csn 71	Peter Esqr.	Yrk 628
Pyeatt, Peter	Csn 169	Richard R.	Ker 401
Pyland, George	Sum 597	Quinney, Rigdon	Bft 130
Isham	Sum 597	Samuel	Ker 411
James	Sum 595	Quinton(?), John	Chr 89
Pyle, Leonard	Fai 194	Quinton, James	Chr 94
Pyles, Abner	Lrs 29	Saml.	Uni 247
John	Lrs 42		
Reubin Esq.	Lrs 43		

R

Q

		R---, Michl.	Col 387
		R---, Philip	Edg 170
Qiblong, Henry	Csn 147	R---, W---	Col 407
Quattlebaum, see		Rabb, John	Fai 214
Quartelbum, Quaddlebum		Robert	Fai 197
Quaddlebam, John	Lex 564	Rabon, William	Edg 183
Matthias	Lex 568	Raborn, George	Sum 591
Qualls, Elizh.	Spa 173	Rabourn, John	Sum 612
David	Spa 173	Rachet(?), Nathaniel	Csn 92
Moses	Spa 173	Rackly, Mills	Uni 217
Wm.	Spa 195	Radcliff, Thomas Sr.	Csn 100
Wm.	Spa 196	Radcliffe, Thos.	Col 391
Quarles, David	Edg 150	Radford, John	Csn 65
James	Edg 172	John Senr.	Csn 71
Richard	Edg 173	Radish, Thomas	Ora 509
Samuel	Edg 141	Rae, Josiah	Geo 389
William	Edg 151	Raffield, William Sen	Sum 604
Quarrell, Joseph	Fai 213	William Junr.	Sum 604
Quartelbum, Mathias	Lex 497	Raffle, Agnex	Lan 8
Quartemus, Wm.	Bft 120	Raford, Philip	Edg 183
Quarterman, Thomas	Ora 537	Ragan, Joseph	Nby 92
Quatlebum, Peter	Nby 90	Rachel	Nby 91
Quash, Robert	Csn 136	Reason	Nby 91
Quay, Alexander	Chr 94	Thomas	Nby 91
Quattlebum, John	Edg 163	Ragin, Elizabeth	Nby 92
Queen, John	Pen 163	Jesse	Edg 162
Thomas	Uni 222	John	Nby 92
Quenan, Dennis	Csn 89	Larkin	Pen 114
Querless, Sarah	Geo 368	Reason	Nby 92
Querry, John	Csn 154	Thomas	Nby 92
Quick, Annice	Mbo 57	William	Nby 92
Aquilla	Mbo 57	Ragins, John	Gvl 256
George	Mbo 57	Ragland, Benjn.	Gvl 283
Levi	Mbo 57	John	Gvl 283
Moses	Mbo 57	William	Nby 92
Solomon	Mbo 57	Raglin, Sarah	Pen 141
Stephen	Mbo 57	Ragsdale, Benjamin	Chr 82
Thomas	Mbo 57	Benjamin	Pen 118
Zach	Mbo 57	Edmond	Gvl 272
Quider, Frances	Csn 153	Elijah	Gvl 272
Quiggin, David	Csn 80	Hezekiah	Uni 222
Quigly, Esther	Csn 146	John	Uni 229
Quin, James	Csn 75	Peter	Pen 130
John	Col 399	Richard	Lrs 44
Quinby, Joseph	Csn 87	Wm.	Uni 222
Quinn, Blackburn	Spa 172	Raiford, Phillip	Fai 200
Daniel	Yrk 628	William	Fai 200
Hugh	Yrk 628	Railey, William	Csn 65
James	Spa 173	Rails, Thomas	Geo 385
James	Yrk 626	Raimey, Thomas	Lex 576
John	Uni 245	Faimick, Peter	Lex 573
John	Yrk 628	Raines, Arail	Gvl 259

James	Nby 91	John	Spa 174
Job	Bar 49	Thomas	Spa 184
John	Bar 62	Reese, see also Rece	
John	Nby 91	Reese, David	Ker 427
John	Spa 197	George	Pen 131
Reubin	Bar 49	Hubert	Sum 585
Thomas	Bar 62	Jacob	Pen 139
Redden, John	Sum 610	James	Pen 112
Reddick, Lamuel	Sum 600	Peter	Pen 108
Shadrach	Cfd 106	Rose	Pen 114
Thomas	Cfd 106	Scarborough	Sum 587
Reddin, Samuel	Pen 161	Widdow	Pen 141
Redding, John	Bft 102	William	Sum 585
Jno	Bft 132	Reeve, William	Abb 17
Thomas	Lrs 40	Reeves, Abner	Yrk 619
Reddish, George	Fai 200	Allen	Yrk 619
Wm.	Fai 232	Burgess	Pen 154
Reddon, James	Gvl 249	Burrell	Pen 130
Redfearn, Solomon	Cfd 106	Enos	Csn 139
Redford, Robert	Pen 162	Frederick	Yrk 619
Redhimer, John	Csn 65	George	Pen 131
Peter	Csn 108	Hardy	Yrk 618
Reding, Robinson	Lrs 38	John	Cfd 106
Sidney	Pen 127	John	Fai 225
Redlick, William	Csn 129	John	Pen 154
Redman, James	Csn 140	John	Uni 246
James	Gvl 261	Joseph	Cfd 106
John	Lex 562	Presley	Ker 409
John	Spa 189	Reubin	Cfd 106
John	Spa 191	Robert	Dtn 115
Saml.	Pen 123	Stephen	Ker 405
William	Gvl 260	Wiley	Yrk 619
Redmond, John	Ora 537	William	Cfd 106
Nancy	Ora 501	William	Sum 593
Zackariah	Ora 523	Will.	Lan 6
Redout, Mathew	Bft 122	William Senr.	Yrk 618
Reead(?), Nathan	Gvl 269	Register, James	Dtn 120
Reease, Henry	Gvl 278	Jesse	Dtn 120
Travis	Gvl 277	Joshua	Dtn 120
Reece(?), George	Pen 121	Joshua Jr.	Dtn 120
George	Mbo 57	Thomas	Dtn 122
Reed, Daniel	Nby 92	Reid, George	Csn 130
David	Nby 91	Hugh	Abb 8
Elizabeth	Pen 110	Hugh	Wil 469
George	Pen 145	James	Abb 38
Hamilton	Pen 114	John	Csn 151
Hugh	Chr 77	John	Csn 153
James	Pen 114	John	Uni 248
Jehu	Pen 152	Joseph	Spa 171
Joseph	Chr 88	Mary	Wil 466
Joseph	Pen 136	Mathew	Abb 37
Margarett	Yrk 629	Robert	Bft 81
Nathl.	Pen 109	Robert	Yrk 620
Nathl.	Pen 141	Samuel	Abb 8
Owen	Lan 4	Thomas	Spa 207
Reubin	Pen 114	Wm.	Uni 249
Robert	Abb 4	Reiley, George	Ora 535
Sarah	Bar 58	Robert	Csn 98
Will	Cfd 106	Susannah	Ker 425
William	Bar 54	Terrence	Csn 135
William	Pen 110	Thomas	Csn 80
William	Pen 133	Reily, Samuel	Sum 600
Reeder, Joshua	Pen 117	Rekambekar, Jacob	Ora 525
Reedy, John	Chr 77	John	Ora 539
Rees, Elijah	Gvl 250	Rely, Charles	Fai 218

Martin	Ora	551	Thos.	Fai	200
Nathan	Nby	92	Thos.	Fai	210
Othniel	Pen	159	William	Edg	182
Right	Ora	513	William	Lan	4
Shadk. Junr.	Mrn	437	William	Sum	587
Thos.	Gvl	271	Wm.	Gvl	279
William	Edg	137	Wm.	Gvl	280
Zeri	Abb	20	Richarson, Jonadab	Nby	91
Rich., Christopher	Csn	179	Richborough, Jas.	Csn	72
George	Csn	179	Henry Jur.	Sum	603
Obediah	Spa	173	Henry Senr.	Sum	602
Wm.	Spa	173	James	Sum	604
Richard, William	Abb	9	John Junr.	Sum	604
Richards, John	Pen	126	John Senr.	Sum	604
Michael	Uni	248	Nathaniel Junr.	Sum	604
Reuben	Spa	172	Nathaniel Senr.	Sum	604
Robert	Pen	151	William	Sum	603
Saml.	Csn	142	Riche, Robirt	Nby	92
Thomas	Nby	91	Richerson, Amos	Bar	49
William	Nby	91	Elisabeth	Bar	60
William	Pen	135	Richeson, Amos	Pen	141
Richardson, --onathan	Edg	147	Richey, Andrew	Abb	18
Abell	Gvl	279	Anthony	Wil	475
Abram	Sum	593	James	Wil	475
Amos	Edg	158	James Junr.	Abb	18
Ann	Sum	585	Jesse	Edg	173
Aron	Bft	90	John	Pen	131
Asariah	Bar	67	Nancy	Pen	131
Charles	Sum	585	Robert	Abb	37
Charles	Sum	604	Thomas	Abb	39
David	Edg	158	William Senr.	Abb	18
David	Edg	182	Richmond, Andrew	Abb	26
Edward	Sum	602	Charles	Bar	62
Eliza	Fai	235	James	Abb	26
Francis	Sum	587	John	Abb	26
George	Ker	407	Mathew	Fai	218
Harry	Lan	3	Mathew	Fai	224
Henry	Csn	179	Richoso, David	Csn	144
Isaac	Col	399	Rickanbaker, see also		
Jacob	Ora	511	Rekambekar		
James	Csn	151	Rickanbaker, John	Ora	555
James	Sum	593	Nicholas	Ora	553
James B.	Sum	604	Ricker, Benjn.	Col	387
John	Bar	67	Fras.	Col	387
John	Csn	132	Rickey, Alexander	Yrk	617
John	Lan	3	Ricksey, John	Edg	139
John	Sum	604	Rickman, John	Spa	170
Jno	Bft	92	Wm.	Spa	169
Joseph	Dtn	121	Ricord, John	Lex	570
Joseph	Dtn	127	Riden, James	Pen	146
Joseph Junr.	Edg	185	Rider, Christopher(2)	Pen	142
Joseph Senr.	Edg	185	Thomas	Uni	221
Laurence	Nby	91	Riddle, George	Yrk	632
Mathias	Pen	103	James	Ker	411
Peter	Nby	91	John	Ker	407
Richard	Sum	602	John	Lrs	15
Robt.	Fai	200	Joseph	Abb	5
Robt.	Fai	210	Margt. Est.	Csn	65
Robert Senr.	Edg	137	Thomas	Pen	130
Solomon	Dtn	118	William Powel	Lex	566
Thomas	Csn	149	Riddlespurger, C.	Col	407
Thomas	Dtn	121	Ridlehoober, George	Nby	92
Thomas	Dtn	127	Ridgell, Jacob	Ora	505
Thomas	Ora	505	Joel	Mrn	454
Thomas	Pen	109	Ridgeway, James	Sum	601

Ruston, John	Ora 529		S		
Joseph	Ora 525				
Ruth, Abraham	Bft 86				
Elizabeth	Nby 91	Sabb, William		Ora 555	
Godfrey	Fai 236	Sabert, Wm.		Col 387	
Rutherford(?), Joseph	Edg 178	Sadale, Richard		Pen 146	
James	Edg 174	Sadler, David		Yrk 617	
James	Edg 181	Isaac		Edg 174	
Robert	Edg 180	Isaac		Yrk 617	
Robert	Nby 91	Isaac, Junr.		Yrk 617	
William	Nby 91	Jeremiah		Lrs 32	
Rutland, Cullen	Ora 519	John		Edg 174	
James	Fai 192	John		Lrs 34	
Jesse	Ora 523	Richard (Stiller)		Yrk 617	
Rutledge, ---	Csn 71	Richard Junr.		Yrk 617	
slaves of	Geo 374	Richard, Senr.		Yrk 617	
Chas.	Csn 171	William		Lrs 34	
Edward	Csn 71	Wm.		Chr 86	
Edward	Ker 421	Sailor, Esaies		Lex 561	
Fredk.	Csn 113	Jacob		Lex 561	
Fredrick	Csn 179	John		Pen 149	
Frederick	Csn 71	Phillip (2)		Pen 155	
H. M.	Col 391	Sainsing, Charles		Yrk 630	
Henry M.	Csn 95	Saint, Thos		Fai 227	
Hugh	Col 371	Saintjohn, Lewis		Edg 150	
Judge Hugh	Csn 135	William		Edg 150	
James	Ora 537	Saixas, Isaac		Csn 112	
Jessey	Abb 17	Sale, John		Yrk 623	
John	Csn 145	Sales, John		Edg 175	
John	Ker 401	Sally, Henery		Ora 529	
John Junr.	Ker 421	Jacob		Ora 529	
Joseph	Abb 18	John		Pen 164	
Mary	Csn 115	Keziah		Ora 555	
Jno	Bft 116	Luke		Ora 525	
Peter	Gvl 250	Salmon, George		Gvl 247	
Wm.	Csn 159	James		Spa 204	
Ryal, Jas	Edg 179	Jeremiah		Spa 183	
John	Nby 92	John		Gvl 245	
Joshua	Nby 92	Thomas		Lrs 33	
Ryall, William	Csn 191	Walker		Gvl 246	
Ryan, Benjn. Junr.	Edg 133	William		Lrs 33	
Elizabeth	Csn 78	Wm.		Gvl 285	
John	Edg 137	Salomon, Levi		Geo 362	
John	Nby 91	Salsberry, John		Csn 72	
Ryce, Micajah	Lrs 38	Salter, John		Uni 225	
Ryckbosh, Mrs.	Csn 146	Saltus, Francis		Bft 83	
Rye, Solomon		Salvage, Robert		Uni 224	
Rykard, Thomas	Nby 92	Salyers, Charles		Gvl 268	
Ryle, Elizabeth	Nby 91	James		Gvl 268	
Hezekiah	Nby 92	John		Gvl 267	
John	Nby 91	Levy		Gvl 267	
Thomas	Nby 91	Samory, Chaudius		Csn 152	
Ryley, Eliphas	Lrs 26	Sample, Alexander		Abb 22	
James	Lrs 26	Jefrey		Abb 31	
James	Lrs 43	John		Chr 94	
Jeremiah	Nby 91	Mathew		Abb 37	
John	Lrs 35	Robert		Abb 22	
John	Lrs 43	Samuel		Abb 22	
Martin	Lrs 43	William		Abb 22	
Michel	Ora 553	Sams, Mrs.		Bft 83	
Patrick	Lrs 43	Francis		Csn 189	
Phillip	Fai 235	Polley		Spa 198	
Sarah	Bft 98	Wm.		Bft 82	
William	Lrs 34	Samson, Daniel		Mrn 454	
William	Lrs 43	Samuel, Robert		Edg 149	

Sance(?), Jacob	Pen	115	Sandifer, Peter	Fai 237
Sandeford, Benjamin	Chr	88	William	Fai 197
Nightengale	Chr	88	Sandiford, Ann	Csn 192
Peter	Chr	80	Sandifur, Philip	Yrk 620
Robert	Chr	81	Sandhill, John	Sum 605
Saml.	Chr	81	Sandlin, John, Junr.	Yrk 627
Sandel, Henry	Ora	543	John, Senr.	Yrk 627
Sanderdale, John	Pen	111	Jonathan	Yrk 627
Sanders, Aaron	Gvl	262	Lewis	Yrk 629
Ambros	Edg	140	Littleton	Yrk 629
Ann	Spa	180	Randolph	Yrk 629
Sanford, Asa	Gvl	265	William	Yrk 629
Sanders, Blansett	Ora	519	Sandling, James	Uni 230
Christopher	Edg	144	Jesse	Uni 228
Demsey	Pen	155	Sandridge, David	Bft 104
Ezekiel	Chr	83	Sandyford, Peter	Bar 55
George	Gvl	259	Saner, John	Edg 172
Isaac	Pen	107	Sanford, Ann	Col 371
James	Gvl	282	Lavina	Lex 571
James	Ker	417	Mary	Gvl 265
James	Spa	177	Sansberry, Daniel	Dtn 119
John	Abb	14	Sansom, James	Edg 181
John	Bar	48	Sante, Angel	Csn 137
John	Gvl	260	Santee Canal Company	Csn 72
John	Mrn	445	Sapp, Jesse	Ora 549
John	Nby	94	Sarbrough, William	Bar 64
John	Ora	517	Sargeant, Elizabeth	Csn 151
John	Spa	181	Sarratt, John	Spa 169
John	Uni	219	Sarter, John P.	Uni 226
Joseph	Abb	6	Sartor, Wm.	Uni 228
Joseph	Gvl	277	Sarvice, John Junr.	Geo 386
Joseph	Ker	417	John Senr.	Geo 386
Lewis	Uni	239	Sass, Jacob	Csn 138
Luis	Chr	85	Satcher, Amos W.	Edg 145
Mary	Bft	108	Emanuel(?)	Edg 145
Mary	Gvl	257	Jiles	Edg 167
Nathaniel	Bar	48	Saterfield, Catherine	Pen 103
Patrick (2)	Spa	206	James	Spa 180
Peter	Mrn	445	Laurence	Cfd 108
Reuben S.	Lex	571	Wm.	Spa 180
Robert	Sum	595	Saterwhite, Bartlet	Nby 93
Simon	Dtn	113	John	Nby 93
Thomas	Chr	82	John Senr.	Nby 94
Thomas	Lex	566	William	Nby 93
Thomas	Ora	517	Satourfield, William	Gvl 258
Thomas	Sum	604	Satterfield, James(2)	Pen 107
W. Est.	Col	381	Jeremiah	Pen 106
Waddle	Mrn	452	John	Nby 94
William	Bft	96	Robert	Pen 107
William	Ora	517	Thomas	Pen 115
William	Sum	595	William	Pen 107
William Junr.	Sum	595	Satterwhite, Bartlet	Nby 94
Wm. (2)	Chr	92	Saturfield, Edward	Lrs 24
Wm.	Spa	176	Sauls, Abraham	Dtn 118
Wm.	Spa	206	Abraham	Dtn 126
Wilson	Lrs	34	Benjamin	Bft 98
Wilson	Ora	519	Holladay	Bft 98
Zachariah	Edg	160	Isaac	Bft 88
Sanderson, John	Ker	403	Meredith	Bft 90
Robert	Chr	84	Saulter, John	Edg 176
Sandford, Jesse	Edg	178	Saun, Stephen	Pen 112
Sandifford, James	Ora	513	Saunders, Elias	Fai 196
Joseph	Ora	511	Elizabeth	Csn 100
Samuel	Ora	507	James	Edg 168
Sandiford, Abrm.	Fai	214	James	Yrk 621

Jesse	Gvl 267	Thomas	Edg 180
John	Gvl 267	Sea, John	Lex 566
John	Lan 9	Mary	Lex 559
John	Pen 119	Michael	Lex 566
John (2)	Pen 148	Philip	Lex 559
John	Wil 463	Susanna	Lex 568
John	Wil 473	Seaborne, James	Gvl 265
John	Wil 475	Seabrook, Benjamin	Csn 185
John	Yrk 623	Benjn.	Csn 126
John, Est. of	Wil 470	Gabriel	Csn 185
Joseph	Bft 82	John	Csn 189
Joseph	Dtn 128	Joseph	Csn 185
Joseph	Wil 470	Joseph Junr.	Csn 185
Josh	Bft 130	Joseph S.	Csn 189
Margarett	Yrk 625	Robert	Csn 185
Moses	Bft 104	Sarah	Csn 185
Moses	Bft 118	T. B.	Csn 185
Patrick	Lrs 24	Thos. W.	Bft 126
Reuben	Sum 584	William	Csn 185
Robert	Pen 118	Seaburn, George	Gvl 259
Robert Capt.	Lrs 23	Seachler, Adam	Lex 569
Samuel	Abb 4	Seagler, George	Fai 212
Samuel	Gvl 267	Geo. Junr.	Fai 212
Samuel	Lrs 39	Seago, William	Cfd 106
Samuel	Yrk 623	Seahorn, Nicholas	Yrk 625
Saml.	Mrn 449	Seal, Anthony	Fai 224
Stephen	Bar 65	Daniel	Fai 225
Thomas	Fai 235	Elijah	Fai 225
Thomas	Lrs 31	Enoch	Fai 224
Thomas	Mrn 438	Seals, William	Mrn 451
Thomas	Wil 464	Sealy(?), Edwin	Chr 83
Thomas Junr.	Wil 466	Sealy, Benjamin	Edg 145
Thomas G.	Bft 81	Seamore, Isaac	Csn 118
W. Est.	Csn 171	Stephen	Csn 115
William	Abb 24	Searcey, Jeremiah	Uni 223
William	Bar 65	Searson, John	Bft 90
William	Bft 104	Thomas	Bft 128
William	Csn 159	Seastrong, Samuel	Lex 487
William	Fai 211	Searver, Benjamin	Lan 5
William	Sum 607	Seawar, Abraham	Csn 87
William	Yrk 623	Seawright, John	Abb 7
Wm.	Gvl 269	John	Lex 561
William Junr.	Bar 65	Robert	Ora 541
Scottow, Susanna	Csn 100	Seay, Gideon	Spa 203
Scouler, Jasper	Csn 59	James	Spa 204
Thomas	Csn 59	Reuben	Spa 203
Screven, Benjamin	Bft 132	Syrus	Spa 203
Scrimsure, John	Pen 156	Sebben, Sebbe	Csn 126
William	Pen 122	Seborah, Michl.	Col 401
Scrimzeour, C.	Csn 131	Secrets, Martin	Csn 82
J.	Csn 131	See, Demcey	Sum 589
James	Bft 126	Seely, Samuel	Chr 83
Scriven, Benja.	Geo 363	Saml.	Chr 85
Richard	Bft 83	Seeright, William	Pen 144
Thomas	Csn 128	Sees, Leonard	Bar 69
Thos. Junr.	Csn 63	Segar, John Jr.	Dtn 122
Thos Senr.	Csn 63	John Sr.	Dtn 122
Scruggs, Drury	Spa 175	Mathew	Dtn 121
James	Gvl 279	Winborn	Dtn 122
Jesse	Edg 163	Segars, William	Dtn 121
Matt	Edg 163	Segrist, Jacob	Ora 539
Richd.	Gvl 278	Seibles, Jacob	Lex 571
Scuddey, John	Abb 33	Seiglar, George	Bar 61
Scurry, Jesse	Edg 182	Seigler, William	Nby 93
Mary	Edg 180	Seignior, George	Lex 561

Wm.	Chr 80	Sherod	Ker 423
Siddle, Jesse	Pen 105	William	Fai 235
Siffritt, Adam	Ora 541	William	Pen 133
Daniel	Ora 551	Simons, Edward	Fai 195
Sightler, see Siteler		Frances	Csn 122
Sigby, George	Lan 10	Francis	Csn 189
Sigler, Rachel	Edg 150	Henry	Col 407
Sigley, Matthew	Lan 10	James	Csn 140
Silberg, Nicholas	Csn 95	James	Csn 171
Silliman, John	Yrk 617	John	Geo 369
Sills, Samuel	Abb 38	Kating	Csn 72
Silly, John	Lex 493	Keating	Csn 115
Vendel	Lex 493	M.	Col 385
Silver, George	Edg 172	Maurice	Geo 364
Simerton, Jno	Fai 208	Robert	Col 407
Simes, John	Pen 103	Shadrack	Geo 371
Simis, James	Csn 66	Thomas	Csn 189
Simisson, Elizabeth	Uni 228	William	Col 371
Simkins, Arthur	Edg 139	Simpkins, Gideon	Lan 6
Elizth.	Mrn 456	John	Edg 187
Thomas	Mrn 455	Simpson, Agness	Chr 79
Simmeral, James	Yrk 620	Alexander	Lrs 29
Simmerlin, Mary	Lex 483	Alexander (big)	Lrs 29
Simmerly, Margaret	Lex 576	Baxter	Pen 104
Simmons, Ace	Bft 84	Benjamin	Lrs 23
Allen	Bft 84	Elijah	Pen 154
Benjamin	Csn 82	Elisabeth	Chr 90
Benjn.	Uni 231	Hugh	Pen 153
Charles (big)	Lrs 37	Hugh	Yrk 621
Charles (little)	Lrs 37	James	Abb 37
Frederick	Dtn 118	James	Lan 10
Elizabeth	Lrs 37	James	Lrs 28
Isham	Gvl 259	James	Yrk 618
Isham Senr.	Gvl 260	Jas.	Csn 159
James	Gvl 261	Jane	Lrs 22
James	Lrs 42	Jesse	Chr 87
James	Ora 513	John	Abb 2
James	Pen 131	John	Abb 11
John	Bft 132	John	Col 407
John	Fai 225	John	Chr 79
John	Gvl 244	John	Csn 72
John	Gvl 259	John	Csn 79
John	Lrs 37	John	Lan 2
John	Ora 511	John	Lrs 17
John	Pen 112	John	Pen 134
John	Uni 223	John	Pen 151
Joseph	Uni 223	John	Pen 153
Luka	Gvl 260	John	Sum 595
Mordecai	Bft 86	John Senr.	Lrs 28
Nat	Uni 223	John Maj.	Lrs 28
Randolph	Fai 225	Joseph	Chr 81
Richard	Bft 84	Joseph	Yrk 630
Richard	Ora 505	Leonard	Pen 152
Richd.	Gvl 262	Magnes	Uni 227
Robert	Abb 15	Margaret	Csn 128
Sarah	Bar 58	Margaret	Csn 189
Theophilus	Ora 525	Mary	Pen 158
William	Bft 96	Nancy	Lrs 31
William	Csn 103	Richard M.	Pen 149
William	Csn 106	Robert	Yrk 629
William	Lrs 37	Samuel	Lrs 17
William	Lrs 41	Saml.	Uni 236
Simms, Edward	Fai 226	Sarah	Gvl 246
Elliott	Ker 421	Thomas	Lrs 17
Rebecca	Cfd 106	Thomas	Ora 547

James	Lrs	33	John	Spa 185
James	Mrn 461		John	Spa 196
James (2)	Nby	93	John	Spa 199
James	Pen 104		John	Spa 200
James	Pen 105		John	Spa 201
James	Pen 116		John	Spa 205
James	Pen 140		John	Spa 208
James	Spa 180		John	Spa 209
James	Spa 195		John	Sum 589
James	Spa 200		John	Sum 602
James	Spa 201		John	Sum 607
James	Uni 226		John	Uni 227
James	Uni 229		John	Uni 238
James	Uni 250		John	Yrk 620
James	Yrk 625		John	Yrk 629
Jeremiah	Gvl 266		John	Yrk 630
Jesse	Col 403		John Capt.	Cfd 106
Jesse	Gvl 277		John Col.	Dtn 116
Jesse	Pen 142		John (joiner)	Yrk 629
Jesse	Spa 185		Jno. Mrs.	Csn 113
Jesse	Uni 229		John Junr.	Fai 224
Jessee	Geo 384		John Junr.	Lrs 33
Job	Bft 112		John Senr.	Lrs 33
Job	Pen 118		John Senr.	Mrn 461
Joel	Spa 198		John Senr.	Ora 529
John	Abb 21		John C.	Csn 137
John	Abb 24		Jno C.	Csn 149
John	Bar 44		John M.	Edg 166
John	Cfd 106		John M.	Mbo 59
John	Csn 83		John Press	Cns 159
John	Csn 96		John R.	Col 371
John	Csn 108		John Ward	Mrn 456
John	Csn 135		Jonathan	Pen 156
John	Csn 143		Jos. Est.	Col 381
John	Dtn 115		Jos: A.	Csn 171
John	Dtn 121		Joseph	Gvl 259
John	Dtn 125		Joseph	Gvl 260
John	Dtn 126		Joseph	Lex 571
John	Edg 139		Joseph	Pen 103
John	Edg 172		Joseph	Pen 117
John	Edg 181		Joseph	Pen 126
John	Fai 195		Joseph	Uni 225
John	Gvl 273		Joseph	Yrk 617
John (2)	Gvl 275		Joseph A.	Geo 374
John	Lan 10		Joshua	Chr 92
John	Lex 484		Joshua	Ora 521
John	Lex 571		Joshua	Pen 104
John	Lex 575		Joshua	Uni 229
John	Mbo 57		Josiah	Csn 137
John	Mrn 436		Josiah	Yrk 629
John	Mrn 458		Josua	Bar 48
John	Mrn 460		Judith	Lrs 41
John	Nby 93		Kellet	Uni 237
John	Ora 507		Kitt	Lrs 41
John	Ora 529		Laban	Yrk 621
John	Ora 531		Latitia	Csn 85
John	Ora 553		Leonard	Uin 216
John	Pen 111		Lewis	Bft 96
John	Pen 115		Lillis	Yrk 618
John	Pen 116		Lovet	Edg 164
John	Pen 120		Luke	Nby 93
John	Pen 131		Luke	Pen 143
John	Pen 142		M.	Col 403
John	Pen 146		Malcomb	Dtn 116
John	Pen 159		Margaret	Csn 145

Mary	Col 379	Robert	Uni 223	
Mary	Ora 545	Robert	Uni 244	
Mary	Pen 143	Robert	Yrk 625	
Mary	Yrk 622	Robert Junr.	Fai 217	
Massey	Uni 234	Rodger Senr.	Csn 102	
Mathew	Dtn 125	Roger	Csn 65	
Matthew	Nby 94	Roger	Csn 171	
Matthew	Wil 476	Roger M.	Col 371	
Maurice	Geo 383	Rucker	Uni 230	
Mical	Abb 37	Samuel	Bft 98	
Michael	Pen 119	Samuel	Bft 112	
Millington	Spa 196	Samuel	Csn 78	
Moses	Abb 8	Samuel	Edg 163	
Moses	Abb 20	Samuel	Edg 183	
Moses	Bar 61	Samuel	Edg 185	
Moses	Chr 92	Samuel	Fai 226	
Moses	Edg 136	Samuel	Geo 366	
Moses	Mrn 457	Samuel	Ker 409	
Moses	Nby 95	Samuel	Lan 7	
Moses	Pen 136	Samuel	Mrn 461	
Myhil	Yrk 629	Saml.	Csn 120	
Nathl.	Fai 197	Saml.	Csn 128	
Noah	Wil 468	Saml.	Spa 200	
OBrian	Csn 126	Saml.	Uni 245	
OBrien	Col 399	Sarah	Col 391	
Paul	Ker 396	Sarah	Csn 63	
Peter	Col 401	Sarah	Csn 125	
Peter	Csn 65	Sarah	Mrn 437	
Peter	Csn 135	Savage	Geo 362	
Peter	Csn 171	Simeon	Edg 134	
Peter	Lrs 33	Simeon	Edg 155	
Peter	Mrn 454	Simon	Mbo 57	
Peter	Spa 201	Slocum	Geo 380	
Peter Esqr.	Csn 114	Soloman	Spa 192	
Phillip	Bar 48	Solomon	Lan 4	
Phil:	Col 379	Solomon	Pen 113	
Rachel	Bar 62	Spencer	Spa 200	
Rachel	Bft 114	Stephen	Abb 32	
Rachel	Nby 93	Stephen	Bar 54	
Rachel	Pen 163	Stephen	Edg 160	
Rachel	Yrk 617	Stephen	Fai 226	
Ralph	Geo 392	Stephen	Gvl 261	
Ralph	Yrk 629	Stephen	Lrs 31	
Rebecca	Csn 139	Summerland	Sum 612	
Rheuben	Gvl 261	Thomas	Bft 100	
Rhueben Junr.	Gvl 278	Thomas	Csn 65	
Rhoda	Yrk 629	Thomas	Gvl 249	
Richard	Cfd 109	Thomas	Lex 484	
Richd.	Mrn 456	Thomas	Lex 575	
Rigdon	Edg 165	Thomas	Mrn 460	
Robert	Abb 3	Thomas	Nby 93	
Robert	Abb 11	Thomas (2)	Nby 94	
Robert	Abb 20	Thomas	Nby 95	
Robert	Bar 60	Thomas	Ora 503	
Robert	Chr 87	Thomas	Pen 110	
Robert	Csn 75	Thomas (2)	Pen 145	
Robert	Csn 145	Thomas	Spa 200	
Robert	Csn 159	Thomas	Spa 201	
Robert	Fai 216	Thomas	Wil 471	
Robert	Gvl 250	Thomas	Yrk 630	
Robert	Lan 5	Thos.	Geo 392	
Robert	Lrs 32	Thos. Junr.	Col 371	
Robert	Ora 555	Thomas Junr.	Sum 607	
Robert	Pen 124	Thos. Senr.	Col 407	
Robert	Pen 159	Thomas Senr.	Sum 607	

Thos. Aiken	Geo 383	Wm.	Uni 237
Thomas B.	Csn 111	Wm.	Uni 249
Thos. B.	Csn 95	William Esqr.	Yrk 623
Thos R.	Col 391	William Junr. (2)	Lrs 33
Thomas R.	Csn 113	Will S.	Csn 120
Turner	Edg 145	Zopher	Spa 200
Valentine	Spa 198	Smithart, Derby	Mbo 57
Whiteford	Csn 83	John	Geo 389
Wilkin	Edg 170	Smithson, Bartlett	Pen 126
Willeford	Mbo 61	Isaiah	Pen 126
William	Abb 14	Marsin	Pen 128
William	Abb 21	Smoke,	
William	Abb 29	see Rouch, Rauch	
William	Bar 47	Smothers, George	Edg 188
William	Bar 48	Smylie, Andrew	Csn 133
William	Bar 58	Susanna	Csn 114
William	Bar 69	Smyrl, Thos. Junr.	Ker 407
William	Bft 81	Thos. Senr.	Ker 407
William	Bft 98	Smyth, John	Csn 101
William	Bft 112	John	Csn 111
William	Cfd 106	Joseph	Ora 541
William	Csn 66	Smythe, Bartlee	Fai 212
William	Csn 90	Snead, Israel	Mbo 57
William	Csn 91	Sneed, Pleasant	Uni 246
William	Csn 96	Snelgrove, Barnet	Lex 579
William	Csn 100	Hillary	Nby 93
William	Dtn 120	John	Lex 568
William	Edg 140	Mary	Lex 567
William	Edg 171	Myer	Lex 568
William	Edg 181	William	Lex 580
William	Fai 200	Sneling, Henry	Bar 44A
William	Fai 202	Snell, Frederick	Ora 553
William	Fai 212	James	Abb 15
William	Fai 223	Snellgrove, Barruck	Lex 497
William	Geo 375	Edward	Lex 497
William	Geo 386	Elsey	Lex 497
William	Gvl 267	Jaremiah	Lex 489
William	Lex 565	Snelling, Henry Junr.	Bar 53
William	Lrs 17	John	Bar 54
William	Mbo 57	Snetter, Charles	Csn 124
William	Mrn 453	Snider, George	Lex 560
William	Mrn 457	Henry	Csn 181
William	Nby 92	Henry	Lex 572
William	Nby 93	Jacob	Lex 564
William	Nby 94	Snipes, Benjamin	Csn 96
William	Pen 124	Benjn.	Csn 65
William	Pen 125	Cathe.	Col 379
William (2)	Pen 136	Henry M.	Col 371
William	Pen 159	William	Geo 372
William	Wil 467	William	Mrn 456
William	Wil 472	Snither, George A.	Bar 68
William	Wil 477	Snoddy, John	Spa 168
William	Yrk 629	Saml.	Spa 123
Willm.	Csn 132	Snookes, David	Bft 118
Wm.	Chr 86	Snow, James	Abb 25
Wm.	Chr 89	Mark	Gvl 279
Wm. (2)	Spa 196	Moses	Gvl 276
Wm.	Spa 197	Nathaniel	Wil 464
Wm.	Spa 200	Rachel	Spa 191
Wm.	Spa 201	William	Geo 381
Wm.	Spa 207	Snowden, Charles	Csn 79
Wm.	Uni 218	Saml.	Wil 471
Wm.	Uni 225	Snyder, John	Bft 100
Wm.	Uni 234	Levittia	Lex 483
Wm.	Uni 235	Soah, Lucretia	Geo 387

Socks, Cutlip	Lex 572	Sowler, Joseph	Gvl 279
Solan, Timothy	Csn 72	Spann, Charles	Sum 589
Soldan, Herman	Lex 491	Eliza	Edg 148
Sollee, John	Csn 117	Henry	Edg 146
Soles, Crissey	Mrn 447	Jeremiah	Uni 217
Soloman, Joseph	Csn 146	Jesse	Spa 197
Philip	Edg 184	John	Edg 146
Solomons, J.	Col 401	Spar, William	Mbo 61
Somarsall, Willm.	Csn 130	Sparkes, Josiah	Spa 170
Somers, Martha	Col 371	Trulove	Spa 210
Mary	Col 407	Sparks, Jesse	Gvl 282
Susan	Col 407	John	Gvl 257
Sommarssall, Thomas	Csn 130	John	Uni 218
Sommer, Frances	Lex 568	Josiah	Uni 238
William	Lex 580	Leonard	Uni 239
Sommers, John A.	Lex 569	Martha	Dtn 125
Sommerwall, Wm.	Bft 94	Mathew	Spa 192
Son, Andrew	Lex 491	Mathew	Spa 210
Soncleer, George	Pen 139	Nancey	Spa 189
Sondley, see Sundly		Saml.	Spa 211
Sones, Henry	Sum 595	Saml.	Uni 236
Song, Christian	Lex 487	Stephen	Nby 93
Songwell, Samuel	Ker 401	Thomas	Csn 138
Soragins, Thomas	Edg 136	William	Lrs 21
Sorrels, John	Edg 139	Zach.	Spa 174
Richard	Edg 139	Sparrow, Daniel	Sum 608
Sorter, Peter	Gvl 261	James	Csn 107
Sosberry, William	Fai 217	Spaulding, Thomas	Sum 611
Sosebay, Job	Spa 174	Speak, John	Nby 93
Sotherlin, George	Edg 160	Speake, Hezekiah	Nby 92
Soujourner, Bridges	Ora 515	Spear, Elizabeth	Edg 142
Gabriel	Ora 521	Spearman, James	Nby 94
Radick	Ora 513	Spears, David	Mbo 60
Souter,		Dempsy	Dtn 122
see also Souther		James	Csn 94
Souter, Casper	Lex 573	James	Mbo 57
South, Benjamin	Lrs 42	Joel	Dtn 121
James	Lrs 42	Mason	Sum 589
John	Lrs 42	Robt.	Geo 378
Joseph	Lrs 42	William	Bar 58
William	Lrs 42	William	Ker 423
William Senr.	Lrs 41	William Junr.	Ker 423
Souther, George	Nby 93	Speed, Michael	Pen 135
Gasper	Lex 483	Robert	Pen 124
Martin	Nby 93	Speer, Andrew	Lrs 21
Southerland, Joshua	Lrs 21	David	Lrs 21
Southerlin, see also		Elizabeth	Lrs 21
Sutherland		Robert	Nby 95
Southerlin, Philip	Gvl 255	Speice, Amos	Spa 178
Southern,		Speight,	
see also Suthern		see also Spoight	
Southern, John	Pen 130	Speight, John	Dtn 114
Saml.	Pen 130	Speirin, Patrick	Csn 101
Southward, William	Edg 133	Speirs, John	Spa 197
Southwell, Edward	Bar 62	John	Uni 248
William	Bar 64	William	Uni 248
William	Bar 62	William Junr.	Uni 248
Sowel, Charles	Gvl 257	Speissegger, John	Csn 90
Mary	Gvl 265	Spelee, John	Spa 184
Richd.	Gvl 260	Spell, J.	Col 401
Sowell, John	Ker 413	Jonas	Col 401
Lowery	Ker 413	M.	Col 401
Worley	Ker 413	Spence, Alexander	Abb 28
Worley	Ker 425	Andrew (2)	Nby 94
Sowers(?), Winifred	Nby 95	Charles	Abb 5

John	Edg 166	Stephen, John	Lex 572
Stedim, Henry	Nby 95	Stephens, Ann (2)	Mbo 57
Stedman, Edward	Chr 73	Daniel	Csn 111
Michael	Yrk 618	Elisha	Gvl 260
Samuel C.	Lrs 29	Isaak	Gvl 258
Steed---, Zachary	Lex 577	Jacob	Nby 93
Steedham, George	Lex 578	James	Lrs 42
Steedley, David	Ora 507	James	Mbo 57
James	Ora 511	Job	Lan 5
Steeful, George	Abb 28	John	Bar 67
Steeher, Christopher	Csn 109	John	Lrs 31
Steel, Archibald	Yrk 617	John	Lrs 42
David	Abb 23	John	Lrs 44
David	Bar 68	John	Nby 94
Francis	Fai 237	John	Pen 111
George	Lex 566	Joseph	Pen 114
Henry	Abb 33	Joshua	Lan 6
Isaac	Sum 593	Josiah	Mbo 59
James	Abb 4	Needham	Dtn 120
James	Fai 230	Samuel	Pen 113
James	Yrk 618	Silas	Bar 66
John (2)	Bar 56	Thomas	Cfd 108
John	Chr 81	William	Csn 94
John	Nby 94	William	Csn 98
John	Yrk 618	William	Nby 95
Michael	Pen 150	Stephenson, Alexander	Yrk 633
Peter	Csn 181	Andrew	Yrk 620
Rebekah	Yrk 618	Caleb	Sum 591
Robert	Chr 80	David	Yrk 623
Robert	Nby 93	Ephraim Junr.	Sum 591
Robert	Yrk 617	Jeptha	Dtn 127
Samuel	Nby 95	John	Fai 195
Thomas	Chr 91	Matthew, Capt.	Yrk 621
Thomas	Fai 223	Moses	Lan 8
Thomas	Wil 474	Robert	Pen 162
William	Lrs 34	Thomas	Chr 77
William	Uni 220	Thomas	Dtn 128
William	Yrk 617	William	Yrk 621
Will.	Lan 3	William	Yrk 627
Steele, Abner	Pen 134	Sterling, Isaac	Bar 46
John	Dtn 118	John	Cfd 106
William	Csn 189	John	Nby 92
William	Pen 129	Robert	Spa 200
Steen, John	Uni 240	Thos.	Spa 203
John	Uni 241	Sterne, Joseph	Yrk 621
Patsey	Uni 240	Sterns, Aron	Uni 237
Richd.	Uni 224	John	Chr 87
Thomas	Uni 225	Levi	Nby 94
Wm.	Uni 236	Slider	Uni 237
Steene, Joseph	Yrk 628	Stetham, Charles	Abb 31
Steenson, James	Chr 88	Stevens, Abner	Chr 87
Robert	Chr 81	Agnes	Abb 4
Wm.	Chr 92	Ann	Col 399
Stegall(?), Samuel	Nby 95	Charles	Ora 517
Steinmetz, ---	Csn 117	Cotton	Csn 192
Steinmier, George	Csn 98	Daniel	Bft 83
Stenson, John	Abb 35	Daniel	Spa 183
Stent, Ann	Csn 171	David	Chr 76
Ann	Csn 192	David	Pen 115
John	Csn 171	Ebinitus	Edg 159
John	Csn 192	Elisha	Edg 134
Mary	Csn 124	Elisha	Geo 381
Step, Colbay	Pen 142	Fielding	Abb 21
Jesse	Pen 142	George	Abb 21
William	Pen 142	George	Bft 83

Gideon	Edg 157	Ann	Csn 149
Henry	Uni 230	Archd.	Geo 376
Hughstress	Geo 387	Charles	Csn 112
Isac	Edg 157	Charles	Dtn 120
James	Fai 219	Charles	Geo 370
Jemima	Pen 141	Clement	Ker 415
Jerves Hy.	Csn 113	Clement Junr.	Ker 417
Jesse	Mrn 445	David	Mbo 57
Jesse	Ora 517	David	Uni 228
John	Edg 140	Edward	Gvl 248
John	Edg 157	Edward	Spa 181
John	Edg 176	Francis	Lrs 21
John	Lan 5	George	Ker 403
John	Spa 185	Hardy	Mbo 57
Jos:	Col 407	Henry	Csn 144
Joshua	Spa 177	Hugh	Chr 94
Joshau	Spa 211	James	Chr 74
Josiah	Edg 141	James	Chr 84
Mark	Ker 425	James	Dtn 120
Meal	Lan 6	James	Dtn 125
Micajah	Abb 21	James	Ker 397
Oneall	Csn 59	James	Nby 95
Oneil G.	Col 371	James	Ora 555
Rachel	Cfd 106	James	Pen 140
Reuben	Mrn 460	James Junr.	Gvl 247
Richard	Geo 380	James Senr.	Gvl 247
Sarah	Lan 4	Jesse	Fai 210
Syllas	Ora 501	John	Abb 36
Thomas	Csn 150	John	Cfd 106
Thomas	Lan 5	John	Csn 147
Thomas	Pen 113	John	Dtn 114
William	Abb 21	John	Geo 379
Will.	Lan 4	John	Gvl 258
Wm.	Ora 517	John	Nby 95
Willm. S. Doctr.	Csn 118	Joseph	Nby 95
Stevenson, Alexr.	Pen 146	John (2)	Pen 150
Benjamin	Pen 141	John	Wil 467
David	Pen 150	John Jr.	Dtn 120
Ephraim	Sum 591	Joseph	Gvl 258
George	Col 407	Martha	Csn 130
George	Pen 147	Martin	Abb 37
Hugh	Spa 177	Nathaniel	Gvl 248
James	Abb 5	Robert	Csn 147
James	Abb 26	Robert	Dtn 120
James	Pen 119	Robert	Lrs 33
James	Pen 146	Robert	Nby 94
James	Pen 158	Robert	Nby 95
Jane	Csn 116	Robert	Pen 139
Jane	Pen 158	Samuel	Abb 24
John	Lan 8	Samuel	Nby 95
John R.	Bft 98	Saml.	Spa 182
Mary	Pen 150	Thomas	Csn 133
Mary	Sum 591	Walter	Lrs 26
Nathanl.	Lan 2	William	Abb 14
Thomas	Wil 471	William	Geo 372
Thos.	Col 371	William	Gvl 247
Thos.	Csn 66	William (2)	Pen 140
William	Pen 149	William	Sum 591
William	Pen 152	Wm.	Chr 93
Steward, John	Nby 93	Wm.	Gvl 259
John	Ora 511	Wm.	Spa 193
Stewart, Adam	Sum 609	William Senr.	Gvl 258
Alexander	Ker 403	Stewrd, John	Bar 50
Alexr.	Csn 119	Walter	Bar 44A
Alexr.	Gvl 258	Stigler, James	Gvl 284

William	Ora 547	John Senr.	Ker 405
Summer, see also		Jonathon	Yrk 623
Sumer, Sommer		Jordan	Ora 511
Summeral, David	Cfd 106	Mary	Csn 89
Levi	Cfd 108	Phinehas	Edg 144
Moses	Cfd 106	Robt.	Wil 476
Thomas	Cfd 106	Thomas	Bar 46
Thomas Jr.	Cfd 110	William	Ora 511
Summerford, Abraham	Bar 51	Swadley, Mark	Spa 209
Edward	Yrk 626	Swafford, Aaron	Gvl 254
Joshua	Mbo 57	Abraham	Gvl 259
Sarah	Mbo 57	Jacob	Gvl 253
William	Yrk 626	James	Gvl 254
Summerlin, Jacob	Edg 169	James	Pen 155
Lazorous	Gvl 279	John	Gvl 250
Summers, Geo	Fai 236	Swaford, Moses	Lrs 31
James	Edg 180	Thomas	Lrs 31
Jesse	Edg 180	Swain, John	Abb 20
John	Nby 93	Joseph	Csn 91
Joseph	Nby 93	Luke	Csn 130
William	Nby 93	Robert	Abb 20
Summerville, James	Ker 419	Swales, Joseph	Dtn 118
Matthew	Ker 419	Joseph	Dtn 127
Sumner, Benjamin	Abb 21	Swan, George	Chr 82
Milly	Uni 217	James	Fai 198
Nazary	Lrs 17	James	Pen 121
Sumter, Thomas	Sum 587	Rebecca	Pen 119
Thomas Junr.	Sum 597	Rebekah	Nby 93
Sun, Andrew	Lex 569	Swancy, John	Pen 133
Sundly, Richard	Nby 94	Swann, John	Yrk 617
Suolon, Henry	Sum 593	Swansey, John W.	Abb 22
Surburns, Joseph	Ker 401	Rosannah	Abb 22
Surgener, John	Lex 558	Samuel	Abb 22
Surges, John	Uni 248	Swearengin, ---	Edg 147
Surman, Jonathan	Bar 63	Swearingen, Nail	Edg 188
Surratt, James	Spa 200	Swearingin, ---y	Edg 147
Saml.	Spa 169	Frederick	Edg 146
Wm.	Sap 169	Thomas	Edg 146
Surrencey, John D.	Sum 603	Sweat, Ann	Gvl 264
Jacob	Bft 110	Caleb	Chr 81
James	Bft 110	Ephraim	Gvl 264
Surrett(?), Allin	Spa 168	Gilbert	Gvl 264
Susworres, Jacob Junr	Csn 120	James	Bar 64
Suthard, William	Gvl 246	William Junr.	Bft 106
Sutch, Ann	Geo 372	William Senr.	Bft 110
Sutherland, Daniel	Pen 122	Wm.	Gvl 275
Francis	Abb 3	Sweet, Anthony Junr.	Mrn 435
Francis	Csn 76	Anthony Senr.	Mrn 459
Sutherlin, Charles	Gvl 252	Gosspero	Mrn 435
James	Spa 184	Sylvanus	Mrn 435
John	Spa 169	Sweetenburgh, William	Lex 569
Philip	Gvl 252	Sweeter, Mary	Mbo 60
William	Pen 109	Sweeting, Lewis	Bft 81
Suthern, Delpha	Gvl 265	Sweetman, James	Csn 66
Suthwell, Thomas	Bar 55	Swelen, George	Edg 173
Sutley, James	Edg 153	Swellivant, Hughlett	Gvl 272
Sutliffe, Eli	Csn 142	Swenson, John	Pen 152
Suttle, Mary (2)	Gvl 264	Swetman, Luke	Sum 607
Suttles, John	Pen 124	Swicard, John	Lex 487
Sutton, Benjn.	Edg 160	Swicord, Barbara	Lex 491
Edward	Mbo 60	Barbary	Lex 574
James	Gvl 264	Christian	Lex 484
John	Gvl 255	Elisabeth	Bar 54
John	Ora 513	Elizabeth	Lex 570
John	Pen 105	George	Lex 493

George	Lex 569	Mary	Csn 122
John	Lex 483	Taggart, James	Lrs 45
John	Lex 575	John	Lrs 45
John Jr.	Lex 484	Tair, Robert	Csn 143
John Senr.	Lex 489	Tait(?), Hannah	Geo 366
John Junior	Lex 576	Talbert, John	Edg 139
Michael	Bar 53	Talbird, John Junr.	Bft 82
Swicort, John	Lex 570	John Senr.	Bft 82
Swidle, George	Lrs 41	Thomas (2)	Bft 82
Swift, John	Col 371	Talbirt, James	Csn 159
Swilavant, Moses	Gvl 272	Talbot, Lewis	Yrk 620
Pleasant	Gvl 271	Samuel	Yrk 623
Swillivant, Nathaniel	Gvl 271	Talford, Saml.	Chr 82
Swilvant, Charles	Gvl 271	Taliaferro, Richard	Yrk 629
Swindersine, Andw.	Col 371	Zachariah	Pen 105
Swindle, George	Abb 7	Talineau, Francis	Bft 126
Swindler, Joseph	Nby 93	Tallard, James	Chr 81
Swindol, Michael	Lrs 41	Talley, Henry (2)	Yrk 630
Swinford, John	Nby 93	Mary	Yrk 630
John	Nby 94	Nathan	Edg 163
Philip	Nby 93	Tallont, John	Pen 137
Samuel	Nby 94	Tally, Anderson	Nby 95
Swink, Lewis	Uni 215	Tamplat, John	Geo 367
Swinney, John	Mrn 451	Mary	Geo 365
Swinton, Alexr.	Geo 368	Thomas	Geo 367
Hugh	Csn 150	Tan---, Anthony	Csn 66
Hugh	Csn 159	Tankersley, Charles	Gvl 251
Switenbergh, Everard	Lex 493	George	Gvl 264
William	Lex 495	Henry	Gvl 251
Switzer, John R.	Csn 148	John	Gvl 254
Swoards, William	Gvl 268	Roland	Pen 104
Swords, John	Yrk 624	Wm.	Gvl 283
Swygert, see also		Tankesley, Bennett	Pen 153
Swicord		Tanner, Benjamin	Mrn 442
Sygar, John	Csn 108	David	Spa 203
Sykes, Henry	Fai 236	Edward	Csn 72
Syler, Wimer	Pen 133	Robert	Bft 106
Sylly, Mary	Lex 483	Thos. K.	Uni 233
Sylvester, Asa	Sum 587	Zopher	Pen 157
Syme, John M. D.	Csn 159	Tannyhill, Andrew	Pen 116
Symmes, Daniel	Pen 116	Tap, Vincent	Spa 204
Symonds, Frances	Csn 132	Tapley, Hosea	Pen 123
James	Csn 94	John	Pen 124
Symons, Sampson	Csn 144	Tara, Andrew	Lex 483
Samuel	Csn 143	Tarbirt, Robert	Nby 96
Synes, John	Csn 63	Tarbox, Susanah	Geo 368
Synum, Mary	Sum 585	Thomas	Geo 368
Synith, Francis	Geo 382	William	Geo 368
Willm.	Geo 389	Tarbrough, John	Bar 59
Synum, William	Sum 584	Thomas	Bar 59
		Tarbrouk, West	Bar 57
		Tarleton, Zion	Yrk 620
T		Josiah	Mrn 451
		Tarrant, Anna	Gvl 251
		Benj.	Ora 539
T--p, John	Edg 185	Benjn.	Gvl 266
T---r, Stephen Senr.	Edg 171	James	Gvl 265
Tabor, Simon	Csn 93	Larkin	Gvl 266
William	Pen 137	Leonard	Gvl 266
Tacket, Phillip	Spa 171	Reuben	Pen 113
Tackett, John	Spa 187	Rheuben	Gvl 266
William	Pen 142	Roland	Gvl 265
Tadd, James	Pen 146	Terry	Gvl 266
Tadlock, James	Cfd 110	Tarrar, Andrew	Lex 573
Thomas	Cfd 108	Andrew	Lex 575

Fedrick	Nby 96	James	Edg 181
Tarrell, Lewis	Bft 114	James	Gvl 261
Tarrence, John	Edg 137	James	Lan 6
Tart, Enos	Mrn 452	James	Lex 560
John	Mrn 452	James	Pen 129
Jonathan	Mrn 445	James	Spa 188
Tarver, John	Csn 142	Jeremiah	Fai 195
Tarwaters, John	Gvl 250	John	Bar 48
Tatam, Edward	Pen 113	John (2)	Edg 143
Jesse	Pen 113	John	Edg 156
Luke	Pen 113	John	Fai 197
Tate, Andrew	Pen 163	John	Geo 367
Elizabeth	Ker 397	John	Lan 8
Elizabeth	Spa 170	John	Lex 577
James	Pen 128	John	Lrs 14
James	Pen 145	John	Lrs 42
James	Uni 231	John	Ora 545
James	Yrk 621	John	Pen 117
Jane	Ker 399	John	Pen 135
Jas. Capt.	Csn 132	John	Pen 155
Jesse	Spa 170	John	Pen 158
John	Spa 189	John	Yrk 628
Nat	Uni 220	John Senr.	Lex 577
Perreyman	Spa 190	John Adam	Lex 577
Richard	Edg 179	John N.	Geo 362
Robert	Pen 145	John V.	Edg 157
Samuel	Fai 216	Jonathan	Lrs 22
Samuel	Pen 144	Jonathan	Nby 96
William	Yrk 633	Jonathen	Nby 96
Wm.	Spa 190	Joseph	Csn 88
Wm.	Uni 238	Joseph G.	Csn 97
Tatem, Bernard	Yrk 631	Josiah	Dtn 124
Tatm, Edward	Pen 113	Lamuel	Wil 468
Tatman, Venice	Bft 128	Leonard	Fai 220
Tatom, William	Abb 39	Leroy	Edg 142
Tauneyhill, James	Abb 3	Lewis	Mrn 445
Taylor, Aaron	Lex 577	Margaret	Csn 112
Abraham	Lex 578	Martin	Nby 96
Aggy	Bar 52	Mary	Uni 237
Alexander	Csn 92	Matthew	Ora 501
Alexander	Lrs 14	Meredith	Fai 211
Archabald	Gvl 254	Michael	Nby 96
Archd.	Geo 367	Moses	Edg 143
Benjn.	Edg 136	Nancy	Lrs 22
Billington	Sum 589	Paul	Csn 59
Catharine	Lex 566	Paul	Csn 107
Champ	Pen 104	Paul	Csn 110
Daniel	Nby 96	Richard	Lrs 21
Edward	Gvl 261	Richd.	Mrn 450
Elinor	Pen 129	Robert	Dtn 119
Elisha	Mrn 448	Robert	Lrs 21
Ellenor	Lrs 13	Ruffin	Geo 373
George	Cfd 107	Saml.	Geo 363
George	Col 401	Sampson	Fai 226
George	Lan 10	Samuel	Pen 129
George	Lrs 33	Samuel	Lrs 21
George	Nby 96	Samuel	Nby 96
George	Yrk 628	Sukey	Spa 186
Henry	Fai 205	Theophilus	Cfd 107
Henry	Lan 8	Thomas	Abb 17
Hy.	Bft 90	Thomas	Abb 18
Isaac	Chr 75	Thomas	Dtn 114
Isaac	Chr 83	Thomas	Edg 173
Isaac	Nby 96	Walter	Edg 153
Isham	Edg 170	Will.	Lan 6

William	Bft 96	John Capt.	Lrs 26	
William	Bft 116	Margaret	Yrk 622	
William	Csn 110	Robert	Lrs 27	
William	Edg 136	William	Yrk 622	
William	Edg 152	Tenile, Richmond	Lan 9	
William	Lex 560	Tennant, Alexr.	Fai 208	
William	Lex 577	William	Csn 66	
William	Nby 95	William P.	Edg 138	
William	Sum 606	Tennessee, Zach.	Uni 247	
William Junr.	Lrs 21	Tennis, Melcajah	Gvl 256	
William Senr.	Edg 136	Teraff, Philip	Csn 93	
William Senr.	Lex 564	Terral, Edmond	Cfd 106	
William Senr.	Lrs 21	Jonathan	Cfd 106	
Winney	Lrs 44	William	Dtn 120	
Wm.	Gvl 261	Terrell, Aaron	Pen 128	
Wm.	Gvl 261	Joel	Pen 112	
Wm. D.	Bft 128	John	Mbo 58	
Wm. M.	Csn 171	Joshua	Dtn 127	
Wm. M.	Csn 192	Richmond	Mbo 58	
Tayne, Dedarick	Sum 611	William	Pen 105	
Teague,		Terrey, Jerry	Abb 34	
see also Tegue		William	Abb 31	
Teague, Abner	Lrs 28	Terry, Benjamin	Abb 10	
Abraham	Nby 95	James	Wil 476	
Elijah	Abb 26	John	Chr 86	
Elijah	Lrs 22	John	Edg 137	
Irail	Lrs 22	John	Lrs 16	
Isaac	Nby 96	Joseph	Abb 34	
Joshua	Lrs 22	Joseph	Sum 601	
Mary	Mbo 59	Mumphard	Gvl 252	
Samuel	Nby 96	Soupt	Gvl 252	
William	Lrs 28	Stephen	Edg 166	
Teal, see also		Stephen	Fai 208	
Teale, Teele		Thos.	Gvl 274	
Teal, Theophilus	Ker 413	William	Fai 217	
Teale, Edward	Dtn 123	William Junr.	Lrs 15	
William	Dtn 116	William Senr.	Lrs 15	
William Jr.	Dtn 115	Wm.	Chr 88	
Team, Adam	Cfd 110	Wm.	Gvl 265	
Teams, Zachariah	Edg 148	Tew, Charles	Csn 145	
Tear, John	Bar 64	Tezeker, Michael	Lex 559	
Richard	Edg 179	Th---, Robt.	Csn 66	
William	Cfd 107	Thacker, Joel	Abb 40	
Teasdale, John	Csn 130	Nathaniel	Abb 7	
John	Sum 591	Thackston, James	Gvl 278	
Hadley	Sum 591	Thames, John Junr.	Sum 603	
Pleasant	Sum 591	John Senr.	Sum 602	
Teddens, John	Edg 188	Tharp, Eleaser	Edg 184	
Tedder, William	Csn 66	William	Pen 103	
Tedford, Elizabeth	Gvl 262	Thaxton, Thos.	Pen 159	
Simon	Lrs 24	Theames, Amos	Bft 110	
Teele, see also		Themis, Jeremiah Junr	Sum 603	
Teal, Teale		Jeremiah Senr.	Sum 603	
Teele, Christopher	Dtn 113	Theus, James	Csn 72	
Tegue, James	Nby 96	Rosanna	Csn 149	
Telph, Ann	Lrs 41	Sarah	Geo 366	
Telfare, Mrs.	Bft 130	Semion	Csn 137	
Telfer, William	Fai 221	Simeon	Csn 171	
Temple, Austin	Dtn 116	Simeon	Csn 192	
Templeman, Aron	Spa 173	Thomas	Csn 189	
Templeton, David	Lrs 27	Theyer, Ebenr.	Csn 114	
David Senr.	Lrs 27	Thexenin, Pieze	Csn 149	
James	Lrs 21	Thigpen, Hardy	Sum 602	
James	Yrk 626	John	Sum 602	
Jno	Fai 214	Thina, Caleb	Ora 519	

Samuel	Abb	30	Light	Mbo	58
Sims	Abb	25	Thomas	Mbo	58
Tomson, Herod	Edg	155	William	Mbo	58
John	Abb	33	Toy, Charles	Edg	175
William	Geo	365	Richard	Edg	174
Toney, Timothy	Pen	104	William	Edg	179
William	Bar	54	Tracey, Thomas	Uni	224
William	Pen	141	Trader, Susanna	Dtn	118
Tonge, Edwd.	Col	373	Trail, Bazel	Spa	200
S. Mrs.	Csn	127	David	Spa	199
Susan	Col	409	David	Uni	243
Tony, Benjamin	Bar	48	Wm.	Uni	243
Phillip	Bft	98	Trainer, John	Pen	151
Tool, Esekiah	Bar	50	Trainum, John	Gvl	282
Isaac	Bar	49	Obediah	Uni	230
Luke	Bar	51	Tramell, Wm. Junr.	Gvl	283
Toole, John	Csn	132	Tramill, Wm. Senr.	Gvl	282
Toomer, Anthony	Geo	363	Trammel, Dennis	Abb	2
Anthony Mrs.	Csn	114	Isaac	Uni	228
Torrans, James	Csn	84	Jared	Uni	227
Torrence, Andrew	Uni	250	Thomas	Abb	14
Tosh, James	Uni	219	Trammell, Benjn.	Gvl	251
Tottey, Wm.	Uni	246	Daniel	Pen	116
Totty, Abner	Uni	249	Jesse	Gvl	251
Ollise	Uni	246	Sampson	Pen	115
Toubert, Philip	Lex	573	Shadarack	Gvl	282
Touchberry, see also			Trammil, Samson	Spa	174
Tuchbery			Trantham, John	Ker	421
Touchstone, see also			Martin	Ker	417
Tuchstone			Maybin	Ker	411
Touchstone, Frederick	Ora	513	Robert	Ker	417
Henery	Ora	519	Zack	Ker	417
Jesse	Ora	513	Tranum, David	Gvl	271
John	Ora	509	Trap, William	Pen	137
Jonas	Ora	509	Trapier, Elizabeth	Geo	367
Martha	Ora	513	Paul	Geo	367
Stephen	Ora	513	Trapp, Thomas	Fai	224
Touchtone, Mary	Bar	69	William	Fai	210
Toushier, Margt.	Csn	127	Travers, John	Ors	503
Towers, Isaac	Gvl	277	John	Yrk	624
John	Gvl	276	Traverse, Barret	Edg	154
William	Pen	125	Travey, James	Spa	206
Towers(?), Winifred	Nby	95	Travis, John	Abb	31
Towey, Henry	Csn	87	John	Abb	32
Towles, Manning	Edg	181	John	Lrs	14
Townes, Samuel	Gvl	263	Trayler, Hyrum	Pen	111
Thomas	Gvl	266	Joel	Spa	210
Towneyhill, James	Abb	33	Traylor, Carey	Spa	209
James Senr.	Abb	34	Jesse	Spa	209
Townley, Henry	Pen	162	Joel	Spa	203
Towns, Peter	Abb	33	John	Spa	182
Townsand, William	Mrn	460	Reuben	Spa	209
Townsen, Sussannah	Abb	16	Richd.	Spa	182
William	Pen	157	Thomas	Edg	149
Townsend, Andrew	Yrk	618	Wm.	Spa	182
Daniel	Csn	185	Traywick,		
John	Uni	234	see also Treyweek		
Martha	Uni	232	Traywicks, William	Mrn	453
Martha	Uni	235	Treadaway, Elsha	Bar	60
Tabitha	Uni	233	Richard	Bar	60
Wm.	Uni	220	Treadcaft, Bethel	Csn	137
Townshend, Benja.	Mbo	60	Treadwell, Reuben	Dtn	118
Benjn.	Gvl	271	Treazvant, Isaac	Bft	130
John	Gvl	271	Isaac S.	Bft	132
John	Mbo	58	Tredwell, Adonian	Csn	72

238

Willis	Sum 608	John	Uni 247
Willm.	Mrn 444	John	Yrk 626
Turbeville,		John Junr.	Mrn 462
see Troublefield		John Senr.	Mrn 459
Turk, Ezara	Spa 201	Jonathan	Bar 44
Mary	Csn 82	Jonathan	Spa 196
Turley, Ignatius	Spa 186	Joseph	Bar 50
John	Ker 411	Joseph	Csn 140
Paul	Spa 186	Joseph	Gvl 245
Peter	Ker 409	Joseph	Lrs 35
Wm.	Spa 186	Joseph Jur.	Bar 51
Turnage, Eliza	Edg 150	Josiah	Nby 96
John	Pen 122	July	Lrs 43
William	Cfd 111	Lewis	Uni 247
Turnbough, Samuel	Gvl 283	Mary	Ker 405
Turnbull, Gavin	Csn 141	Mary (2)	Nby 95
James	Abb 34	Mary	Nby 96
Robt. J.	Csn 124	Mathew	Bar 50
Turner, Abednigo	Abb 8	Mathias	Spa 179
Abisha	Edg 167	Moses	Mbo 58
Alexander	Abb 25	Mthias	Pen 132
Amos	Mrn 457	Nathan	Pen 114
Amy	Mbo 60	Nathan	Pen 115
Andrew	Fai 231	Noel	Bar 49
Asa	Lrs 38	Pierce	Yrk 625
Benja.	Wil 467	Rebecca	Nby 96
Benjamin	Gvl 246	Reuben	Ker 427
Benjamin	Pen 139	Reuben	Mrn 462
Benjn.	Gvl 262	Reubin	Sum 612
Champness	Lrs 33	Rhoday	Mbo 59
Danl. W.	Csn 118	Robert	Ker 399
David	Yrk 621	Robert	Ker 427
David	Yrk 632	Robert	Yrk 632
Derby	Spa 202	Saml.	Spa 174
Edward	Pen 139	Saml.	Spa 202
Elijah	Uni 247	Samuel	Yrk 626
Elisabeth	Bar 49	Sanders	Spa 196
Elizabeth	Nby 96	Sion	Gvl 266
Fielding	Lrs 33	Thomas	Bar 50
George	Bar 49	Thomas	Csn 144
George	Lex 572	Thomas	Csn 152
George	Wil 467	Thomas	Lrs 32
Hannah	Spa 170	Thomas	Mbo 58
Henry	Spa 201	Thomas	Nby 96
Jacob	Bar 59	Thomas	Yrk 624
James	Fai 241	Thomas	Yrk 626
James	Lex 487	Thomas Jr.	Mbo 58
James	Lex 574	Vincent	Fai 192
James	Lrs 33	Wilkinson	Yrk 628
James	Mbo 58	William	Bar 65
James	Pen 151	William	Csn 106
James	Spa 176	William	Nby 95
James	Uni 223	William	Pen 107
John	Bar 59	William	Pen 151
John	Bar 60	William	Wil 467
John	Dtn 128	William Junr.	Gvl 246
John	Fai 231	William Senr.	Gvl 244
John	Fai 237	William G.	Gvl 246
John	Gvl 257	Willm.	Geo 384
John	Nby 95	Wm.	Spa 170
John	Nby 95	Wm.	Spa 202
John	Nby 96	Turnipseed, Bartw.	Fai 236
John	Nby 96	Jacob	Fai 236
John	Pen 132	Turpin, Hanna	Csn 132
John	Spa 170	William	Csn 66

Joseph	Chr	78	Right Junr.	Mrn	435
Joseph	Edg	145	Right Senr.	Mrn	435
L.	Col	401	Thomas	Mrn	461
Laurence	Ora	537	Wallace, Widow	Pen	118
Lavinia	Bft	98	Aaron	Dtn	115
Mansfield	Lrs	34	Alexander	Csn	151
Mary	Spa	169	Benjn.	Csn	67
Mary	Uni	238	David	Cfd	107
Mason	Uni	248	George	Edg	153
Molley	Spa	184	James	Csn	123
Nat.	Spa	181	James	Lrs	28
Nathan	Ora	507	Jesse Senr.	Lrs	19
Nathaniel	Ora	509	John	Edg	140
Philip	Bar	66	John	Lrs	20
Rebeckah	Chr	86	John	Lrs	44
Robert	Bar	67	John	Pen	162
Robert	Chr	77	John	Uni	226
Robert	Chr	77	John Junr.	Lrs	19
Robert	Csn	95	Jonathan	Lrs	20
Robert	Csn	115	Joseph	Edg	140
Robert	Uni	249	Joseph	Uni	239
Robert Boyd	Yrk	617	Joshua	Abb	16
Saml.	Chr	92	Michael Senr.	Lrs	19
Samuel	Edg	135	Samuel	Edg	161
Samuel	Gvl	261	Rachel	Mbo	59
Sarah	Lrs	30	Richard	Edg	162
Silvanus Junr.	Lrs	38	Robert	Abb	20
Silvanus Esq.	Lrs	30	Robert	Edg	163
Solomon	Abb	32	Thomas	Csn	153
Susanah	Lrs	24	Thomas	Lrs	40
Tandy	Lrs	30	Wm.	Uni	218
Terry	Abb	31	William	Abb	16
Thos.	Gvl	251	William	Edg	179
Thos.	Gvl	265	Walldon, William	Ker	403
Thomas	Chr	85	Walldrum, Joseph	Pen	137
Thomas	Chr	88	Walle, Jesse	Chr	76
Thomas	Csn	146	Wallen, William	Bar	51
Thomas	Edg	157	Waller, Benjamin	Abb	8
Will.	Lan	4	John	Abb	8
Will.	Lan	4	John N.	Abb	8
Will	Lan	4	Leonard	Abb	7
Wm.	Chr	93	Samuel	Ora	519
Wm. G[ay]	Chr	86	Samuel	Yrk	631
William	Bar	67	William	Geo	386
William	Csn	146	Wallern, see Wallon		
William	Edg	164	Walley(?), George	Csn	67
William	Edg	164	Walley, John	Mrn	462
William	Lrs	30	Walling, Robert	Nby	97
William	Ora	529	Wallis, Elias	Yrk	622
Willis	Uni	221	Guy	Lan	8
Wall, Benjamin	Mrn	436	Hugh	Chr	87
Bird	Chr	81	James	Chr	93
Charles	Chr	80	James	Yrk	627
Drury	Bft	120	James, Capt.	Yrk	618
Dudley	Pen	137	Jesse	Chr	90
Elisha	Bft	120	Jesse	Fai	227
Hardy	Bar	61	John	Fai	217
Howell	Bft	120	John	Nby	98
John	Chr	80	Joseph	Yrk	625
Jonathan	Spa	178	M'Caslin	Yrk	625
Joseph	Pen	136	Robert	Yrk	627
Mary	Chr	80	Thomas	Chr	94
Michael	Mrn	462	Thomas	Yrk	625
Nancy	Mbo	58	William	Nby	98
Richard	Csn	75	Wallon, Fedrick J.	Nby	98

Walls, Charles	Edg 138	Joshua	Csn 189
John	Edg 186	Joshua	Geo 377
William	Edg 135	Mark	Pen 144
William	Edg 179	Mary	Fai 199
Wally, Thomas	Mrn 443	Micajah	Abb 22
Walpole, Richard	Edg 138	Micajah	Sum 589
Thomas	Edg 138	Michal	Abb 4
Walsh, Daniel	Mbo 58	Michael	Sum 608
Henry	Dtn 117	Milly	Mrn 439
Henry	Mbo 59	Nathan	Spa 172
James	Mbo 58	Nathan	Spa 205
Mary	Mbo 59	Richd.	Gvl 256
William	Cfd 109	Samuel	Pen 107
Walston, Elias	Cfd 107	Shadrack	Edg 170
Thomas	Cfd 108	Soloman	Spa 205
Thomas	Cfd 110	Theophilus	Dtn 117
Waltee, Alexander	Chr 80	Thomas	Dtn 120
Walter(?), Jacob	Col 381	Thomas	Nby 98
Walter, Isaac	Col 409	Thomas Junr.	Abb 33
J. S.	Col 387	Thomas Senr.	Abb 33
John	Csn 163	Walter	Abb 4
John Est.	Col 381	Will.	Lan 6
Jude	Col 409	William	Abb 33
P.	Col 379	William	Dtn 124
Walters,		William	Edg 182
see also Waters		William	Gvl 244
Walters, Jacob	Wil 463	William	Gvl 260
Joshua	Cfd 107	William	Mrn 439
Mary	Col 409	Warden, John	Abb 3
Zadrack	Ora 545	Wardlaw, Hugh	Abb 9
Walton, Enoch	Edg 136	James	Pen 114
John	Edg 162	James	Pen 159
John	Edg 185	Nancy	Abb 9
Moses	Edg 182	William	Abb 9
Samuel	Edg 182	William	Pen 159
Waltroop, Grafton	Dtn 117	Wardlow, Hugh Esq.	Abb 38
Waly, John	Bar 66	James	Abb 40
Wamach, William	Pen 126	John	Abb 9
Wammock, Sarah	Pen 121	John Junr.	Abb 13
Wande, Thomas	Edg 134	John Junr.	Abb 40
Wannamaker, Jacob	Ora 521	Samuel	Abb 10
Jacob	Ora 533	William	Abb 22
Jacob	Ora 553	Ware, David	Dtn 121
Ward, Christopher	Edg 159	Edmond	Abb 10
Daniel	Csn 161	Edward	Gvl 257
Daniel	Edg 153	Francis	Gvl 258
Frederick	Edg 174	Henry	Edg 172
H. D.	Ora 539	Henry Junr.	Edg 144
Howell	Yrk 622	James	Cfd 111
James	Gvl 266	Jane	Abb 15
James	Lrs 33	John	Cfd 111
James	Spa 205	Moss	Pen 122
James	Wil 477	Robert	Edg 160
James	Yrk 622	Thomas	Pen 156
James Esqr.	Csn 116	Will	Lan 2
Jeremiah	Abb 24	William	Abb 11
Jessey	Abb 25	Warham, Chas. Est.	Csn 171
John	Csn 152	Mary	Csn 139
John	Dtn 120	Warhurst, Timothy	Pen 143
John	Geo 377	Waring, Daniel	Csn 97
John	Lex 565	J. Est.	Col 409
John	Spa 184	Jos.	Col 409
John	Spa 186	Morton	Csn 119
John	Sum 612	Richard	Col 409
Joshua	Csn 123	Richd. Est.	Col 409

Dempsy	Mbo 58	James	Pen 151	
Edward	Gvl 259	Samuel	Abb 38	
Elias	Dtn 114	William	Lex 567	
Elijah	Edg 156	Watters(?), Nathaniel	Ora 543	
Elijah	Lrs 32	Watters, Mary	Sum 587	
Ezekiel	Lan 10	Wattles, Benjamin	Ker 413	
George	Cfd 107	Watts(?), John	Nby 98	
George	Yrk 623	Watts, Andrew	Lrs 44	
Harrison	Mrn 438	Charles	Csn 151	
Henry	Abb 35	Christopher	Geo 373	
Henry	Dtn 123	David	Nby 98	
Hezekiah	Edg 134	Edward	Fai 194	
Hulda	Edg 156	George	Fai 225	
James	Abb 24	George	Lrs 30	
James	Sum 585	George	Pen 151	
James	Yrk 625	James	Abb 10	
James	Yrk 630	James	Lrs 32	
James, Junr.	Yrk 626	Jarrett	Pen 136	
John	Csn 109	John	Geo 365	
John	Csn 117	John	Lrs 41	
John	Edg 177	John	Pen 151	
John	Edg 180	John Capt.	Lrs 32	
John	Fai 224	Joseph	Lan 5	
John	Gvl 258	Joshua	Ker 413	
John	Gvl 262	Julius	Sum 587	
John	Lrs 38	Otteryon	Nby 98	
John	Wil 472	Peter	Lan 3	
John	Yrk 625	Rachel	Lan 2	
John, Esqr.	Yrk 621	Richd.	Geo 378	
Jonathan	Pen 163	Robert	Csn 136	
Joshua	Lex 560	Thomas	Pen 117	
Lewis	Lrs 38	William	Geo 373	
Mark	Mrn 439	William	Ker 399	
Meredith	Geo 388	Wattson, Archibald	Ker 403	
Nat	Spa 190	Edward	Ker 403	
Nat	Spa 192	Jacob	Pen 138	
Nathan	Lrs 18	James	Pen 120	
Peter	Yrk 626	John	Pen 133	
Richman	Edg 134	John	Pen 151	
Robert	Fai 208	Thomas	Pen 138	
Robert	Spa 193	William	Pen 137	
Samuel	Edg 177	Watwood, George	Cfd 107	
Samuel Colol.	Yrk 621	Waugh, John	Fai 240	
Samuel Esqr.	Yrk 625	Robert	Pen 141	
Samuel, Junr.	Yrk 621	Way, Amos	Bar 57	
Scace: B:	Mrn 438	Joseph	Sum 608	
Simeon	Uni 239	Peter	Mbo 58	
Stephen	Abb 21	Richd.	Col 409	
Stephen	Abb 38	Samuel	Bar 56	
Stephen	Abb 38	Samuel	Bar 56	
Tapely	Fai 229	Wayne, William	Geo 365	
Valintine	Spa 181	Waysinger, Susannah	Lex 497	
Violet	Yrk 625	Weakfield, Alexr	Spa 167	
William	Cfd 107	Josiah	Spa 168	
William	Csn 150	Moses	Spa 182	
William	Edg 177	Weaks, Arthur	Bar 65	
William	Fai 191	Wear, Andrew	Abb 36	
William	Lrs 32	David	Fai 237	
William	Mrn 438	James	Fai 237	
William	Nby 98	Weatherall, John	Abb 38	
William	Sum 597	Weatherby, Gideon	Bar 51	
William	Yrk 626	Weatherford, Elisha	Abb 23	
William	Yrk 630	John	Edg 148	
William Senr.	Edg 149	Weatherington,	Dtn 122	
Watt, James	Csn 127	William		

Weatherley, Isaac	Csn	148	Andrew	Lex	576
Weatherly, Isaac	Mbo	58	John	Lex	484
Thomas	Mbo	58	John	Lex	575
Weathers, Thomas	Lrs	35	Martha	Abb	2
Thomas	Csn	87	Martha Junr.	Abb	7
Weathersby, Lewis	Bar	52	Weedingman,	Edg	157
Mary	Bar	59	Christopher	Edg	157
Stephen	Bar	50	Weekly, George	Bft	98
William	Bar	51	John	Bft	96
Weaver, Benjn.	Edg	135	John Junr.	Bft	100
Daniel	Pen	109	Thomas	Bar	44
Daniel Jr.	Pen	110	William	Bar	69
David	Lex	577	Weeks, Benjamin	Nby	98
David	Pen	110	Charles	Nby	98
Demsey	Edg	184	David	Pen	139
Francis	Cfd	107	James Jur.	Sum	601
George	Lex	564	James Ser.	Sum	601
Henry	Lex	567	John	Uni	218
Henry	Lex	578	Levi	Bft	92
Henry	Nby	98	Luke	Lrs	21
Jesse	Cfd	110	Mary	Uni	217
John	Edg	134	Phillip	Sum	601
John	Lan	2	Theophilus	Bft	96
Jonathan	Edg	183	Thomas	Fai	230
Kate free black	Wil	478	Wm.	Spa	208
Milly	Lan	2	William	Edg	141
Morris	Fai	193	William	Edg	158
Nichl. Junr.	Ora	549	William	Sum	601
Nicholas Senr.	Ora	549	Weems, Bartholomew	Abb	26
Peter	Csn	105	Elizabeth	Abb	6
Peter	Pen	111	George	Abb	26
Samuel	Cfd	110	Henry	Abb	6
Samuel	Lex	564	James	Abb	26
Weavor, John	Mrn	460	John	Abb	2
Weavour, Thos.	Gvl	258	Margret	Abb	26
Webb, Andrew	Abb	9	Samuel	Abb	26
Benjn.	Col	383	Thomas	Abb	6
Chas.	Col	381	William	Abb	24
Chas.	Uni	222	Weir,		
Elizabeth	Bft	116	see also Were		
Hannah	Csn	181	Weir, David Senr.	Fai	218
Hendley	Edg	133	James	Fai	229
Henry	Sum	600	Jane	Fai	201
James	Yrk	631	John	Fai	201
John	Csn	148	Letty	Lrs	19
John	Edg	174	Samuel	Fai	201
John	Ker	413	Samuel	Lrs	31
John	Sum	600	Thomas	Lrs	28
Robert	Edg	155	Weissinger, John	Csn	101
Theoderick	Yrk	631	Welch,		
Thomas	Bft	82	see also Wilch		
William	Col	401	Welch, Daniel	Lrs	22
William	Fai	202	Daniel	Nby	97
Webber, Wm.	Spa	207	David	Pen	103
Webster, James	Mbo	58	Elizabeth	Lrs	19
Roddy	Pen	162	George	Gvl	276
William	Nby	97	James	Ora	505
Wecker, John	Lex	495	James	Ora	519
Uriah	Lex	495	James Junr.	Sum	611
Wedgeworth, Esther	Abb	22	James Senr.	Sum	611
James	Abb	22	John	Bar	46
Joseph	Abb	21	Mses	Bar	61
Richard	Abb	22	Nicholas	Pen	157
Wedingman, David	Nby	99	Richard	Sum	612
Weed, Andrew	Lex	484	Stephen	Mrn	450

Thomas	Sum 611	James	Edg 154
Wm.	Gvl 276	John	Csn 88
William	Edg 163	John	Lan 10
William	Edg 164	Nicholas	Lan 5
William	Pen 104	Robert	Csn 181
William	Pen 162	Robert	Lan 10
Welchel, Francis	Uni 239	Robert	Yrk 626
Martha	Uni 239	Saml.	Uni 246
Weld, Edward	Csn 91	Thomas	Lan 10
Weldon, Isaac	Abb 19	William	Lan 5
James	Sum 591	Were, Elizabeth	Chr 74
Saml.	Fai 208	George	Chr 80
Welken, John H.	Csn 74	Hugh	Chr 91
Well, Thomas	Csn 67	James	Chr 73
Wellimson, Adam	Pen 162	John	Chr 75
Welloon, Meridith	Nby 85	Mary	Chr 73
Wells, Mrs.	Bft 134	Samuel	Chr 93
Abigal	Nby 97	Werly, Peter	Sum 603
Abner	Uni 249	Wernandau, Henery	Ora 531
Arnold	Csn 161	Thomas	Ora 531
Clement	Lrs 35	Wernandaw, Samuel	Ora 523
Edward	Dtn 126	Werts, Henry	Nby 98
Edward	Sum 587	Wesbury, Thos.	Col 409
Elijah	Dtn 117	Wescoat, Mary	Csn 185
Elizabeth	Gvl 264	Randall	Csn 185
Esther	Cfd 109	Thomas	Csn 185
George	Cfd 107	William	Csn 185
George	Ker 417	Wessinger,	
George	Nby 97	see Waysinger	
George	Uni 249	Wessinger,	
Hardy	Dtn 114	see Weysinger	
Hardy	Dtn 125	Wessinger, John	Lex 573
Henry	Spa 205	John	Lex 576
Horatia	Csn 79	Matthias	Lex 575
Hugh	Yrk 617	Matthias	Lex 576
James	Lrs 36	Michael	Lex 576
Jane	Lan 6	Susanna	Lex 573
Jesse	Spa 205	West, Alexander	Gvl 246
John	Cfd 107	Alexander	Nby 99
John	Cfd 109	Alexander, Senr.	Gvl 249
John	Csn 181	Benjamin	Abb 17
John	Edg 135	Benjamin	Gvl 255
John	Edg 143	Benjamin	Sum 603
John	Fai 234	Berry	Lrs 39
John	Spa 189	Catharine	Csn 86
John	Sum 601	Celia	Geo 384
Jones	Edg 179	Elizabeth	Nby 98
Josiah	Bft 132	Elizabeth	Pen 119
Joseph	Ker 403	Hannah	Pen 133
Lewis	Gvl 278	Hezekiah	Chr 83
Moses	Lrs 35	Isaac	Gvl 265
Pheobe	Csn 103	Isaac	Spa 178
Redman	Geo 377	Isaac Junr.	Gvl 244
Robert	Edg 186	Isaac Senr.	Gvl 244
Samuel	Csn 87	James	Gvl 258
Samuel	Ker 405	James	Gvl 265
Samuel	Nby 99	James	Ker 411
Thomas	Fai 239	James	Spa 211
Thomas	Spa 172	James	Sum 584
Wm.	Spa 205	James Doctr.	Csn 117
Willm. H.	Csn 181	Jean	Edg 176
William	Ker 403	Jennet	Spa 210
Welsh, Charles	Csn 75	Joel	Ker 411
Edmond	Csn 134	John	Gvl 258
George	Csn 105	John	Ker 411

Daniel	Spa 178	Joseph	Geo 368
Daniel	Spa 201	Joseph	Lan 3
Daniel	Uni 235	Joseph	Lrs 41
David	Spa 183	Joseph	Mrn 443
David	Sum 600	Joseph	Pen 137
Edward	Yrk 619	Luke	Ker 403
Elicha	Lan 5	Martha	Csn 96
Elizh.	Geo 386	Martin	Lex 491
Francis	Abb 21	Mary	Bar 50
George	Abb 39	Mary	Col 409
George	Dtn 117	Mathew	Bft 124
George	Dtn 127	Moody	Sum 608
George	Lan 2	Moses	Gvl 257
George	Lan 7	Moses	Lan 2
George	Lan 8	Nancey	Spa 205
George Estate	Csn 161	Nathan	Edg 141
Gideon	Mrn 449	Patrick	Pen 150
Henry	Bft 96	Robert	Abb 22
Henry	Sum 601	Robert	Edg 188
Hugh	Chr 78	Robert	Ker 399
Hugh	Fai 219	Robert	Pen 143
Hugh	Uni 243	Robert	Uni 217
Hugh Esqr.	Yrk 630	Robert	Uni 243
Isaiah (2)	Uni 245	Robert Junr.	Lan 6
Isaiah	Uni 247	Saml.	Spa 204
James	Bar 47	Stephen	Spa 210
James	Col 401	Thos.	Uni 244
James	Csn 76	Thomas	Abb 37
James	Ker 397	Thomas	Chr 78
James	Lan 2	Thomas	Chr 80
James	Lrs 36	Thomas	Chr 88
James	Mrn 450	Thomas	Lan 7
James	Ora 527	Thomas	Uni 245
James	Pen 119	Thos. Junr.	Geo 374
James	Pen 145	Vincent	Edg 159
James	Pen 150	Wm.	Chr 77
James	Spa 178	Wm.	Gvl 275
James	Sum 604	Wm.	Uni 224
James	Uni 215	Wm.	Uni 244
James	Uni 244	Wm.	Uni 246
James	Uni 245	William	Abb 38
Jane	Abb 6	William	Bft 104
Jesse	Gvl 255	William	Cfd 107
Jesse	Sum 601	William	Csn 131
John	Abb 34	William	Csn 141
John	Cfd 107	William	Edg 172
John	Cfd 110	William	Geo 378
John	Cfd 110	William	Gvl 255
John	Chr 84	William	Ker 417
John	Csn 98	William	Mrn 450
John	Csn 185	William	Pen 127
John	Edg 161	William	Pen 143
John	Ker 411	William	Pen 150
John	Ker 411	William	Pen 151
John	Lan 2	William	Uni 246
John	Lan 2	Whitefield, William	Mbo 58
John Senr.	Lan 6	Whiteford, David	Lrs 35
John	Lan 9	Whitehead, Daniel	Lrs 35
John	Pen 141	Jacob	Edg 145
John	Spa 195	James	Edg 145
John	Spa 199	John	Mbo 58
John	Spa 200	William	Lrs 35
John	Uni 243	Whitehouse, Cath:	Csn 59
John	Uni 246	Whiteman, Jacob	Ora 551
John	Yrk 630	William	Csn 151

Whiten, Philip	Gvl 268	Whittimore, Abram	Spa 185
Whites, Martin	Lex 568	John	Spa 185
Whiteside, Hugh	Chr 91	Whittington,	Mbo 58
Whitesides, Hugh	Yrk 619	Elizabeth	Mbo 58
James	Yrk 619	Ephraim	Mbo 58
Mary	Csn 163	Francis	Mbo 58
Mary J.	Yrk 630	John	Sum 585
Sarah	Csn 163	Moses	Mbo 61
Thos.	Csn 163	Nath	Mbo 59
Thomas	Yrk 619	Nathl. G.	Mrn 444
Whitfield, Geor.	Csn 131	Noah	Mbo 58
Mary	Pen 103	William	Mbo 61
William	Mrn 452	Whittle, James	Edg 155
Whiticut, Hugh	Abb 31	Joseph	Edg 155
Whitington, Greeff	Mrn 446	Whitton, Charles	Nby 99
Nathl.	Mrn 444	Moses	Nby 99
John	Mrn 445	Lindsy	Nby 99
Whitler, William	Edg 172	Rachel	Nby 99
Whitley, Moses	Pen 156	John	Nby 99
William	Sum 609	Elijah	Nby 99
Alexander	Sum 610	Jonathon	Uni 232
John	Edg 174	Whitworth, Jacob	Lrs 33
John	Edg 184	Samuel	Pen 122
Stephen	Edg 136	Whorton, Benjamin	Pen 138
Whitlock, John	Uni 225	Whright, John	Pen 148
James	Edg 186	Robt. M.	Pen 148
W--dfrey	Edg 149	Wiatt, Abraham	Spa 174
Wm.	Uni 224	Edward	Spa 170
Thomas	Uni 224	Isham	Spa 174
Robert	Uni 224	Leonard	Spa 169
Betsey	Uni 224	Susanna	Spa 174
Susannah	Uni 224	Thomas	Spa 171
James	Uni 218	Vincent	Spa 172
Whitman, Chrisly	Nby 97	Zach	Spa 174
Wm.	Geo 389	Wickelse, John	Csn 102
Peter	Nby 99	Wicker, see Wecker	
Whitmire, William	Nby 98	Adam	Nby 99
Michael	Pen 108	Andrew	Nby 99
William	Pen 139	Gospel	Nby 99
Federic	Uni 232	Henry	Nby 98
Henry	Pen 139	Simon	Nby 99
Stephen	Pen 137	Uriah	Nby 99
Christopher	Pen 137	Wickham, Thomas T.	Mrn 461
Samuel	Pen 136	Wicks, Joseph	Sum 602
Whitmore, Alse	Lrs 26	Wideman, Adam	Abb 6
George Capt.	Lrs 25	Henry	Abb 31
Joseph	Lrs 26	Lenord	Abb 31
Rolley	Uni 250	Mark	Abb 31
Whitner, Joseph	Pen 131	Thomas	Abb 31
Whitney, Francis	Ora 525	Widener, Samuel	Lan 10
Jerimiah	Pen 134	Widner, Jacob	Fai 201
John	Pen 135	Wiel(?), Richard	Chr 89
Whitney, Makeon	Bar 50	Wigfall, Constantia	Csn 97
Joseph	Fai 207	Levi	Csn 161
Whitsell, F. Est.	Col 379	Samuel	Csn 181
John	Col 379	Thomas	Csn 161
Whitson, David	Uni 226	Wigg, H.	Bft 94
Whitted, John	Chr 76	Leatitia	Bft 94
Whitten, Phillip	Lrs 26	Wm. H.	Bft 82
Joel	Lrs 26	Wm. H., Mrs.	Bft 82
Austin	Edg 143	William	Bft 132
Moses	Edg 143	Wiggens, Daniel	Dtn 127
John	Gvl 256	Assail	Lrs 35
Lydia	Geo 367	Daniel	Dtn 122
Whitter, Jane	Csn 189	Elisha	Csn 67

Eliza	Uni 227	Wilkey, James	Chr 77
Jesse	Mrn 443	Wilkie, William	Csn 98
John	Col 401	William	Yrk 628
Jonathan	Mrn 443	Wilkins, Isaac	Gvl 284
Lewis	Mrn 443	Benjamin	Yrk 628
Mary	Dtn 121	Benjamin Junr.	Yrk 628
William	Mrn 443	James	Spa 172
Wight, John	Lan 5	John	Bft 126
Jonathan	Edg 186	Saml.	Spa 172
Wighton, Charles	Pen 104	Terrel	Spa 207
Wiginton, George	Gvl 249	Willm.	Csn 118
John	Gvl 248	Wm.	Bft 82
Wigley, Allin	Spa 201	Wilkinson, ---mas	Edg 147
Wilbanks,		Carey	Lan 9
see also Woolbanks		Dorcas	Ora 515
Wilbanks, Evey	Uni 233	Elizabeth	Ora 515
Gillum	Uni 237	James	Mbo 60
Jos.	Uni 233	John	Bar 49
John	Uni 234	John	Bft 116
Marshal	Uni 233	John	Csn 80
Wm.	Uni 237	John	Edg 188
Wilburn, Aaron	Pen 160	John	Mbo 60
Elijah	Uni 221	John Junr.	Bar 49
Epheraim	Uni 223	M. Est.	Col 373
James	Pen 159	Margaret	Pen 121
John	Uni 223	Mary	Mbo 60
Joshua	Uni 222	Mary	Mbo 61
Wm.	Uni 223	William	Mbo 60
Wilch, William	Nby 97	William Jr.	Mbo 60
Wilcox, Jeremiah	Csn 152	Wilks, Abner	Chr 83
Wilcuts, Thomas	Mbo 58	Francis	Cfd 107
Wildair, Vincent	Sum 585	Francis	Chr 82
Wilder, Jesse	Sum 604	Hardy	Geo 368
Stewart	Sum 604	Richard	Chr 83
Wm.	Spa 194	Rubin	Chr 83
Wildredge, Gibson	Abb 11	Thomas	Lrs 29
John	Abb 11	Wm.	Chr 76
Wilds, George	Dtn 124	Will, Philip	Csn 95
Mary	Dtn 113	Willard, Bard	Uni 220
Samuel	Dtn 125	James	Uni 220
Samuel Jr.	Dtn 113	John	Lrs 39
Wiley, David	Abb 29	John	Uni 220
Francis	Chr 93	Willbanks, Richard	Pen 116
James	Chr 94	Willcox, William	Bft 120
James	Yrk 619	Willenhoup, John	Edg 149
John	Abb 22	Willes, George	Col 387
John	Chr 78	Willey, George	Ker 405
John	Chr 88	Williams, ---	Csn 163
John	Pen 149	Abilimilech	Geo 381
John	Yrk 631	Abner	Csn 140
Joseph	Fai 219	Abraham	Ora 529
Richard	Yrk 624	Absolom	Sum 591
Robert	Yrk 619	Ailes(?)	Pen 126
Samuel	Pen 150	Allen	Bft 124
Thomas	Abb 28	Ann	Csn 131
Wm.	Chr 86	Anne	Ora 515
Wm.	Chr 92	Arthur	Abb 27
Wilhelm, Peter	Nby 98	Arthur	Edg 159
Wilkel, John	Uni 238	Arthur	Ker 425
Wilkens, Micajah	Geo 364	Augustine	Fai 236
Wm.	Spa 207	Benjamin	Bar 49
Wilkerson, Dunkin	Gvl 255	Benjamin	Lrs 36
Michael	Bar 49	Benja.	Mbo 58
Robert	Bar 49	Benjn. P.	Csn 66
Mathew	Bar 62	Brooks	Spa 175

Butler	Edg 138	Jas.		Col 381
Caleb	Pen 134	Jeremiah		Lex 565
Charles	Csn 123	Jesse		Dtn 119
Charles	Edg 141	Jesse		Ker 425
Charles	Pen 134	Jno		Col 383
Charles	Wil 464	Joel		Spa 170
Christean	Ker 425	John		Abb 19
Colden	Lan 6	John		Abb 40
Daniel	Abb 27	John		Bar 59
Daniel	Fai 220	John		Bar 62
Daniel	Lrs 34	John		Bft 88
Daniel	Nby 98	John		Bft 92
Daniel	Nby 99	John		Bft 94
Daniel	Pen 155	John		Cfd 109
Daniel	Yrk 623	John		Cfd 110
David	Dtn 122	John		Cfd 110
David	Geo 382	John		Dtn 123
David	Lan 6	John		Dtn 125
Davis	Edg 142	John		Edg 135
Denis	Bar 54	John		Edg 187
Edward	Bft 116	John		Gvl 245
Edward	Bft 122	John		Gvl 276
Edward	Ker 415	John		Lan 6
Edward	Pen 130	John		Lex 566
Edward	Pen 143	John		Nby 97
Elihu	Edg 153	John		Nby 97
Elijah	Pen 116	John		Spa 205
Elizabeth	Lex 565	John		Sum 587
Elizabeth	Ora 529	John		Wil 476
Elizth.	Geo 392	John (Free)		Geo 373
Enoch	Pen 106	John Junr.		Lrs 40
Ephram	Bar 54	John Senr.		Lrs 40
Evin	Bar 69	John Lieut.		Lrs 13
Febe	Nby 99	Joseph		Chr 82
Frederick	Edg 158	Joseph		Edg 134
Frederick	Edg 170	Joseph		Gvl 244
Fredk.	Lan 6	Joseph		Edg 175
Fredk.	Lan 11	Joseph		Lex 565
Freeman	Bar 54	Joseph		Lrs 41
Gabriel	Edg 169	Joseph		Mbo 61
George	Spa 174	Joseph		Pen 107
Hannah	Geo 368	Joseph		Pen 142
Henry	Mrn 459	Joseph		Sum 595
Hillary	Nby 98	Joshua		Gvl 255
Hiram	Chr 80	Joshua		Pen 127
Hopkin	Nby 98	Jourdan		Yrk 628
Humphrey	Yrk 619	Laurence		Ker 401
Isaac	Bar 65	Lewis		Gvl 268
Isaac	Fai 240	Luke		Spa 193
Isaac	Spa 168	Mamariah		Edg 166
Isham	Csn 91	Margt.		Col 373
Isham	Gvl 281	Marmaduke		Dtn 119
Izaah	Gvl 244	Martin		Gvl 268
J---	Gvl 276	Martin		Pen 142
Jacob	Geo 383	Mary		Sum 585
Jacob	Lrs 38	Membrance		Dtn 114
James	Abb 37	Micajah		Dtn 116
James	Bar 49	Moses		Chr 89
James	Csn 80	Naomi		Mbo 61
James	Dtn 123	Nathaniel		Abb 37
James	Gvl 256	Peter		Edg 172
James	Nby 99	Philip		Ora 543
James	Ora 509	Presley		Uni 230
James	Pen 104	Providence		Nby 97
James A.	Lrs 31	Reuben		Bft 126

255

Rignal	Lex 578	Elizabeth	Nby 98
Robert	Ker 411	George	Ora 525
Robt.	Gvl 258	George	Yrk 620
Roger	Edg 132	Henry	Spa 195
Roland	Bar 47	Humphrey	Edg 157
Rowland	Edg 156	James	Dtn 115
Rubin	Abb 27	James	Abb 37
Saml.	Spa 198	James Junr.	Yrk 618
Samuel	Abb 5	James, Senr.	Yrk 618
Samuel	Edg 161	John	Csn 84
Samuel	Edg 187	John	Lex 563
Samuel	Gvl 269	John	Nby 99
Samuel	Ker 425	John	Ora 527
Samuel	Lrs 43	John	Spa 193
Samuel Senr.	Lrs 45	John	Spa 193
Seth	Dtn 113	John	Sum 587
Simion	Abb 27	John	Yrk 618
Soloman	Ker 409	Moses	Sum 613
Solomon	Lan 3	Rolling	Fai 210
Stephen	Dtn 126	Samuel	Yrk 618
Stephen	Lan 11	Sarah	Dtn 128
Stephen	Lex 564	Shad Jr.	Dtn 128
Stephen	Lex 577	Shadrack	Dtn 126
Stephen	Lrs 45	Stephen	Mrn 462
Stephen	Nby 98	Stephen	Pen 161
Thomas	Abb 27	Thomas	Dtn 128
Thomas	Edg 176	Thomas	Spa 184
Thomas	Fai 229	Thomas Jr.	Dtn 128
Thomas	Pen 135	Thomas Junr.	Lrs 42
Thomas	Spa 198	Thomas Senr.	Lrs 42
Thomas	Wil 463	Vincent P.	Edg 188
Thomas	Yrk 621	Walker	Spa 193
Thomas M.	Mbo 61	William	Abb 32
Thos.	Geo 381	William	Dtn 116
Thos. Senr.	Fai 204	William	Uni 244
Washington	Lrs 32	Wm. H.	Bft 84
William	Dtn 123	Wm., Jr.	Dtn 116
William	Edg 148	Williford, Britain	Spa 198
William	Geo 383	Wyley	Spa 198
William	Geo 366	Williman, Chrst.	Csn 171
William	Lrs 41	Christopher	Csn 147
William	Lrs 45	Jacob	Col 409
William	Mbo 58	Jacob Junr.	Csn 148
William	Mrn 460	Willimon, Jacob	Csn 103
William	Ora 509	Willingham, Christr.	Geo 369
William	Pen 140	Edward	Fai 240
William	Yrk 628	Jno	Fai 220
William	Yrk 631	Jos.	Csn 66
Wm.	Chr 81	Wm.	Fai 233
Wm.	Gvl 272	Willis, Britton(?)	Pen 152
Wm.	Spa 168	Daniel	Pen 123
Wm.	Uni 227	James	Ker 407
Wm.	Uni 230	John	Spa 187
Willis	Bft 82	Richd.	Spa 187
Willis	Bft 86	Robert	Edg 135
Zadock E.	Bar 66	Willison, Robert	Pen 137
Williamson, Abram	Csn 107	Willis, Samuel	Edg 152
Amelia	Csn 86	Stephen	Pen 153
Andrew	Yrk 620	Wm.	Spa 171
Benja.	Geo 365	William	Csn 98
Benajah	Bar 63	William	Ora 543
Celia	Geo 387	Willison, Samuel	Edg 188
Danl.	Fai 239	Willow, Daniel	Pen 105
David	Bft 90	Wills, John	Nby 98
Eliza	Col 373	Willis	Sum 604

John	Edg 143	Wish, Catharine	Csn 135
John	Pen 121	William	Csn 154
Joseph	Csn 141	Wishby, Thomas	Edg 139
Lettice	Abb 34	Wisher, John	Yrk 622
Minor	Fai 214	Wit, John	Edg 168
Minor	Spa 204	Wite, William	Bar 47
Minor Junr.	Fai 195	Witherington, Wm.	Dtn 124
Richard	Fai 206	William Jr.	Dtn 126
Rosey	Fai 195	Withers, Frances	Csn 181
Samuel	Abb 33	Francis	Geo 373
Thomas	Abb 22	James	Geo 364
Thomas	Abb 32	John	Geo 379
Zachariah	Dtn 114	Mary	Geo 375
Winningham, Joseph	Csn 66	Robt. F.	Geo 373
Joseph	Ora 549	Witherspoon, David	Sum 608
Roland	Csn 67	Elizth.	Wil 464
Thomas (2)	Pen 159	Gavin	Mrn 446
William	Ora 541	Gavin	Wil 473
Winnright, John	Lex 558	James	Sum 607
Winnum, John	Edg 153	James, slaves of	Wil 474
Winsloe, John	Yrk 630	John	Mrn 446
Winsor, Thomas	Csn 96	John	Wil 470
Winsrett, John	Pen 103	John Junr.	Sum 609
Winstanley, Thomas	Csn 111	John Senr.	Sum 609
Winston, William	Bft 88	Joseph	Wil 471
Winter, Hugh S.	Csn 67	Robt.	Wil 474
Hugh Est.	Csn 67	Robert	Sum 610
John	Wil 466	Sarah	Wil 473
Winters, George	Abb 16	Thos.	Wil 464
James	Wil 463	Wm.	Fai 198
Leonard	Abb 16	Wm.	Fai 222
Winthrop, Joseph	Csn 66	Wm.	Csn 67
Joseph	Csn 113	Witsell, Lawrence	Bft 94
Wiott, William	Pen 113	Witt, Michael	Nby 98
Wirey, Harman	Fai 236	Wittel, Thomas	Bft 82
Wirey, Michael	Fai 236	Wittemore, Reline(?)	Csn 89
Wirick, Harman	Fai 195	Witten, Peter	Csn 72
Nichs.	Fai 211	Witter, Jonathan	Bft 132
Wirodisk, Andrew	Ora 549	Norwood	Csn 171
Wise, Ambrous	Mrn 439	Norwood	Csn 192
Benjamin	Sum 605	S.	Csn 192
George	Lex 484	William	Csn 192
George Junr.	Lex 484	Wittich, Charles	Csn 124
George Junr.	Lex 567	Wittler, Elizabeth	Ker 411
George Senior	Lex 567	Wittner, Jacob	Ora 539
Henry	Sum 601	Witzell, Elizabet	Ora 551
John	Lex 484	Woddrop, John	Csn 129
John	Lex 567	Wofford, Benjn.	Uni 223
John Junr.	Sum 603	James	Spa 191
John Senr.	Sum 603	James	Spa 199
Michael	Lex 559	Jeremiah	Spa 196
Nathan	Sum 605	John	Spa 200
Robert	Sum 603	John	Spa 211
Step	Sum 603	Joseph	Spa 196
Thomas Junr.	Sum 603	Nathaniel	Spa 191
Thomas Senr.	Sum 603	Sarah	Spa 173
William	Sum 603	Wagan, James	Csn 114
Wiseman, Hugh	Nby 99	Wolbanks, Daniel	Gvl 244
Hugh	Nby 99	Joseph	Gvl 277
Thomas	Edg 155	Woldrige, Edward	Gvl 285
Wisener, Jacob	Lrs 42	Wolf, ---	Csn 181
Wisenhunt, George	Yrk 628	Christian	Ora 555
John	Yrk 628	George	Csn 90
Nicholas	Yrk 628	George	Gvl 248
Nicholas Junr.	Yrk 628	Jacob	Gvl 280

Jacob	Ora 541		Obediah	Gvl 267
Jacob	Ora 555		Oliver	Pen 155
John	Ora 539		Pennuel	Spa 190
John	Ora 539		Penwell	Gvl 277
Joseph	Ora 555		Peter	Gvl 249
Margaret	Csn 75		Robert	Csn 66
Wolfe, John Junior	Lex 560		Robert	Pen 155
John Senior	Lex 560		Robert	Spa 190
Wolff, John F. Col.	Lrs 19		Robert	Spa 202
Wolly, Sarah	Bar 51		Saml.	Uni 247
Womble, James	Cfd 108		Samuel	Edg 165
Wommack, Cloe	Spa 186		Samuel	Nby 99
Wood, ---	Csn 181		Stephen C.	Gvl 284
Aaron	Yrk 632		Thomas	Dtn 117
Adam	Bar 52		Thomas	Lan 7
Augustin	Uni 249		Thomas	Lrs 37
Belfield	Pen 139		Thomas Junr.	Lrs 40
Benjamin	Nby 98		Thomas Senr.	Lrs 40
Benjn.	Spa 189		Thos.	Gvl 251
Bennett	Spa 190		Thos.	Gvl 272
Christopher	Dtn 116		Will.	Lan 6
Daniel	Lrs 34		William	Bar 52
Edmon	Spa 202		William	Csn 140
Elias	Pen 129		William	Csn 141
Elizabeth	Gvl 283		William	Edg 169
Elizabeth	Pen 117		William	Gvl 253
Francis	Uni 247		William	Lrs 19
Frederick	Dtn 123		William	Lrs 20
George	Lex 563		William	Pen 158
Gideon	Uni 248		Willm.	Wil 474
Henry	Spa 189		William Estate	Csn 185
Henry M.	Gvl 246		Wm.	Chr 92
Iham(?)	Uni 229		Wm.	Col 383
James	Chr 79		Writ	Pen 153
James	Lrs 20		Zadock	Lrs 23
James	Lrs 38		Woodall, John	Pen 130
James	Nby 99		John	Pen 134
James	Spa 202		John	Pen 144
Jesse	Mrn 444		John	Pen 153
Jethro	Bar 58		Joseph	Pen 140
Joel	Pen 144		Joseph	Pen 146
John	Bar 53		Woodard, Charles	Ker 411
John	Edg 179		James	Sum 609
John	Gvl 244		Woodbury, Elizth.	Mrn 458
John	Lrs 20		Richd.	Mrn 460
John	Mrn 437		Wooddruffe, Edwd.	Csn 131
John	Mrn 450		Wooddy, Henry	Spa 177
John	Spa 202		John	Lrs 18
John	Spa 202		Woode, Wm.	Spa 211
John G.	Mrn 457		Woodham, Alis	Dtn 121
John W.	Gvl 245		Aris	Dtn 127
Jonathon	Abb 34		Edward	Dtn 121
Joseph	Bar 65		Edward	Dtn 127
Joseph	Dtn 122		Woodle, John Anthy	Csn 128
Joseph	Dtn 128		Woodman, Edward	Csn 90
Joseph	Lrs 23		Woodruff, John	Spa 185
Joseph	Pen 111		Joseph	Spa 189
Josias	Uni 229		Josiah	Spa 184
Lazarous	Gvl 285		Nat	Spa 188
Lot	Uni 248		Saml.	Spa 185
Mary	Uni 229		Saml.	Spa 186
Michael	Spa 190		Saml.	Spa 189
Moses	Gvl 259		Thomas	Spa 187
Nancey	Spa 206		Thos.	Spa 184
Nathaniel	Edg 159		Woods, John	Spa 207

James	Bar	61	William	Sum 587
James	Lrs	25	William	Yrk 623
James	Nby	99	William Junr.	Yrk 618
Jane	Fai	237	William Senr.	Sum 595
Jane	Mrn	451	William Senr.	Yrk 618
Jemima	Nby	99	Wright	Lrs 38
Jeremiah	Wil	470	Wrotton, Henery	Ora 505
Jesse	Pen	112	Isaiah	Ora 503
Jno	Bft	94	James	Ora 501
John	Dtn	123	Nehemiah	Ora 501
John	Chr	85	William	Ora 505
John	Edg	139	Wulmer, John Junr.	Lex 495
John	Fai	218	John Senr.	Lex 495
John	Gvl	248	William	Lex 495
John	Lan	2	Wurdeman, John G.	Csn 76
John	Lrs	20	Wyan, George	Csn 105
John	Lrs	46	Wyatt,	
John	Nby	98	see also Wiott	
John	Spa	185	Wyatt, Peter	Csn 104
John	Ora	555	James	Abb 32
John	Yrk	617	James	Dtn 116
John	Yrk	618	Richard	Csn 81
Jonathan	Dtn	123	Violetta	Csn 81
Jonathan	Dtn	127	Wyld, Clevious D.	Bar 46
Joseph	Abb	30	John C.	Bar 43
Joseph	Ker	401	Wylder, George	Ora 525
Joseph	Mbo	58	Wylds, Magdalen	Ora 539
Joseph	Nby	98	Wylie, James Docr.	Yrk 628
Joseph	Nby	99	Wymer, John	Ora 533
Joseph	Pen	126	Mary	Ora 533
Joseph	Sum	595	Wyngate, Planner	Yrk 630
Joseph	Yrk	631	Wynne, Mathew	Gvl 243
Mary	Lrs	40		
Mary	Sum	595		
Mesheck	Edg	153	**Y**	
Moses	Pen	112		
Nathan (2)	Nby	99		
Pleasant	Abb	4	Yager, John	Lrs 41
Randolph	Fai	215	Samuel	Lrs 41
Rebecca	Csn	121	Yandle, Andrew	Gvl 278
Richard	Chr	76	Yantz, Mathias	Lex 497
Richard	Nby	99	Yarboro, George	Fai 213
Robert	Abb	17	John	Fai 206
Roderic	Uni	227	Owen	Fai 196
Roderick	Yrk	622	Rachel	Fai 200
Saml.	Chr	86	Yarborough, see also	
Samuel	Yrk	622	Yerborough, Yerber	
Samuel	Yrk	625	Yarborough, Eliza	Cfd 107
Samuel	Yrk	627	John	Edg 157
Sarah	Lrs	39	Joel	Cfd 109
Solomon	Dtn	123	John	Chr 80
Solomon	Lan	2	Lewis	Lrs 26
Stephen	Bar	54	William	Abb 37
Thomas	Nby	92	William	Gvl 254
Thomas	Nby	99	Wm.	Chr 80
Thomas	Spa	211	Yarbro, Asa	Mrn 450
Thomas	Sum	597	Yarbrough, Jilson	Edg 138
Thomas	Uni	238	Yateman, John	Pen 156
Thomas	Yrk	620	Yates, D.	Csn 123
Thompson	Yrk	621	James	Pen 115
William	Abb	26	Jeremiah	Csn 123
William	Dtn	115	Yancy, Lewis	Lrs 31
William	Edg	144	Yates, Seth	Csn 128
William	Mbo	58	Yeadon, Richard	Csn 118
William (2)	Nby	98	William	Csn 139

William	Dtn 114	Wm.	Dtn 117
William	Dtn 128	Zin, Jacob	Edg 152
William	Fai 193	Zinn, Jacob	Edg 153
William	Gvl 245	Zorn, Henery	Ora 505
William	Ker 407	Henery	Ora 507
William	Lex 577	John	Ora 543
William	Lrs 28	Nicholas	Ora 507
William	Pen 149	Nicholas	Ora 509
Willm. P.	Csn 120	Zucker, Michael	Csn 108
Wm.	Chr 83	Zuill, James	Wil 470
Youngblood, Andrew	Edg 164	Zylk, John	Csn 100
Eli	Pen 116	Zylstra, Peter	Csn 79
George	Edg 146		
J. Est.	Col 385		
John	Abb 12		
Joseph	Bar 66		
Lewis	Abb 9	ADDENDA	
Lewis	Edg 136		
Mary	Col 385		
P. Est.	Col 385	Dale, William Senr.	Abb 37
Samuel	Abb 10	Daniel, James Senr.	Edg 172
Terry	Edg 134	Holly, Martha	Gvl 253
Thomas	Edg 157	Johnson, George	Edg 163
Younge, Daniel	Uni 234	Land, Jacob	Spa 201
Henry	Spa 178	Pullium, James	Abb 8
James	Spa 179	Rose, John	Col 407
Jesse	Uni 235	Steward, Thomas	Fai 218
John	Spa 177	Wharton, Barnard	Gvl 282
John (2)	Spa 195		
Joseph G.	Spa 195		
Nat.	Spa 196		
Robert	Spa 177		
Thomas	Uni 220		
Wm.	Spa 195		
Wm.	Spa 211		
Wm.	Uni 234		
Younginger, Jacob	Lex 483		
Jacob	Lex 576		
Mathias	Lex 484		
Sebbastian	Lex 483		
Yowell, David	Pen 141		
James	Pen 141		
Joel	Pen 141		

Z

Zachary, Benjamin	Ora 501
John	Ora 523
Wm.	Ora 523
Zaler, Jacob	Col 403
Zauler, Eve	Bft 100
Azvencroft, --lliam	Edg 147
Zealor, Joseph	Csn 119
Zeigler, Godfrey	Ora 535
John	Ora 511
Michel	Ora 501
Michel Junr.	Ora 503
Nicholas	Ora 535
Zeizey, Mark	Lex 493
Zeller, Jacob	Bft 98
Ziles, Christian	Nby 100
Zilk, John	Csn 72
Zimmerman, Jacob	Bft 108

CPSIA information can be obtained
at www.ICGtesting.com
Printed in the USA
LVHW082204051121
702580LV00011B/85

9 780806 308845